Reclaiming Our Children

Also by Peter R. Breggin, M.D.

———◆———

Your Drug May Be Your Problem: How and Why to Stop Taking Psychiatric Medications (with David Cohen, Ph.D.), 1999

Talking Back to Ritalin: What Doctors Aren't Telling You About Stimulants for Children, 1998

The War Against Children of Color: Psychiatry Targets Inner City Youth (coauthor, with Ginger Ross Breggin), 1998

The Heart of Being Helpful: Empathy, and the Creation of a Healing Presence, 1997

Brain-Disabling Treatments in Psychiatry: Drugs, Electroshock, and the Role of the FDA, 1997

Psychosocial Approaches to Deeply Disturbed Persons (coeditor, with E. Mark Stern, Ed.D.), 1996

Talking Back to Prozac: What Doctors Aren't Telling You About Today's Most Controversial Drug, 1994

Beyond Conflict: From Self-Help and Psychotherapy to Peacemaking, 1992

Toxic Psychiatry: Why Therapy, Empathy, and Love Must Replace the Drugs, Electroshock, and Biochemical Theories of the "New Psychiatry," 1991

Psychiatric Drugs: Hazards to the Brain, 1983

Electroshock: Its Brain-Disabling Effects, 1979

Reclaiming Our Children

A Healing Solution
for a Nation in Crisis

———✦———

Peter R. Breggin, M.D.

PERSEUS BOOKS
Cambridge, Massachusetts

Many of the designations used by manufacturers and sellers to distinguish their products are claimed as trademarks. Where those designations appear in this book and Perseus Books was aware of a trademark claim, the designations have been printed in initial capital letters.

CIP information for this book is available from the Library of Congress.

ISBN: 0-7382-0252-5
Copyright © 2000 by Peter R. Breggin

Perseus Books is a member of the Perseus Books Group

Text design by Cynthia White
Set in 10-point Janson Text by the Perseus Books Group

1 2 3 4 5 6 7 8 9 10—03 02 01 00 99
First printing, December 1999

Perseus Books are available at special discounts for bulk purchases in the U.S. by corporations, institutions, and other organizations. For more information, please contact the Special Markets Department at HarperCollins Publishers, 10 East 53rd Street, New York, NY 10022, or call 1-212-207-7528.

Find us on the World Wide Web at
http://www.perseusbooks.com

To the Board of Directors, Advisory Council, and general
membership of the International Center for the Study
of Psychiatry and Psychology (ICSPP),
who have given enormous support to me,
to my wife, Ginger, and to each other in
our mutual efforts on behalf of America's children

Contents

Acknowledgments

———◆———

Members of the Board of Directors and Advisory Council of the International Center for the Study of Psychiatry and Psychology made numerous contributions to this book. I interviewed or received commentaries from a number of them during the writing of the manuscript, including Fred Bemak, Ed.D.; Brian Berthiaume, M.Ed.; Paula Caplan, Ph.D.; Roland Chrisjohn, Ph.D.; David Cohen, Ph.D.; Ty Colbert, Ph.D; Charles Collier, M.A.; Sharon Collins, M.D.; Ronald David, M.D.; William Glasser, M.D.; Richard Goodman, Ph.D.; Ron Hopson, Ph.D.; Linda Jessup, R.N., M.P.H.; Jake Johnson, Ed.D.; Pax Linson, M.A.; Jeffrey Moussaieff Masson, Ph.D.; Kevin McCready, Ph.D.; Barry Mehler, Ph.D.; Loren Mosher, M.D.; David Oaks; Sue Parry; Vance Sherman, M.D.; Doug Smith, M.D.; Tony Stanton, M.D.; and Sharon Morrison Velasco, Ph.D. Not everyone's interview is quoted in the book, but each person's ideas made a contribution. Drs. Caplan, Hopson, and Smith read the manuscript to provide overview comments and Dr. McCready generously provided both his insights and invaluable, time-consuming detailed editing.

Michael DeHart, the headmaster of the Thornton Friends School of Maryland and Virginia, graciously allowed me to visit his school and interview him. He also read the chapter on schools. My wife Ginger's wonderful mother, Jean Ross, also helped with editing. I also want to thank Frank van Meerendonk of the Netherlands for the stream of useful information that he generously provides.

I want to thank my editor at Perseus, Marnie Cochran, who has given uncommon support to this writer. Marnie's capacity to bring out my best—and to gently push aside my worst—is quite remarkable. She enhances my creative work without in any way impeding it.

Perseus is a fine press. I also value my association with senior publicist Sharon Rice and project editor Marco Pavia. Andrew Blauner, my literary agent, has been more successful on my behalf than anyone who came before him.

Each time I have written a new book in the past sixteen years, I have been confronted with the increasingly difficult task of communicating the depth of my indebtedness and gratitude to my partner and wife, Ginger Ross Breggin, in every aspect of my personal and work life. During the past two years, when my schedule became unusually busy and intense, Ginger not only provided research help, editorial assistance, and direction and inspiration to my writings—she took charge of many personal and family activities to provide me the time to write. While doing all that, Ginger also managed and directed the International Center for the Study of Psychiatry and Psychology, organized two international professional conferences, produced and edited the Center's newsletter, increased the organization's membership, and originated the concept for and managed the Center's journal, *Ethical Human Sciences and Services.* And all of that, believe it or not, hardly captures what she has accomplished in these recent times, including the loving support she gives to our children, her mom and dad, and our friends and colleagues!

Unless otherwise designated, none of the vignettes in this book is an exact portrait of any individual person or family. To protect anonymity, I combined and modified the stories of different children and their families. A lengthy piece of dialogue from my practice might, for example, be a very close approximation to events that actually took place, but the names, ages, background, or even gender of the participants will have been changed. All of the dialogues are reconstructions from memory or notes. None are verbatim. It is best to view the vignettes as dramatic illustrations of experiences that I have on a regular basis in my practice rather than as exact case histories.

The International Center for the Study of Psychiatry and Psychology can provide the names of consultants who would be able to help communities, schools, churches, private practice groups, clinics, hospitals, and other organizations to develop their own drug-free relationship-based treatment programs for children and youths, as well as adults. See Appendix B for further details.

Reclaiming Our Children

1

Defining Moments for the Future of Our Children

---·•◦•·---

The year 1999 saw two defining moments for the future of America's children, one a tragedy and the other an attempted national solution that created an even greater threat to our children.

The tragedy occurred on April 20, 1999, when eighteen-year-old Eric Harris and his friend and cohort, seventeen-year-old Dylan Klebold, led an assault on their own high school in Littleton, Colorado, killing or wounding thirty-five students and one teacher.[1]

The second defining moment—the attempted solution—took place several weeks later, on June 7, 1999, the opening day of the White House Conference on Mental Health in Washington, D.C.[2] The President and Vice President of the United States along with their wives came together with leading figures from the media and the field of psychiatry. They were mindful of the Littleton tragedy, as well as the subsequent May 20 school shooting of six classmates by fifteen-year-old T. J. Solomon at Heritage High School in Conyers, Georgia.

Mrs. Clinton introduced the two psychiatrists who were showcased at the opening session, both of them biological psychiatrists, or biopsychiatrists. Biopsychiatrists believe that all serious emotional problems have a physiological cause and can be treated with medication. First one and then the other doctor informed us that our chil-

1

dren suffer from genetic and biological brain diseases that cause many millions of them to be mentally distressed and potentially violent.

The child psychiatrist specifically rejected any possibility that "bad childhood traumas," "inadequate parenting," or even "absent fathers" could lie at the root of the suffering displayed by so many of our 70 million infants, children, and youths under eighteen, including 52 million schoolchildren.[3] These extraordinary pronouncements rendered parents irrelevant, gutted family life of any meaning, and rejected common sense as well as an enormous array of scientific research confirming the overwhelming importance of childhood trauma in the development of childhood emotional problems.[4]

Seemingly enamored with the psychiatrists, the Clintons and the Gores wholly endorsed the biological view of our children's suffering as well as the resort to psychiatric drugs as the inevitable solution.

President Clinton concluded the White House Conference by announcing a new multi-agency federal initiative aimed at providing training programs to all of America's schools and communities "to help us identify troubled children, and provide them better school mental health services." The President and the other speakers urged America to use the nation's schools to identify greater numbers of children as potentially violent or otherwise in need of psychiatric treatment.

Meanwhile, no one mentioned that the school shooters Eric Harris in Colorado and T. J. Solomon in Georgia were already receiving psychiatric drugs when they became violent. Harris was prescribed a Prozac-like drug called Luvox and Solomon was being given the stimulant Ritalin. Both boys were described as receiving psychiatric treatment for depression.[5]

The speakers at the White House Conference ignored the fact that schools are already vigorously identifying children and referring them for psychiatric evaluation. They did not acknowledge that several million children are already being subjected to stimulants like Ritalin, Dexedrine, and Adderall, as well as Prozac-like "antidepressants"* and other drugs.

The first defining moment, the violence at Columbine High School in Littleton, as tragic as it was, could have inspired us as adults

---

*The concept of "antidepressant" drugs is now being scientifically challenged (see Chapter 7).

to examine our own consciences and to transform ourselves for the better. It could have motivated us to place a higher priority on our children's needs, especially their desperate cries for more meaningful relationships with us. A lot depended on the leadership provided to the nation by the kind of people gathered at the White House Conference.

Despite its political thrust, the second defining moment, the one in Washington, D.C., could have put the needs of children at center stage. Instead, the White House Conference shut the door on children. By advocating a congressionally funded program for identifying children in need of psychiatric interventions, the administration provided a windfall to the psychiatric and the health professions, to the pharmaceutical industry, and cover for schools and communities that want to control children without providing for their genuine needs. By locating our children's problems in their supposedly flawed brains rather than in our obviously flawed society, the White House Conference took adults off the proverbial hook, while dangling our children on its point.

Witnessing Littleton

As we watched the events at Columbine High School in Littleton, Colorado, unfold on television, most of us felt confused, helpless, and angry. We also had a sense of sharing these feelings with millions of other Americans.

There had been school shootings before Littleton. During the five years ending in 1997, more than a dozen episodes of multiple murders had been committed by children in American schools.[6] There had also been numerous examples of adults "going berserk" and attacking people in their workplace. But this school assault grabbed our attention as had no previous mass shooting. There were two boys involved in the killing spree at Columbine High School, they seemed so prepared and purposeful, and so many were killed and wounded. We could hear the terrified victims screaming for help on cell phones while gunshots sounded in the background, we were shocked by the images of children fleeing with their hands on their heads as if themselves surrendering, and frightened that it could take place in such a typical American suburb. And the dreadful events dragged on for so many hours on television. The extensive coverage indicated our fascination with the lives of children and young people, at least when observed from afar—but did it show concern and love for them?[7]

What we watched unfolding became much more than a case of two distraught or disturbed high school seniors shooting up their own school, killing twelve students, a teacher, and then themselves. It became a metaphor for our inability, or unwillingness, to give our children what they need from us—even to rescue them when their lives are threatened. For me as a parent and a psychiatrist who often works with children and their families, it renewed my determination to engage the issues of what's being done to our children—and not being done for them.

From the way the police responded to the crisis inside the school to the later disclosure that one of the boys was taking a psychiatric drug, I kept seeing images of an America that does not put children first, an America whose adults elevate their own safety and well-being above that of their children, and an America in which bureaucratic rules take precedence over courage and creativity in caring for our children.

Parents, teachers, religious officials—all the caregivers of our society—have been indoctrinated to turn to specialists to handle difficult children. When children present us with serious problems, many of us quickly turn to the police or to medical doctors instead of to our own resources as caregivers. As a nation, we have made this a policy. Both the criminal justice system and psychiatry have taken under their control ever greater numbers of our children. As the power of these institutions has escalated, parents, teachers, and other caregivers have been disempowered, losing their place in the center of our children's lives.

In the Littleton disaster, the police quickly attempted to take control of the situation. When the police were done, psychiatry took over, calling for the early identification and treatment of potentially troubled and troublesome children. But can the criminal justice system and psychiatry really identify and solve the problems of our children?

The Police Respond to Desperate Cries from Columbine High School

At approximately 11:15 A.M. on the morning of April 20, 1999, students and teachers began phoning to alert police of a shooting going on at Columbine High School. From within the school library, a teacher on a cell phone desperately pleaded for rescue with the police as she simultaneously shouted at her students, "Kids, under the table. Kids, stay on the floor . . . Oh God, oh God—kids, just stay down."[8] The sound of gunshots could be heard exploding in the hallway a few feet beyond the library door. The officer on the other end of the line kept repeating, "Help is on the way!"

But was it? The first SWAT team entered the building about 12:30 P.M., one hour and fifteen minutes after the initial phone calls. Two hours later, at 2:30 P.M., they began to locate pockets of students in hiding and continued to do so for another hour.

Although the police knew exactly where the massacre was taking place, minutes and then hours passed before rescue teams worked their way to the library. They arrived at the center of the carnage at approximately 4:00 P.M.—four hours and forty-five minutes after the initial alarm—and found twelve bodies: three girls and nine boys, including the two gunmen.[9]

As much as any of the events, the teacher screaming into the phone for help and the lack of any effective response epitomized the situation of children everywhere in our society. So many are in desperate distress, so many are signaling their suffering in so many ways, with hardly anyone taking notice, let alone responding effectively.

Parents, some in four-wheel-drive cars and probably armed with guns, tried to break through the police blockades to rescue their children. Parents anywhere in the country would have wanted to rescue their children, but in Colorado—land of the Rocky Mountains, outdoor sports, and hunting—many parents would have been especially prepared to mount an independent rescue. But they never got the opportunity.

What if one of your children or my children had been in that building? What if we were being forced to stand outside while the explosions and gunshots persisted and the minutes and hours ticked by?

The scene was like a caricature of what goes on all the time in schools all over the country as they keep out parents and other valuable community resources. From retired people, who would volunteer as class aides and hallway monitors, to representatives of business, the professions, and homemaking, who could inspire the students' career interests, our children would benefit from interacting with adults from the world outside the school. Meanwhile, administrators and teachers try to cope in isolation with many hostile students, with students dealing and abusing drugs, with students humiliating and bullying each other unmercifully, with students who obviously feel depressed, suicidal, and alienated.

After more than an hour, SWAT teams cautiously began working their way through Columbine High toward the center of the carnage in the library area. They stopped to rescue pockets of students in hiding. When students were found, the SWAT team would hunker down while some of the officers escorted the students back to safety outside the building. This caused long delays. Meanwhile, hundreds of police officers, including other SWAT teams, stood around with nothing to do outside the building but watch and wait for orders.

Schooled by action movies where heroes come to the rescue, many of us waited expectantly for someone to come forward to rescue the children. Instead, we witnessed a seemingly endless bureaucratic process slowly unfolding.

A wounded youngster was shown on TV hanging out the top of a shattered library window beside a large sign that begged, "Help, I'm bleeding to death." But except for the rolling cameras, nothing else was moving.

Of all the images from that awful day, the image of the boy in the window is the one that many found most heart-rending and frustrating. "My God," we gasped around the nation, "the boy has hung out a sign. Do something!" The SWAT teams, we were told, were afraid that the sign was a setup, a trap created by the shooters. "What if it is?" many of us must have responded. "Can't they see that the boy is dying? Aren't they *paid* to risk their lives for our children?"

Inside the building, two boys stayed behind in the hallway with their wounded teacher while other students fled or hid out of sight. Their teacher's face was shattered, and they were trying to comfort him and to stop his bleeding. They remained alone with him for three harrowing hours—without trying to flee the building—while they tried to stanch his bleeding. When a SWAT team finally reached them between 3:15 and 3:30 P.M.,[10] the officers forced the two youngsters to evacuate the building against their wishes, leaving behind their teacher, who was bleeding profusely.

As the immediate crisis subsided, details of the heroism surfaced: The teacher was the basketball coach Dave Sanders. At his funeral, students spoke about how he had saved many lives by going through the building warning them to hide or to flee.[11] Aaron Hancey, a junior with Boy Scout first aid training, was one of the boys who stayed in the treacherous hallways to administer to the injured, including Mr. Sanders, while getting medical advice relayed to him from a phone hookup with paramedics.[12] He had volunteered to stay behind but was not allowed to remain when the SWAT team arrived. The officers later explained that they did not know that Klebold and Harris were no longer a danger. Mr. Sanders died by the time paramedics reached the scene a short time later.[13]

When seventeen-year-old Cassie Bernall was confronted by one the shooters, she closed her eyes and clasped her hands in prayer. He asked her if she believed in God, and she replied "Yes." Then he killed her. She is admired as a martyr and an inspiration by religious youngsters around the nation.[14]

The young man with the sign, "Help, I'm bleeding to death," finally managed to pull himself so far out the window that he was in danger of plunging two stories to the ground. SWAT team members, frustrated by the restraints imposed on them, demanded the opportunity to rescue him. Standing on a truck, they let him drop into safety in their arms.

We waited breathlessly as the rescue at the window played out on our televisions. Surely the SWAT team—their truck parked at the window with the pitiful sign—would send men bursting through the window to save any other youngsters or teachers dying or hiding in terror in the room. Instead, they retreated as if under a withering hail of bullets.

Fortunately, the student survived. His name was Patrick Ireland and he had been shot twice in the head and once in the foot before dragging himself to the window.[15] He will have a long, slow recovery from brain injury.[16]

It's unclear when the shooting finally stopped inside the school. Many media reports failed to mention or discuss this aspect of the chronology. Others stated that the shooting could be heard for about one hour, until about 12:30 p.m. However, a story in the *Columbia Journalism Review* drew on extensive interviews with the local media and concluded, "As late as 3:45 P.M., news crews report shots can be heard inside the school."[17] If this indicates that the killers continued to rampage all afternoon, the slow movement of the SWAT teams becomes even more tragic.

Eric Harris and Dylan Klebold, as noted earlier, finally ended the mayhem by killing themselves in the library, where they were found sometime around 4:00 P.M.

For those of us watching on television, or holding vigil in Littleton, the tragedy did not end with the death of Eric and Dylan. Terrified parents, not knowing whether or not their children were alive, waited a seeming eternity before the police completed their painstakingly slow search of the building for victims living and dead. By now, most of America was asking, "Why is this taking so long? What is the matter here?"

Who's to Blame?

Individual police officers should not be blamed for any failure to act more rapidly or courageously. This could not have been a matter of personal cowardice on the part of so many men and women. Some of the officers had their own children in the school; they would have chosen to risk death for them. Whatever held them back, it was not lack of motivation or courage. It was something else—something that disconnected them from their natural relationships to the children inside the building.

From civilians to police and firefighters to the National Guard, Americans commonly risk their lives for strangers, pulling them from icy waters and burning buildings, shoring up their levies, using their own bodies as shields to protect children and older people from falling debris, even at times risking death to save animals from fire and flood.

Somehow, the structure of authority at the Littleton tragedy kept them from acting with the individual heroism characteristic of many adults in rescuing children. Afterward, law enforcement representatives around the nation defended the Columbine SWAT teams as, in effect, going by the book. Unfortunately, but predictably, it was not a book about adults putting the lives of children ahead of their own.

The police took an *adult*-centered approach to the situation, protecting themselves and parents rather than mobilizing in a single-minded effort toward rescuing as many children as possible as quickly as possible. To be *child*-centered often requires reframing what we've been trained to do as professionals in order to focus on what children really need from us at that very moment in their lives. Sometimes this means sacrificing our own comfort, safety, or cherished beliefs in order to respond directly to what we're hearing from children. This did not happen at Columbine. The police responded the way they have been taught to respond in our society. Rescuing the children was not the one and only priority on their list. The entire process became an allegory for the failure of society to respond to the needs of its children and their families.

Embarrassed by public criticism, the police and the SWAT team leaders tried to justify their behavior to the press. They explained, "There were unexploded bombs everywhere"; "We had to look out for booby traps"; "We were afraid to get caught in friendly cross-fire if we sent in too many men"; "Doors were open everywhere down the hallways exposing us to ambush." Using words with a dreadfully familiar ring from Vietnam, some said, "We couldn't tell which of the students were the killers."

There were additional problems that did make the situation difficult for the SWAT teams. The SWAT team expert Peter Kraska attributed the problems to lack of appropriate training: "Where they know people are being killed inside, it's not a hostage situation and they have to go in and hunt people down. They really aren't trained to do that."[18] Conditions were not only frightening, they were confusing and disorienting. The fire alarms were deafening, sprinklers were pouring water down on the SWAT team members' heads, they were uncertain how many people were involved or whom they were dealing with.

Nonetheless, descriptions by the police themselves seem to confirm that the SWAT teams were held up by the dangerousness of the situation. The first policemen had been fired upon and had retreated. Bombs were going off as the SWAT teams entered the building. Was it too dangerous for the adults to charge past open doors, bomb-blast wreckage, and possible booby traps to rescue the children? Meanwhile, no police officers suffered life-threatening wounds. With the exception of those by teachers inside the school, no adult acts of heroism were reported.

Still, the press kept looking for heroes. In an absurd stretch, one interviewer praised the police officer who spent so many agonizing minutes listening on the phone to the distraught teacher in the library. The policeman's frustration was apparent as he explained that he had done nothing to merit any such accolades. Understandably, he seemed deeply distressed by having to keep repeating to the teacher, "Help is coming," when it wasn't.

That police officer was certainly not to blame for the failure to fulfill the promise "Help is coming," but like other aspects of Littleton, this failure was a metaphor for larger failures. For years, society has been promising help to our schools, our teachers, and our children without delivering it.

The Police Are Not to Blame

Heroism isn't limited to those in uniform. When an airplane crashed into a bridge and sank in the freezing waters of the Potomac a few years ago, an ordinary citizen risked his life in the icy waters to save one of the victims. A few days ago, I saw a story about a father who was bleeding profusely from a shark attack but nonetheless stayed in the water until he had hoisted his children to safety on a boat. In a local report, a grandmother was killed by a stray bullet as she shielded three neighborhood children with her body during a street shoot-out in Washington, D.C. Our newspapers and television news stories regularly praise people who put themselves in jeopardy to save strangers, not to mention their own children.

In fact, we have a model of heroism from another school shooting incident in Assistant Principal Cecil T. Brinkley of Heritage High School in Conyers, Georgia. Risking his own life after several people had already been shot, he approached the armed young boy, T. J. Solomon, and convinced him to hand over his .357 magnum revolver. To everyone's good fortune, T. J. complied and collapsed into Brinkley's arms, crying, "Oh, my God, I'm so scared."[19]

In the shooting at Thurston High School in Oregon a year earlier, the attacker, Kip Kinkel, was tackled and disarmed by a seventeen-year-old student whom Kip had shot in the hand and chest.[20]

In a West Paducah, Kentucky, shooting in December 1999, fourteen-year-old Michael Carneal opened fire on an early-morning prayer meeting at his high school. His murder spree was stopped by seventeen-year-old Ben Strong, a senior and leader of the prayer group, who refused to flee, stood his ground, and repeatedly urged Michael to put the gun down. When Michael paused, Ben rushed over and disarmed him. Michael begged, "Kill me, please. I can't believe I did that."

We can be certain that many, indeed most, of the police officers who surrounded Columbine High School were willing to risk "taking a bullet" to save the teenagers inside the building. They must have been held back by their superiors. Their superiors, in turn, must have suffered from a bureaucratic viewpoint that put the safety of adults ahead of rescuing the children.

A Better Scenario

Only July 29, 1999, forty-four-year-old Mark O. Barton entered two brokerage and investment firms in a glitzy, wealthy business district on the edge of Atlanta and killed nine adults in a hail of bullets from two handguns.[21] Television news coverage that evening showed a markedly different scene from the first hours at Littleton.[22] Instead of a boy hanging from a window bleeding to death while no one came to his rescue, windows were smashed and people inside hurriedly pulled policemen *into* the building. Within minutes, police were running full tilt down the halls yelling at people to take cover while they looked for the unknown assailants. Instead of being marched out of the building with their hands over their heads, occupants were allowed to flee for their lives without regard for the possible escape of the killer.

Other adults besides the police also acted heroically. When John Cobrer heard gunshots from across the street, he ran to the building where the shooting was taking place and began ministering to the wounded inside. When emergency medical technicians arrived in a few minutes, they too immediately entered the danger zone. Instead of throwing John out, they asked him to run back and forth to their trucks for supplies.

Granted, the situation was somewhat different from Columbine High School. There were no bombs going off. No one fired at the first policemen to arrive. But John Cobrer, the emergency medical technicians, and the police who broke into the upper stories through the windows did not know how many gunmen were involved or whether they were still in the building. Newspaper descriptions of the scene describe policemen fearing for their lives and those of the people fleeing the building.[23] Heroic actions were being taken by people who were willing to endanger themselves for their fellow citizens. Even though conditions may have been somewhat more terrifying and confusing at Columbine High School, there was another factor in the school situation that should have overridden all fear of known or unknown dangers: There were *children* inside the school.

Nothing is more potentially glib than Monday morning quarter-backing, especially in regard to such a tragic disaster as Columbine High School. But the events surrounding the high school demand a rethinking, not so much of how the police responded but of how our society continues to *fail* to respond to the needs of our children.

There is no way to know with certainty what would have happened if the SWAT teams had reacted with a different set of priorities at Columbine High School—for example, if they had stormed into the building the way citizens, emergency workers, and police did in Atlanta. Perhaps they would have been criticized if some police, good Samaritans, or students had been injured or killed during a rapid rush into the school. But the scenario might have unfolded with much less loss of life.

The adult Atlanta shooter, Mark O. Barton, apparently stopped firing at the day-trader offices and fled the building when the police began to arrive. Perhaps Eric Harris and Dylan Klebold would have ended their massacre sooner if they had heard the footsteps of police bearing down on them. In the best possible scenario, perhaps one or both would have handed over their guns the way T. J. Solomon did when approached by an assistant principal. Or perhaps one of them would have hesitated long enough to be disarmed, like Michael Carneal or Kip Kinkel.

More certainly, if the police had been more daring at Columbine High School, girls and boys would not have been left to fend for themselves, huddled terrified and in hiding for over four hours. Their parents would not have been forced to wait in helpless dread for even longer hours outside the building.

Widespread Resentment and Hatred

Immediately after the Littleton tragedy, it became apparent that the resentment and hatred that motivated Eric Harris and Dylan Klebold were not limited to them, their school, or their community. Several planned school assaults were discovered and aborted without receiving much national attention.

Within a few days of the assault on Columbine High School on April 20, 1999—and too soon to be copycats—five thirteen-year-olds in an accelerated academic program in a Brooklyn middle school were arrested for conspiring to blow up their school.[24] They had drawn diagrams for constructing bombs and made lists of more than a dozen targeted students and teachers.

Another potential bombing was thwarted a few days after Littleton when four fourteen-year-old eighth-graders were arrested in Wimberley, Texas, for plotting to blow up Danforth Junior High. Students had overheard them talking and reported it to school officials. Searches of the boys' homes turned up "several explosive devices, gunpowder, and bomb-making instructions taken off the Internet." Planning for the attack had begun three or four months prior to Littleton.

On April 28, 1999, a high school boy in rural Taber, Alberta, Canada, opened fire with a rifle, killing one student and seriously wounding another at W. R. Myers High School. He reportedly was a frequent target of derision from other students.[25]

On May 4, 1999, four teenagers fifteen to sixteen years old were arrested before they could attack Adams City High School near Denver.[26] The students had detailed written plans and drawings, a map of the school, and planned an assault with guns on May 7.[27] Shortly after this, a fifteen-year-old boy from Kennedy High School in Denver was arrested after telling friends that he planned to handcuff and kill a number of students and teachers.[28]

In mid-May 1999, in suburban Port Huron, Michigan, four boys between twelve and fourteen years of age were arrested for concocting a plot to outdo the catastrophe at Columbine High School. They stole a building plan from the custodian's office of Holland Woods Middle School, drew up a list of 154 targets for rape and murder, and planned to use a gun belonging to one of their parents to hold up a gun store for additional weaponry. They were caught after a classmate reported them to the assistant principal.[29] In what may have been a separate incident, hours after the last child was in custody, a bomb was found and defused outside the school.[30]

Nearly all of these boys were discovered when classmates reported threats made by the students. We are left to wonder whether these threats would have been taken seriously and reported by students prior to Littleton.

After the Columbine High School assault, a deluge of copycat threats followed throughout the nation. A Gallup Poll indicated that more than one third of students had heard of copycat threats at their own schools and that 20 percent had undergone school evacuation.[31] In the Washington, D.C., area there were multiple school evacuations, often several over a few days at the same school. Around the country, students were arrested for planning assaults on their schools with bombs and guns, and innumerable others were arrested for making threats. The media began to ask whether its coverage was encouraging copycat crimes.

Then, on May 20, exactly one month after the Columbine High School tragedy, a fifteen-year-old sophomore fired on his classmates at Heritage High, a highly regarded public school in Conyers, Georgia, on the outskirts of Atlanta. T. J. Solomon entered the school carrying a pistol and a .22-calibre rifle. Intentionally aiming too low to kill, he fired the pump-action rifle until he had wounded six students.

Turning Schools into Prisons: The Limits of the "Law and Order" Response

Schools around the country responded in many different ways to the Littleton and Conyers tragedies. Some took to heart the need for increased communication among the students, teachers, and administrators. Others turned to more simplified responses, often involving more intense policing of the children. Though increasing security is an understandable knee-jerk reaction, it probably fueled the fear and anxiety in and around schools. Armed guards, metal detectors, searches of student lockers, locked doors, passes, surveillance cameras, and stricter dress codes imposed further humiliating restrictions on students, making them feel more like prisoners than students.[32] It is an unfortunate irony that prison is the prototypical institution where alienation and outrage are enforced, and where violence is learned and promoted.

Offhand remarks that would have been ignored before the Columbine shootings now became the subject of FBI investigations, suspensions, and criminal indictments. Teachers untrained to act like security personnel found themselves assigned to the task of monitoring the student body for signs of danger.

In a Ponchatoula, Louisiana, Catholic school, twelve-year-old Michael was tapping on the chair of the girl in front of him to annoy her when she turned around and slapped him.[33] Later he got irritated with some boys ahead of him in a cafeteria line and told them to hurry up or "I'm going to get you." When the principal began asking questions about Michael, other students said that earlier in the year he had made threats to bring a gun or knife to school. Within a week, Michael was locked up in juvenile detention for making "terroristic threats," and there he was still languishing two weeks later.

Mad Monday in the Schools

In Montgomery County, Maryland, where I live, rumors spread that "something was going to happen" on Monday, May 10, 1999, less than one month after the Columbine tragedy. At Sherwood High School, the principal, assistant principal, and three parent volunteers worked all day Sunday and Sunday night checking every locker, every door, and every suspicious corner in the 1,700-student school.

Throughout Montgomery County, police occupied school buildings, bomb squads went on alert, and in some schools nearly half the student body stayed home. One pupil came accompanied by her father. When school was out later in the day, my wife and I chanced to meet members of the "hazardous materials" team in a local pizza parlor. They were remarkably relaxed; the day, to their surprise, had been entirely uneventful. Mad Monday had fizzled—but not before disrupting the school system and throwing countless parents and children into a panic.

The fear struck most dramatically in the largely white suburbs of Maryland and Northern Virginia, where schools became eerily empty. In the District of Columbia—where violence is a daily risk—Mad Monday had no effect on attendance at all.

Clearly, the fear of violence that has cast a shadow over our inner cities for so many years had spread outward into the suburbs. Parents throughout the country realized that even in affluent communities they could not guarantee the safety of their children. A father in my psychiatric practice felt overwhelmed by his inability to protect his two young children in the future, when they entered school. It added to his already depressed state of mind.

There are adults who would do almost anything, including risking their lives, in order to protect or rescue children from the violence and despair that engulfs so many of them. While individual adults can do a great deal for individual children, the overall problems faced by our children cannot be resolved by parents, teachers, or other people acting on their own. The problems lie within our institutions, which increasingly serve adults, often to the detriment or exclusion of children.

Reclaiming Our Children is about changing that attitude—about doing what it takes to make this a better society for our children. To offer our children what they need, we will have to change our attitudes and our priorities. We will need to shift our viewpoint from one that is adult-centered to one that is child-centered. Instead of focusing on how to "fix" our children, *we will have to transform ourselves.*

The changes must take place simultaneously on a national policy and at a personal level. For the sake of our children, we must find new solutions to society-wide crises involving poverty, racism, sexism, and violence, as well as pedism itself—prejudice against children. We must, on this national level, address the reform of our families, schools, churches, police, and other community institutions. Yet solutions on this level will come slowly—while the alienation and suffering of our children require an immediate response. We must begin immediately as individuals to transform our personal relationships with the children in our lives by making them a higher priority and especially by creating meaningful relationships with them. When we practice and experience the kind of meaningful relationships that children really need from us, we will also become more able to guide our communities toward creating a more child-friendly society.

2

Psychiatry and the Government React to Our Children's Violence

---

Should the threat of violence lead the nation to turn its schools into mental hospitals—or are there better approaches to helping troubled and even dangerous young people? A few years ago, this question might have seemed absurd. In mid–1999 it became more than a question; it became a plan. With 5 million or 6 million children already taking psychiatric drugs, the President of the United States implemented plans to spread an even larger psychiatric net over the nation's schools with the aim of drugging increased numbers of pupils.

Showcasing the President's Mental Health Plan

On June 7, 1999, the first-ever White House Conference on Mental Health was convened in Washington, D.C., and was broadcast via the Internet to an estimated six thousand additional conference locations. It featured an astonishing lineup of top Democratic leaders: President Bill Clinton and First Lady Hillary Clinton, and Vice President Al Gore and his wife, Tipper.

This was a major event for the President of the United States. In January 1999 he had announced in his State of the Union address that Tipper Gore would chair the conference. He also appointed her his mental health policy adviser.[1] The Saturday before the conference, President Clinton and Mrs. Gore used the President's weekly radio address to promote the conference and its central theme that mental distress and emotional disorders are physical diseases of the brain that are best treated with drugs.[2] Mrs. Gore estimated that "more than one in five Americans experience some form of mental illness every year, from depression to schizophrenia." She called "mental illness" a "physical disease" and added, "Many mental disorders are biological in nature and can be medically treated." She underscored "new drugs," along with community health services, as mainstay treatments.

The White House Conference also featured the director of the National Institute of Mental Health (NIMH), the psychiatrist Steven Hyman, and other health officials and professionals, as well as Mike Wallace of *60 Minutes*. The President used the conference to announce a nationwide plan for psychiatric intrusions of unprecedented proportions into our schools and communities.

The Columbine High School tragedy and the problems facing our children were repeatedly mentioned by speakers at the conference to underscore the need for increased expenditures for psychiatry and "mental health." Depression, suicide, and violence were repeatedly mentioned as increasing afflictions among our children.

The conference had been orchestrated as a public relations event for biological psychiatry and especially for the use of psychiatric drugs to treat all the emotional and behavioral problems of our children—in effect, all of their individual suffering and all of their conflicts with adults.

One month earlier, Tipper Gore had "come out" as someone whose "clinical depression" in 1989 had been helped by antidepressant drugs.[3] Mike Wallace was also featured as someone who has been long depressed and believes he must take antidepressants for the rest of his life. In fact, the conference presented a stream of people who claimed that psychiatric drugs had helped them or their children.[4]

Another theme that emerged—one closely related to this celebration of psychiatric drugs—was that as parents and interested adults, we have nothing whatsoever to do with our children's suffering. We do not contribute to or cause *any* of their more serious emotional, psychological, or social difficulties—and there's little we can do about our children, except to hand them over to the experts for psychiatric diagnosis and drugging.

The President's Plan Ignores Reality

This renewed emphasis on psychiatrically identifying and treating children came at an odd moment. The speakers had to ignore the reality that youngsters in the two most recent shootings were known to be receiving "mental health care" and psychiatric drugs apparently to no avail.

Eric Harris was taking the Prozac-like drug, Luvox, and T. J. Solomon, who fired on his fellow students at Heritage High School in Conyers, Georgia, was taking the stimulant drug Ritalin, supposedly for depression. Furthermore, Kip Kinkel, a boy who killed his parents and opened fire at his Oregon school on May 21, 1998, had been receiving psychiatric treatment that probably included his taking Prozac sometime in the past and Ritalin at the time of the shooting.[5]

It has also been reported in the press that Mitchell Johnson, thirteen, and Andrew Golden, eleven, may have been taking psychiatric drugs at the time they opened fire on their classmates at Westside Middle School in Jonesboro, Arkansas, in 1998. When asked to confirm the story, their attorney responded, "I think that is confidential information, and I don't want to reveal that."[6]

In a less publicized incident on April 16, 1999, four days before the Columbine tragedy, Shawn Cooper, a fifteen-year-old sophomore at Notus Junior-Senior High School in Notus, Idaho, "fired two shotguns rounds, narrowly missing students and school staff."[7] He was taking Ritalin at the time.

Programs to Save Our Youth

Mrs. Gore, who has no professional qualifications in this field, offered a program for improving the psychiatric well-being of America's children. As the President's mental health policy adviser, she planned to provide "parents and teachers and child care providers and social service workers . . . with education programs about the mental health needs of young children, so that they will intervene." Later in the day, President Clinton would elaborate on these plans.

Mrs. Gore spoke knowingly about "the Decade of the Brain"—a phrase whose acceptance was a public relations coup by adherents of biopsychiatry and the drug companies. As a result of congressional lobbying by these powerful interests, the U.S. Congress mandated the 1990s to be the Decade of the Brain. Notice that the 1990s were not the decade of soul or even of the mind, but of the *brain* as the seat of our psychological, social, and spiritual crisis in America.

In reality, the Decade of the Brain theme epitomizes the problem in America: materialism. Not just materialism in the ordinary sense of a preoccupation with owning wealth and valuable physical objects. The Decade of the Brain is actually a time of moral and philosophical materialism, for psychiatry has convinced a great portion of the public that psychosocial and spiritual suffering has no psychological or spiritual meaning whatsoever but emanates instead from abnormalities in the physiology of the brain.

That concept that people suffer from brain diseases rather than from psychological, social, or spiritual problems was arguably the central theme of the White House conference. A special press release entitled "Myths and Facts About Mental Illness" declared in its first sentence, "Research in the last decade proves that mental illnesses are diagnosable disorders of the brain."[8] The statement is scientifically false: No so-called mental disorder such as depression, anxiety, schizophrenia, or attention deficit/hyperactivity disorder has been proved to be a brain disorder.[9]

The psychiatric/drug company public relations campaign has been so successful that many people, including otherwise devoted and sensitive mothers like Mrs. Clinton and Mrs. Gore, have failed to appreciate the inherent destructiveness of attributing all personal suffering and misconduct to genetics and brain disease. Biological psychiatry disempowers parents while sapping family life of meaning. It reduces our own suffering and misconduct, and that of our loved ones, to mechanical breakdowns in brain chemistry.

Mrs. Gore was impressed with the idea that mental health can be understood through "mapping the architecture of the human brain." Mental suffering, she declared, is "treatable as a disease of a bodily [*sic*] part, namely the brain." The number of people with these diseases, according to Mrs. Gore's estimate, is astronomical: "Fifty-one million Americans will experience a mental issue at some point in their life." Her speech was a public relations blockbuster for biological psychiatry and drugs—and a disaster for America's children.

The Beleaguered Brains of the Children

The psychiatrist Steven Hyman, director of the National Institute of Mental Health (NIMH), informed the conference that "two million children" have depression. What causes it? He said not a word about divorce, absentee fathers, child abuse, peer humiliation, broken love relationships, academic pressure, alienation from school and church, drug and alcohol abuse, and countless other life circumstances that contribute to and cause depression in children and youths. Instead, he claimed that psychiatric disorders are "incredibly genetic" in origin—a speculation lacking scientific confirmation. He showed photographs of brain scans that awed the audience with their seemingly scientific sophistication—without explaining that they prove nothing about the origin of emotional distress.[10] In touting biological psychiatry, Dr. Hyman claimed that our children suffer from "real diseases of a real organ—the brain" that should be treated "like general medical illnesses," meaning with drugs.[11]

Following Dr. Hyman's speech, Mrs. Clinton announced that NIMH was launching new clinical drug trials costing $61 million. The official newspaper of the American Psychiatric Association has reported that some of the studies would focus exclusively on children.[12] In the past, the cost of demonstrating the effectiveness of psychiatric drugs has been borne by the pharmaceutical industry. The new NIMH initiative confirms the administration's determination to help the drug companies expand their market among children and adults.[13]

The Doctor Who Believes That Child Abuse Doesn't Hurt

Mrs. Clinton introduced the child psychiatrist star of the show, Dr. Harold Koplewicz.[14] Because of the prominent role he plays in the administration's health and educational policies, it is important to document his views. His attitudes also epitomize the thinking of the biopsychiatric establishment that has been pushing drugs on America's children.

Dr. Koplewicz exemplifies the new breed of biological psychiatrists who have won over politicians like the Clintons and Gores with slick explanations and solutions. He popularized the biopsychiatric slogan "no-fault brain disease"—meaning that emotional suffering in children has nothing to do with abuses or mistakes committed by the adults in their lives. Instead, the suffering of children, like a tumor or a stroke, emanates from their diseased brains rather than from any environmental condition or occurrence in the child's life.

In the June 17, 1999, issue of the on-line magazine *Salon*, the Internet feature writer Rob Waters reported an interview with Dr. Koplewicz in which the doctor described himself as recommending medication in the first five minutes with a child. "There are five or six million kids who could potentially benefit from [Prozac-like drugs]," Dr. Koplewicz told Waters, and added, "I actually think we're not medicating kids enough."

In his *Salon* interview, Dr. Koplewicz also raised dire threats about the dangers of not medicating children, including the specter of suicide in children not treated with antidepressants. In reality, there is no significant evidence that antidepressants are in any way helpful to children, and they are not FDA-approved for children.[15]

In his book *It's Nobody's Fault*, Dr. Koplewicz made outrageous claims without citing any scientific sources. In a bold new stroke of proof by proclamation, his book contained no scientific citations to back up any of his assertions. For example, without offering a shred of supportive evidence, he stated that "depression is the most common brain disorder in America. . . . One survey found that 19% of all adolescents had experienced an episode." He compared these "brain diseases" in children to "a full-blown infection."[16]

Dr. Koplewicz is so devoted to the biological and genetic model that he entitled a section of his book "Bad Seed."[17] He noted that the concept of a "bad seed" sounded like "the stuff of fiction. . . . But it can also be a fact, if a child has conduct disorder." These children "seem too bad to be true."

Ultimately, Dr. Koplewicz argued that all troubled or troublesome children are the product of defective genes. For example, again without citing a single scientific source he made yet another false claim, that "a gene for Attention Deficit Hyperactivity Disorder has been identified."[18]

The back cover of Dr. Koplewicz's unabashedly pro-drug book contained a twenty-six-page chart of psychiatric medications, including their adverse effects. Despite the comprehensive appearance of the chart, however, he left out many of the most common, and most serious, drug-induced adverse effects that parents need to know about in order to make informed treatment decisions on behalf of their children.[19]

Dr. Koplewicz was given a special award by the National Alliance for the Mentally Ill (NAMI), a very aggressive drug company-funded organization of parents who advocate drugs, electroshock, and even lobotomy—and especially *forced* treatment—for their own adult children.[20] The NAMI leadership, made up almost entirely of parents of profoundly disturbed children and adults, has consistently applauded physicians like Dr. Koplewicz. The doctors in turn have exonerated these parents of any role in or responsibility for causing—or for healing—their children's serious emotional problems.

Mrs. Clinton described Dr. Koplewicz as a man who brought to bear "extraordinary talent and experience on behalf of children as a child psychiatrist." The doctor's opening statement captured the thrust of the White House Conference on Mental Health and its attitude toward the suffering of our children:

> It is hard to believe that until 20 years ago we still believed that inadequate parenting and bad childhood trauma were the cause of psychiatric illnesses. And in fact, even though we know better today, that antiquated way of thinking is out there, so that people who wouldn't dream of blaming parents for other types of diseases, like their child's diabetes or asthma, still embrace the notion that somehow absent fathers, working mothers, over-permissive parents are the cause of psychiatric illness in children. . . . And as Dr. Hyman pointed out, these diseases are physiological, they respond to medicine.

In Dr. Koplewicz's opinion, "absent fathers, working mothers, over-permissive parents" no longer have to face their responsibilities and go through the often painful process of reevaluating their priorities in order to pay more focused and beneficial attention to their children. No longer do we have to be overly concerned about children exposed to "trauma." Even traumatic events, in Dr. Koplewicz's opinion, cannot by themselves cause anxiety, depression, posttraumatic stress disorder, or other "psychiatric disorders" in children.[21]

It was extraordinary for me, as both a parent and a psychiatrist, to hear a colleague claim that an "absent father" played no role in a child's developing serious emotional problems and that even "bad childhood trauma"—including severe physical and sexual abuse—could not cause mental disorders. Have we, as generations of parents, been wasting our time relating to and protecting our children?

I was also shocked that anyone in the mental health field would dare to deny the mountain of clinical and research evidence that confirms the devastating effect of broken relationships and traumatic events on the lives of children. In fact, there is inescapable evidence that trauma, abuse, neglect, and loss of relationship cause severe emotional disturbances that can last a lifetime, especially when inflicted upon children and young people.[22]

Many clinical and epidemiological studies confirm the connection between childhood emotional, physical, and sexual trauma and later adult emotional disturbances. As an example, in a Los Angeles survey of 3,132 men and women, conducted on a scientific basis, 447 reported enduring sexual abuse in the form of forced or pressured sexual contact before the age of sixteen.[23] The victims of sexual abuse suffered from greatly increased rates of adulthood drug and alcohol abuse, mood problems and major depressive disorder, anxiety disorders, phobias, and panic disorder. The men also suffered from increased rates of antisocial behavior. Overall, these disorders were two to ten times more prevalent in adults who reported childhood sexual abuse than in those who did not. Those who reported abuse also suffered from increased levels of anxiety, guilt, anger, and sexual dysfunctions. Once again, this is but one of many studies linking a variety of childhood traumas and stressors to adult emotional problems and disorders.

As Bloom and Reichert observe, "Children are especially prone to post-traumatic stress because they are helpless in most situations."[24] But this knowledge about the vulnerability of children requires us to examine our families, schools, and communities. It provides no easy solutions. And it will not encourage the support of private philanthropic organizations, who commonly receive huge donations from the pharmaceutical industry. Nor will a focus on childhood trauma and stress motivate federal agencies to fund research. Government sponsors prefer to fund more simple-minded, quick-fix approaches.

In claiming that our children are genetically brain-injured, Dr. Koplewicz and Dr. Hyman were not restricting their remarks to a limited number of seriously disturbed children. The conference brochure contained the estimate that there are 13.7 million children with diagnosable mental illnesses. Dr. Koplewicz himself estimated that "12 percent of the population under age 18—that's about 8 million children, teenagers, in the United States today—have a diagnosable psychiatric illness. And that means that about 2 million children have depression." Eight million children and teenagers! That's a lot of genetically induced brain disease—and, of course, a lot of potential business for drug companies and psychiatry.

Children go through enormous stress growing up in the modern world, so it's easy to inflate figures about how many suffer from psychiatric disorders. Probably the great majority of adolescents undergo sufficient suffering that most clinicians, if given the chance, would assign to them a psychiatric diagnosis. But why attach a psychiatric label to their suffering, except to promote psychiatric treatment? The large estimates made at the White House Conference were aimed at promoting organized psychiatry by demonstrating the need for wide-scale biopsychiatric interventions. The extent of the planned interventions became clear when the President spoke at the end of the keynote presentations.

Dr. Koplewicz specifically attributed the violence in Littleton to mental illness in the shooters: "Normal children just don't snap and go out on a shooting spree." His solution? Prevention through early identification and psychiatric treatment. But like the other speakers, he again failed to mention that Eric Harris, T. J. Solomon, and other school shooters were already taking psychiatric drugs at the time they "snapped." He rejected the idea that the increasing violence displayed by children might reflect the conditions of their lives at home and at school as well as a larger social problem requiring national attention.

Whether They Like It or Not

During Dr. Koplewicz's presentation, Mrs. Clinton interjected a brief comment with "the tragedy at Littleton in mind." She voiced an ominous intention to *force* psychiatry on young people. The goal, she said, must be to "identify and get help to children who need it, *whether or not they want it or are willing to accept it.*"[25]

Forced treatment can, of course, be a moot point with small children who are in no position to make up their own minds about the value of medical interventions, such as surgery or vaccination. But for older children, including many preadolescents and all teenagers, respect for their autonomy and decisionmaking is an extremely important component of any proposed psychological or psychiatric help.

The theme of forced treatment was emphasized in the press briefing for the conference, which announced federal aid through Medicaid for Assertive Community Treatment, called ACT.[26] This highly controversial program is based on involuntary outpatient treatment. It promotes forced medication and the threat of hospitalization to control the daily lives of people labeled mentally ill. If an individual gets up late for work, has conflicts with a parent or spouse, or otherwise seems to the ACT personnel to be doing poorly, the ACT program can force the person to take medication. The drug enforcers literally come to the door of the citizen's home to make the individual submit to a long-acting (several weeks or more) injection of mentally paralyzing and neurologically damaging "antipsychotic" medication.[27] The Clinton White House was advocating one of the most serious threats to individual freedom in contemporary American society.

ACT has never been proven effective.[28] There is, in addition, no evidence that forced treatment in general is helpful to people. Besides, to force thousands and even millions of teenagers into psychiatric treatment against their will would not only be unethical, wrongheaded, and useless, it would further humiliate and alienate them.

Mrs. Clinton argued that forced treatment would help to prevent "school shootings." Again she seemed to conveniently forget that many of the shooters were already getting psychiatric treatment and drugs. After her comment, Dr. Koplewicz resumed with his remark that about 8 million children and teenagers have a "diagnosable psychiatric illness." That's a lot of people to treat whether they like it or not.

Who Creates the Stigma?

Destigmatization was a theme at the White House Conference. Interest groups that favor biopsychiatric diagnoses and drugs want to "destigmatize mental illness" in order to encourage more Americans to take psychiatric drugs. If people become more willing to see themselves as "mentally ill" and as suffering from "brain diseases," they will also be more accepting of drug treatment. Not surprisingly, the destigmatization campaign is funded by the drug companies. But who in fact creates the original stigma? The stigma is created and enforced by organized psychiatry and those drug companies that connect emotional suffering to psychiatric diagnoses and brain diseases.

Nothing is more stigmatizing than carrying the label of "mental illness" for the rest of your life. It is especially unfair and demoralizing to tell children that they suffer from "brain diseases," "biochemical imbalances" or "crossed wires" when they simply don't.[29]

To the extent that individuals believe they have "mental disorders" or "brain diseases" that are causing their emotional suffering, they become dependent on experts rather than upon themselves for the "cure." They are further stigmatized by being told they need to take psychoactive (mind-altering) drugs to "make them normal." The process of psychiatric diagnosing and treatment often actually magnifies the patient's feelings of helplessness and futility rather than empowering the patient to personally overcome them.

Psychiatric stigmatization can destroy career opportunities. For example, five days prior to his assault on Columbine High, Eric Harris was rejected from the Marines because of events surrounding his psychiatric treatment. He had not mentioned his use of Luvox on his application but his parents informed representatives of the Marines during a visit to the Harris home.

The *Denver Post* was told by a spokesperson for the Marine Corps that the service had discovered from Harris's parents that he "had a medical disqualification" and that the family was "informed Eric was not eligible for enlistment in the Marines."[30] The articles stated that the Marines would not disclose the nature of the medical disqualification, which presumably could have been either a mental disorder or treatment with psychiatric drugs, or both. According to a *New York Times* report, "Friends said that Eric was crushed by the news, and had been growing increasingly depressed as graduation neared."[31]

Millions of children will be automatically rejected from military service in the future because the Department of Defense has an official policy of turning away all recruits who have taken Ritalin or other similar drugs after the age of twelve.[32] Parents are rarely if ever in-

formed in advance by their doctors about this potential adverse effect
from their children's taking drugs like Ritalin, Dexedrine, and Adderall for behavior control.

The Department of Defense policy also disallows anyone who has
a history of problems with academic skills caused by "mental disorders" if they "interfere with work or school after age 12."[33] By taking
diagnoses of psychiatric problems more seriously than they deserve,
the Department of Defense could end up excluding from military service millions of children diagnosed with attention deficit/hyperactiv-
ity disorder (ADHD) and learning disorders, as well as every other
psychiatric diagnosis, regardless of whether these children have taken
psychiatric drugs.

Psychiatric diagnosis and treatment creates stigma. If, instead, people view themselves as suffering from traumatic experiences, family
conflicts, psychological and spiritual crises, or alienation, they are not
as likely to feel stigmatized. They instead have the opportunity to
overcome these obstacles in their lives through counseling or therapy,[34] improved principles of living, religion, and all the other methods of personal empowerment that are available in the community.

In my own practice, I focus on each person's life story rather than
on prefab diagnoses. As individuals and families unfold an understanding of themselves through the therapy and through their personal efforts, they have no use for a cookie-cutter diagnoses. Instead,
they have written their own autobiography with a self-understanding
of their problems and how to overcome them. Children in particular
begin to do much better as soon as their parents improve their parenting approach.

President Clinton Announces a Dangerous New Policy

President Clinton made the final presentation at the White House
Conference and concluded his speech with a proposal of giant proportions. He introduced the grand scheme by reemphasizing the
claim that "one out of every ten children suffers from some form of
mental illness, from mild depression to serious mental disease. But,"
he said, "fewer than twenty percent receive proper treatment." He
reaffirmed that "the tragedy at Columbine High School, as Hillary
said, was for all of us a wake-up call. We simply cannot wait until
tragedy strikes to reach out to troubled young people."

What was his policy response to the wake-up call? "Today," the President declared, "I'm pleased to announce a new national school safety training program for teachers, schools, and communities, to help us identify troubled children, and provide them better school mental health services."[35]

The first "training session" was planned for a much-publicized kick-off by Vice President Gore and his wife, Tipper, in the fall of 1999, with satellite transmission to more than one thousand schools and communities around the nation. The blueprint aimed at eventually involving "every school district in America."

At first glance, Clinton's proposal might have sounded innocent, benign, and even benevolent—a nationwide training program directed at the schools to help teachers identify children in need of mental health interventions. But in a nation where millions of children are already being aggressively identified by the schools for medical evaluation and drugs, and in which children line up daily to get psychiatric drugs from school nurses, this program sounded like much more of the same.

Many schools already pressure parents to give medications, often under the threat of having their children sent to special classes, and sometimes with the threat of calling in child protective services. The President's program, with Hillary's emphasis on involuntary treatment, raised the specter of the increasing coercion of our children and families.

At least one community already has a closed-circuit television program similar to the one proposed by the Clintons for instructing teachers in how to identify problem children for referral into the mental health system. The program was created by a psychiatric clinic that would benefit from the referrals. To promote itself, the clinic has climbed on the violence prevention bandwagon, claiming that its kind of service could prevent school shootings.[36]

Instead of being a boon to the children it claims to help, Clinton's proposal is a thinly disguised bonanza for biopsychiatry and individual practitioners from many branches of the health profession. Innumerable professionals would be required to provide educational programs, diagnostic procedures, and treatment. The Clinton program would also make it easier and more acceptable for schools to control their classrooms by winnowing out for control even larger numbers of children for medical evaluation and treatment. Finally, it would bestow another financial windfall on the already prosperous pharmaceutical industry.

Touted as the "first-ever" White House conference on mental health, the Clinton-Gore spectacle became the first-ever orchestrated public relations and marketing campaign by the nation's political leadership for the further spread of involuntary biopsychiatric drugging in our schools and communities.

But what about the well-being of our children, families, schools, and society? Increased pharmacological social control is no substitute for identifying and meeting the genuine needs of our children.

Lessons from an Earlier Violence Initiative

Despite all the partisan Democratic fanfare surrounding the White House Conference on Mental Health, biological psychiatry's aims are wholly nonpartisan. In 1992, a very similar proposal for a youth violence prevention initiative—the so-called Violence Initiative—was developed under the administration of President George Bush.[37] It, too, located the cause of violence in genetics and brain disease rather than the environment of the children, and proposed using the schools to identify children at risk.

However, the Bush proposal focused specifically on predominantly black inner-city children. Research would seek a genetic component for violence, the so-called "violence gene," as well as biochemical abnormalities, using intrusive research involving spinal taps and brain scans.

Starting in 1992, my wife, Ginger, and I organized a national effort to resist the Bush Violence Initiative program. As described in *The War Against Children of Color*,[38] we mobilized the International Center for the Study of Psychiatry and Psychology to bring the dangers of the violence initiative to the attention of Congress, the media, concerned professionals, and the public. As a result of this successful campaign, its main proponent, the psychiatrist Frederick Goodwin, the director of the National Institute of Mental Health (NIMH), resigned from the his lifelong career in the government.

In describing the necessity of the Bush Violence Initiative to a government-sponsored meeting of leaders in mental health, Dr. Goodwin had strung together a series of racist metaphors, comparing inner-city children to monkeys living in a jungle who just wanted to kill each other, have sex, and reproduce:[39]

Somebody gave me some data recently that puts this in a perspective and I say this with the realization that it might be easily misunderstood, and that is, if you look at other primates in nature—male primates in nature—you find that even with our violent society we are doing very well.

If you look, for example, at male monkeys, especially in the wild, roughly half of them survive to adulthood. The other half die by violence. That is the natural way of it for males, to knock each other off and, in fact, there are some interesting evolutionary implications of that because the same hyperaggressive monkeys who kill each other are also hypersexual, so they copulate more and therefore they reproduce more to offset the fact that half of them are dying.

Now, one could say that if some of the loss of structure in this society, and particularly in the high-impact inner-city areas, has removed some of the civilizing evolutionary things that we have built up and that maybe it isn't just careless use of the word when people call certain areas of certain cities jungles, that we may have gone back to what might be more natural, without all of the social controls that we have imposed upon ourselves as a civilization over thousands of years in our own evolution.

African American youngsters compared to monkeys living in a jungle? Going backward in evolution? Being hypersexual? Killing each other? Reproducing at a rapid rate? When a black government employee blew the whistle on this dismal appeal to racism, we learned about it on the news. If Goodwin hadn't made racist remarks in support of his proposals, we might never have heard about his plan or been able to mobilize the public against it. The focus on inner-city children and Goodwin's offensive comments enabled us to build an effective coalition with African Americans in Congress, the media, the professions, and the public.

Although Clinton's plan will also threaten inner-city children, it is mainly aimed at preventing violence perpetrated by mainstream white schoolchildren. Because Clinton's program encompasses most of America's schools, the African American community may not feel as motivated to organize against it. Meanwhile, little opposition can be anticipated from middle-class white parents and their political representatives, who as a group have proved all to willing to go along with the psychiatric diagnosing and drugging of millions of white children. Therefore, we fear that the Clinton plan, in the absence of an effective opposition, will further escalate the use of psychiatric drugs for the control and suppression of the nation's children.

Clinton's Vastly Expanded Plan

President Clinton's proposal resurrected the central theme of the earlier Bush initiative: to obtain congressional funding for a multiagency initiative to use schools for the early identification and treatment of children at risk for violence. However, the Clinton version—with its initial pilot program to train one thousand schools by satellite communications—was far more ambitious than anything proposed in earlier years.

Exactly like the Bush version, the Clinton program involves the collaboration of the Departments of Education, Justice, and Health and Human Services. This combination of the Department of Justice, the nation's top law enforcement agency, with health and educational agencies will prove as menacing now as it has in the past, in the Bush violence initiative. Now, as then, it lets social control masquerade as a "public health measure."

If the Justice Department by itself were to declare that it wanted to go into the schools to identify and to drug millions of children into docility and conformity, it would raise a storm of protest about "police-state tactics" across the nation. But when the President announces the same plan as a health measure, it causes not a ripple of criticism.

On the day of the White House Conference, Donna E. Shalala, the secretary of the Department of Health and Human Services (DHHS), announced a new shared effort with the Departments of Justice and Education to make schools safer.[40] Under the new program, $180 million per year would be awarded to "school districts in partnership with local mental health and law enforcement authorities" to promote child development and to "prevent violent behaviors."

President Clinton's proposal did not announce a research component aimed at proving the assertions made by the speakers about the genetic and biological basis of violence and other expressions of suffering among children. This kind of intrusive, dangerous, and speculative research on children had been scientifically and ethically discredited during the controversy surrounding the Bush proposals. However, individual federally funded projects continue to exist and to arouse public controversy. Almost surely, genetic and biological research on children will become a part of the Clinton plan as it gains in momentum and boldness.

Can the Clinton Initiative Be Defeated?

With the current program directed at *all* of America's children, and with mainstream America already accustomed to drugging millions of its children, Clinton's proposed escalation of the psychiatric diagnosing of children seems more likely to succeed than the failed Bush violence initiative, which was vigorously opposed by many African Americans. As already described, mainstream America is less skeptical about the scientific and medical establishment than the minority community, and is far more willing to drug its children than is black America.

Biopsychiatry has been persistent and nonpartisan in its efforts, first convincing one president and then another to develop broad programs for subduing our children's "violence" with psychiatric drugs. Tipper Gore has announced her intention to bring a biopsychiatric thrust to the White House if her husband becomes president, and there's no guarantee that the son of George Bush, should he win the presidency, would be wiser than his father in this regard.

The Futility of Efforts to Identify Individual Children at Risk

At the heart of both the Clinton and Bush proposals, and of biopsychiatry's claim to help children and society as a whole, lies the concept of identifying "children at risk," especially children who are likely to commit violence. But do we need improved techniques for identifying individual children at risk to commit violence, or do we need instead to take more seriously the distress—including anger and hate—displayed by so many millions of our children?

Eric Harris and Dylan Klebold, the Columbine High School shooters, gave innumerable signals of their emotional turmoil and violent intentions. These signals resulted in many missed opportunities to respond to the boys on the part of significant adults in their lives, including professionals in their school, in the criminal justice system, and in mental health services, and probably in their families as well. These repeated missed opportunities say more about the inability of their whole community to respond than about the failings of particular individuals. They exemplify the failure of our society to identify and to meet the needs of all of its children and young people.

In 1998 Randall and Judy Brown, parents of the Columbine student Brooks Brown, informed the sheriff's department that Harris was threatening on his Website to kill their son. They downloaded Harris's Web page and gave the sheriff ten pages of ranting that included "I don't care if I live or die in the shootout, all I want to do is kill and injure as many of you p—— as I can, especially a few people like Brooks Brown." Harris wrote that people he respected would not be "in my line of fire," but "For the rest of you, you all better f—— hide in your houses because I'm comin for EVERYONE soon, and I WILL be armed to the f—— teeth and I WILL shoot to kill and I WILL f—— KILL EVERYTHING."[41] Other passages read, "I live in Denver and god damnit I would like to kill almost all of its residents. . . . I am the law, and if you don't like it, you die. If I don't like you or I don't like what you want me to do, you die. . . . I'll just go to some downtown area in some big ass city and blow up and shoot everything I can. Feel no remorse, no sense of shame."[42]

At a parent-teacher meeting one month before the assault, Dylan Klebold's mother was told about a violent story he had written that ended in a killing.[43] Dylan dismissed it as just a story. Both boys also made violent videos for one of their classes, but the teacher, while rejecting the films as inappropriate for school projects, took no action to warn anyone.

The two boys came to the attention of the law after they broke into a van, on January 29, 1998, and stole $400 worth of electronic equipment. They were put on probation and entered a Jefferson County "diversion" program.[44] (The judge was unaware that Eric Harris had posted threats against his classmates on the Internet.)[45] Youths who opt for the county diversion program can avoid a trial. They can choose from a variety of educational experiences, including anger management, impulse control, self-esteem development, long-term planning skills, and the opportunity to perform community service. The boys also saw a diversion supervisor twice a month during 1998.[46]

The program has been criticized for failing to identify the boys as violence-prone, but its director, Bobbie Spicer, pointed out that Harris was already receiving mental health care. In fact, he was reported still to be seeing a therapist at the time of the shootings and was taking the psychiatric drug Luvox.[47] In addition to the drug therapy and the diversion program, Eric Harris was also in private counseling sessions that started a year before the incident, around the time he began taking Luvox. The sessions began on a weekly basis and then, according to newspaper reports, became monthly around the time of the assault. His violent actions do not argue for the efficacy of identifying youngsters for "mental health interventions." Spicer also correctly observed, "There is no predictor for lethality."[48, 49]

In an early TV interview, the principal of Columbine High School denied ever hearing anything about boys in trench coats parading around his school. He dismissed the possibility of a "trench coat gang" existing without his knowledge! Was he simply covering up? Or was he so removed from the day-to-day functioning of his school community that he wasn't aware of how they played war games in the school corridors and even made videos of themselves with real weapons?

Whether the principal knew about these ominous activities or not, it is misleading to blame him as an individual. His lack of awareness probably says more about the impossibility of adequately administering a school of 1,900 students than about the principal himself. Our giant schools are no longer communities. Schools are no longer places where teachers and administrators have the opportunity to know and care about their students.

It bears repeating that the Littleton tragedy is about missed opportunities to save the children, perpetrators and victims alike. The opportunities were missed in part because so many children in America give so many signals of distress that it becomes difficult to marshal resources in response to any one particular individual. In addition, it is probable that many of the adults in the lives of these boys were insufficiently bonded with them to have a beneficial impact on their conduct at critical moments. This, too, is a society-wide problem. Perhaps most tragic, the mental health system empowered to identify and to help Eric relied upon an ineffective, harmful biopsychiatric intervention in the form of a psychoactive drug, Luvox.

Other school shooters also gave obvious signals of distress that were also missed. Shortly before he killed his parents and began firing on his classmates at Thurston High School in Springfield, Oregon, Kip Kinkel had been expelled from school for bringing in a loaded pistol. The police were called in but returned the boy to the custody of his parents. Kip was also in psychiatric treatment. He was probably taking Ritalin at the time of the shooting and Prozac sometime earlier.

T.J. Solomon, the Conyers, Georgia, shooter, was receiving Ritalin for depression. T.J. was considered a bit "nerdy." In homeroom he would do school work by himself rather than socialize. He was also subjected to ridicule by older, bigger boys. He may have recently broken up with a girlfriend.[50]

Following the shootings, fellow students said in retrospect that T.J. had threatened to "blow up this classroom" during an argument on the previous day. A friend reported that T.J. had told him shortly before the shooting, "I really don't have any reason to live anymore." His friend later explained, "I mean, a lot of kids say stuff like that any never do anything."

T.J.'s friend was right: We're overloaded with signals that our children are hurting. In a review of sixteen school shooters between 1993 and mid-1999 in the United States, the psychologists James P. McGee, Ph.D., and Caren R. DeBernardo, Psy.D., evaluated many of the characteristics of these young boys, whom they called "classroom avengers."[51] They found that fifteen out of sixteen had "verbalized threats" prior to the incident and had been recently disciplined or rejected. Their signals, including the threats of violence on Eric Harris's Web page, should be viewed as unanswered *cries for help*—cries that went unanswered because we live in a society that has grown deaf to the distress of its children.

The failure to intervene effectively to stop Eric Harris, T.J. Solomon, Kip Kinkel, and the other shooters should not be used to justify greater invasive efforts to identify violence-prone children and label them as mentally ill. Instead, it illustrates society's lack of an effective response to the most obvious signs that a child is troubled and even dangerous. In short, as a society we simply are not paying enough attention to or caring enough about our children.

Furthermore, trying to identify especially disturbed children will do virtually nothing to winnow out school shooters. Drs. McGee and DeBernardo (1999b) found that *none* of the school shooters had a "documented history of severe mental illness." None, in their opinion, were psychotic, and none suffered from "mental retardation, severe learning disability, or organically based brain disorder." Only two had a "documented history of extreme violence or substantial police involvement."[52]

Although McGee and DeBernardo suspect that many of the shooters were suffering from a carefully concealed depressed mood, they emphasized that none of the boys showed or complained about typical signs of depression, such as sadness, crying spells, lack of energy, weight loss, or insomnia.

The report by McGee and DeBernardo may have been written before sufficient information was available about Eric Harris, whose Website and diary portrayed his elaborate, grandiose, vengeful, and profoundly disturbed plans for violent retaliation against large numbers of people.

Also, we have insufficient information to evaluate the mental state of the other shooters, including T.J. Solomon and Kip Kinkel, who were in psychiatric treatment and receiving drugs. Indeed, because laws protect the privacy of juvenile offenders, we cannot be certain about the total number of shooters who were being treated with psychotherapy or drugs.

Nonetheless, the point made by McGee and DeBernardo remains valid. From the available evidence, it appears that most of the shooters did not have a diagnosable psychiatric disorder based on *DSM-IV* criteria. There may have been no way to suspect their violent potential on the basis of a typical clinical evaluations in a mental health professional's office. Furthermore, as illustrated by the mental history of several of the shooters, treatment did not prevent their violent outbursts,[53] and instead could have caused or contributed to them.

Meanwhile, there is no evidence that mental health professionals—or anyone else—can predict violent behavior in a particular individual. In rejecting legal responsibility for predicting violence in patients, the American Psychiatric Association (1976) wrote that "study after study" has shown that violence cannot be predicted in advance. The American Psychiatric Association even denied that "mental health professionals are in some way more qualified than the general public to predict future violence." Although that opinion was written more than twenty years ago, it remains valid today, and contemporary textbooks of psychiatry continue to avoid making any claims for violence prediction. The textbooks advise practitioners to rely on common sense and obvious warning signs, such as repeated violent acts or specific plans for injuring an individual.

Anger was the consistent and obvious emotional state expressed by nearly all of the school shooters, and vengeance was their stated aim; but none of them had a prior history of repeated or injurious violence. Their frequent public expressions of violent intent were, however, glaring warnings about their potential dangerousness, but they were largely ignored.

The challenge isn't to identify the most severely mentally disturbed and overtly violent youngsters; certainly they need and deserve help, but these children are not the perpetrators of mass murder. We need to care enough about *all* children to address their widespread problems—to make this a better society for them. We need to give more attention to all of our children rather than a select few whose potential violence we fear. When we begin to take our children seriously—and to spend more mutually rewarding time with them in all aspects of their lives—they will become less violent before they have to be identified.

The most despairing and violent of our children reflect the underlying disorder of the society: the alienation and abandonment of our children. We must utterly reject the idea that the problem lies in our children's brains or bodies, or that we need to focus on diagnosing individual children. Instead we need to identify the breakdown of relationship with our children in our homes, schools, and community, and then to come together as adults dedicated to making ourselves and our institutions more able to serve the needs of our children.

A Grim Future for Our Children

The nation is already subjecting several million of its children to psychiatric diagnosis and drugging. Schools are already comparable to mental hospitals in which the staff keeps a constant eye out for children who need medication. Even without the President's proposed school training programs, millions of children are being stigmatized with psychiatric diagnoses and exposed to the hazards of toxic agents during their growth years. We end up sweeping them under the drug rug, rather than attending to their individual needs. Our children need to be engaged by caring adults in every aspect of their lives. But instead we have turned to medicating them into silence so that we don't have to deal with their pain.

The Inner City Comes to Littleton

Several years ago, African Americans first began telling me how the neglected, abandoned black child foreshadowed the fate of all of America's children. While white Americans almost universally ignored the violent deterioration of inner-city life, African Americans predicted the inevitability of its spread.[54]

After Littleton, it became more apparent to white people that the inner city had spread to the suburbs. Listen to Superintendent of

Schools Paul L. Vance from my wealthy suburban county of Montgomery Maryland: "School violence hitherto was associated with disadvantaged youth. And now, all of a sudden, we're seeing ghastly behavior in what had been the promised land, among people who fled urban violence, in upper-middle-class families. The best and the brightest. That's new and very frightening."[55]

In some ways, Superintendent Vance was mistaken. African American youths have not been massacring their fellow students in indiscriminate assaults. That seems to be a tragic specialty of white suburban boys and country boys. But suburban youths have been bringing guns to school in increasing numbers much as has been happening in the black urban schools. And like urban schools, suburban schools are beginning to fortify themselves with video cameras and a stepped-up police presence.

There is another, yet more disturbing, way in which the events surrounding Littleton are an extension to the suburbs of what has been going on for years in America's inner cities. Perhaps the most disturbing similarity between Littleton and the inner city lies in the reaction of the adults who came streaming onto the school grounds amid the ongoing shooting. As already suggested, their reaction was to seal off the children while they slaughtered one another. This is a metaphor for how we have been treating our urban poor black children for years. Bureaucratic values of safety and caution, the determination to take care of the adults first, came far ahead of the safety or well-being the children cordoned off in the school.

Meanwhile, our nation is trying to address the problem of youth despair and violence among suburban white boys, but is not simultaneously addressing the problem of our inner-city youth, especially African Americans and Hispanics, who suffer much more terribly than suburban whites from the effects of violence in their lives. The media have focused almost exclusively on violent white adolescent males living in the suburbs, not on "the least among us"—our minority children, poor children, and female children.

In the spring of 1999, perhaps for the first time ever, white suburban children went to school amid a fear of impending violence; but it's worth repeating that generations of America's urban black children have lived with this fear throughout their young lives, often ultimately succumbing to violent death. Many not only feel compelled to carry weapons for their own protection but begin planning their funerals as they enter junior high school.

Remember the old philosophical conundrum, if a tree falls in the forest with no one there to hear it, does it make a sound? While many of us have lived in relative safety in predominantly white, affluent suburbs, children have been screaming in despair and falling prey to violent deaths a scant few miles away in the inner cities. Because we cannot hear them, we make believe they are not falling. Actually, they have been falling with a deafening sound, but we have remained unmoved.

Ignoring the plight of America's poor and minority children, we missed the early warning signs of the impending disaster that has begun to afflict all of our children. If we want to know what's wrong in American society, we can examine what we've allowed to happen in America's inner cities. From the dissolution of the family and the decline of the public schools to the glorification of violence, it's now happening everywhere.

Even if our poor urban black children's succumbing to wretched circumstances did not directly affect us, it would remain inexcusable for us to allow it to happen. A moral irresponsibility of such proportions should be unthinkable. A deadening of empathy of such enormity should be incompatible with considering oneself a human being. Indeed, it is exactly this deadening of empathy and caring that distances us from our own children and from each other.

The Larger Meaning of the School Shootings

The violent school tragedies cannot be understood without regard for the relationships in which the perpetrator boys were enmeshed—or from which they were rejected and ostracized. Eric Harris, Dylan Klebold, T.J. Solomon, and other school shooters are the most extreme expressions of the kind of alienation that afflicts millions of our children. More children identify with them than we would want to admit.

Rage and self-hate were growing problems among America's children before the series of school shootings that began in 1996. Four years earlier, in an editorial in the *Journal of the American Medical Association*, the former surgeon general C. Everett Koop (1992) wrote that violence in America had become a "public health emergency." He noted that one million Americans die prematurely each year from homicide or suicide. The figures for young people were escalating in an ominous fashion: Gunshot wounds had become the leading cause of deaths among both black and white teenagers. Suicide had become the third leading cause of death among children and adolescents. Armed assaults in the California schools were sharply increasing. A survey of Illinois high schools showed that one third of students had brought weapons to school for self-defense.

Homicidal and suicidal violence are the extreme expressions of outrage, self-hate, and fear that afflict a much broader range of young people. Although only relatively few of our children become openly violent, many more feel humiliated, frustrated, lonely, frightened, and angry. Too often we send these young people to psychiatrists and other specialists, or into the juvenile or criminal justice systems, where they are treated as if the problem lies in them instead of us and our society.

Questioning Facile Solutions

The White House Conference on Mental Health, ostensibly concerned about violence, depression, and anxiety among our children, handed them over en masse to the psychiatrists for diagnosing and drugging. It blamed our children's brains, exonerating us as adults from any responsibility for their suffering. The conference embodied America's worst attitudes toward our children.

President Clinton's plan brought many basic issues to a head. Should schools and teachers step up their referrals of children for psychiatric diagnosis and treatment—or are the dangers of abuse and social control already too great? Has diagnosing children as "mentally ill" helped to winnow out the violent ones—or has it proved to be a useless but oppressive strategy? Will scrutinizing out children's behavior even more thoroughly on a daily basis oppress them further? Does treatment with drugs reduce violence—or does it in fact increase violence? Will more psychiatric involvement in our children's lives further disempower the family?

Then there are the larger societal questions. Is the focus on mental disturbances and violence in individual children a red herring—a distraction from the real issues? With so many children showing signs of distress, shouldn't we focus on identifying and addressing the societal causes, such as the need for reforming our schools, improving our family life, expanding our health care, eradicating poverty, ameliorating sexism and racism, cutting back on violence in the media, reducing the rates of maiming and death from guns and automobile crashes, and counteracting the rampant abuse of drugs and alcohol?

These questions—which will continue to be addressed throughout the book—were given immediacy and urgency by the White House Conference on Mental Health. The following chapter looks at the kinds of stressors that impinge upon our children and continues to examine the nature of the effort we need to make to rescue and reclaim them.

3

Identifying the Real Risks to Our Children's Well-Being

Following the school shootings in 1999, many experts commented on the importance of identifying children at risk in order to facilitate psychiatric treatment with drugs. At the White House Conference on Mental Health, we saw President Bill Clinton make a national policy of increasing the "mental health" presence in our schools. Yet the basic idea of psychiatrically diagnosing and medicating children is flawed. Instead of finding better ways of meeting the needs of all of our children, we label and drug those who most openly express the distress and anger that so many others suffer in relative silence. It is much more useful and accurate to evaluate our children's situations—the conditions that are confusing, frustrating, and hurting so many of them.

Violent children are simply not a major cause of maiming and death among children. Focusing on the potential Eric Harrises distracts from more real dangers in children's lives such as accidental death from guns, use of illicit and psychiatric drugs, binge drinking, unprotected sex, and especially, traffic crashes, which account for 42 percent of childhood deaths.[1] Moreover, a child's unhappiness should be of concern to us, whether or not the child is "at risk" for hurting someone.

As detailed in Chapter 2, greater sophistication in "recognizing the danger signs" of mental disturbance or violence in our children is not likely to do much good. Many of the school shooters gave patently obvious, multiple signals that failed to result in any effective response from adults.

By the time children do begin to display serious "warning signals," they are often already so alienated from the adults in their lives that, in effect, no one is listening or able to respond to them. The stresses in the family have usually driven parents and children apart. If psychiatric treatment has been sought, the tendency to focus on the child's "disorder" to the exclusion of family conflicts has likely increased the chasm between parents and child.

Creating relationships with all of our children is the key to not only preventing violence but also giving them happier lives. We need to be developing these relationships with our children on a daily basis long before they start giving us signals of impending emotional breakdown.

Genuine Public Health Measures

An analogy to air pollution in the physical environment can help us understand how to help children who react to noxious factors in the human environment. At lower levels of air pollution, the most vulnerable individuals—such as the very old, the very young, and those with cardiovascular and respiratory problems—tend to show obvious ill effects. Other people, of course, are also suffering from the poisonous air, but they're not becoming noticeably ill. As pollution persists or worsens, increasing numbers of people will show serious harmful effects. When pollution reaches very high levels, a code-red warning will be issued for everyone to stay indoors if at all possible.

Of course it is worthwhile to identify and to help especially vulnerable individuals during an air pollution alert. But if public policy focused on the vulnerable individuals to the exclusion of the offending air pollution, the larger problem would go unnoticed while it worsened. In the future, increasing numbers of people would become ill. Soon the pollution would be visibly harming everyone.

In a similar fashion, focusing on individual children who are distressed or violent certainly has the potential to benefit them. But public policy should put more energy into identifying the real risks to all our children, focusing on the larger societal stressors that are harming so many of our children, even those kids who aren't "going crazy" or "going berserk." So many of our children are showing signs of distress—small and large—it's time for us to take notice and to respond to the overall societal emergency.

Besides, the biopsychiatric treatments routinely given to children don't really help them. Psychiatric drugs simply subdue children's signs of suffering. Suppressing our children's emotional signals with toxic agents not only harms them, it delays our recognition of the larger environmental stressors in the family, school, and community. Thus, when we treat children with drugs, we harm them as individuals by suppressing them and we harm the community by overlooking the larger sources of the problems.

Genuine help for individual children requires identifying and meeting their needs for meaningful relationships with adults and with each other at home, in school, and elsewhere in the community. Since the needs of disturbed or angry children do not differ in kind from those of other children, the most fair and effective approach is to improve the human environments in which all of our children live.

Profiling the School Shooter

The emphasis on identifying and treating troubled children, as opposed to identifying societal problems, misses not only the fact that many of the school shooters were already diagnosed and medicated but also the point that they look a lot like the rest of our schoolchildren. Though some of them gave more drastic signals of despair than most children, their backgrounds and their general deportment in public often resembled that of many others.

The three perpetrators of school violence in April and May 1999— Eric Harris, Dylan Klebold, and T. J. Solomon—shared many characteristics with other children who opened fire on their schools earlier in the 1990s. With the exception of one eleven-year-old, they were teenagers. They were white, male, from blue-collar or middle-class families; their average age was sixteen; they were seemingly of average intelligence or better, were Christian,[2] were raised in the suburbs or countryside, and attended public schools.

The psychologists James McGee and Caren DeBernardo confirmed this basic profile in their review of sixteen school shooters from 1993 through T. J. Solomon in May 1999.[3] The two researchers further concluded that *all* of the shooters could be considered social outcasts, but that *none* had a "documented history of severe mental illness"—which echoes the points made in Chapter 2.

The profile of the school shooter—as many have observed—turned out to be that of mainstream America's children. Here is a brief summary of ten school shootings involving twelve shooters from 1996 through mid-1999 in the United States:[4]

February 2, 1996: Barry Loukaitis, fourteen, killed one teacher and two students, and wounded a third student at Frontier Junior High (600 students), Moses Lake, Washington.

February 19, 1997: Evan Ramsey, sixteen, killed the principal and one student, and wounded two others at Bethel Regional High School (600 students), Bethel, Alaska.

October 1, 1997: Luke Woodham, sixteen, stabbed his mother to death and killed two students and wounded seven at Pearl High School (1,000 students), Pearl, Mississippi.

December 1, 1997: Michael Carneal, fourteen, killed three students and wounded five at Heath High School (600 students), West Paducah, Kentucky.

December 15, 1997: Joseph Todd, fourteen, while hiding in a wooded area wounded two students as they entered Stamps High School (350 students), Stamps, Arkansas.

March 24, 1998: Andrew Golden, eleven, and Mitchell Johnson, thirteen, killed one teacher and four students and wounded ten students at Westside Middle School (250 students), Jonesboro, Arkansas.

May 21, 1998: Kipland Kinkel, fifteen, killed his parents, then killed two students and wounded twenty at Thurston High School (1,400 students), Springfield, Oregon.

April 20, 1999: Eric Harris, eighteen, and Dylan Klebold, seventeen, killed themselves, one teacher, and twelve students and wounded twenty-three students at Columbine High School (1,900 students), Littleton, Colorado.

April 25, 1999: Andrew Wurst, fourteen, killed one teacher and wounded two students and a teacher at Parker Middle School (850 students), Edinboro, Pennsylvania.

May 20, 1999: Thomas Solomon, fifteen, wounded six students at Heritage High School (1,200 students), Conyers, Georgia.

Identifying "at-Risk" Children

Identifying children who are at risk is an easy matter: All of our children are at risk. They are endangered by a plethora of stressors, from alienation at home to peer humiliation at school to drug and alcohol abuse to precocious sex to gun-related accidents to car crashes. With all of our children at serious risk from the pitfalls of modern childhood, no parent or caregiver can afford to assume that one or another child is invulnerable.

Does it do us any good to accept that all of our children are at risk? It does. It allows us to put the focus where it belongs: on ourselves, our families, and our communities—on the life conditions we have created around us for our children. In addition to helping children who have come to our attention because of their especially glaring emotional problems, we need to put our energy into identifying the risks in our world that impinge so heavily on every child.

Identifying ourselves as adults at risk of hurting our children is a more useful goal than identifying our children who are at risk of becoming violent or "mentally ill." By focusing on ourselves, we empower ourselves to find new ways to identify and to meet the needs of our children.

Environmental Stressors for Children

Listing the wide range of stressors in the modern child's life reminds us just what they are.[5] This list also reconfirms the need to pay more attention to the conditions under which all of our children live. It is a partial antidote to the biopsychiatric view that trauma and disruptions in primary relationships, however painful, are not the cause of the "mental illness" that biopsychiatrists believe afflicts millions of children. Biopsychiatrists like Harold Koplewicz from the White House Conference on Mental Health would replace the entire list that follows with two concepts: genetics and brain disease.

1. Stressors in the Family

It's not always possible to completely separate stressors within the family from those outside it. For example, parents who maintain a sloppy or disordered home may cause their children to feel ashamed to invite home their peers. Their reluctance to bring children home could lead to impaired relationships with their peers. This also is an example of how stressors are interrelated. Nevertheless, it is useful to discuss stressors originating within the family separately from those originating outside it.

Loss or Lack of Meaningful Relationship with Significant Adults. A meaningful parent-child relationship—where parents give unconditional love and genuine attention to the child—is the single most important factor in providing a child with a secure, emotionally stable life. Conversely, the loss or absence of beneficial relationships with significant adults is the single most important source of suffering in a child's life. Almost all the other causes are derivative: They have their impact by impairing relationships.

Relationships that lack a consistent, firm adult presence cause a great deal of distress in children. Many of the children I see in my practice suffer more from lack of rational discipline than from severe abuse. Often their parents are very successful, but their success has come at the cost of their finding enough time for their children. Although more obvious forms of child abuse are easier to associate with emotional suffering, lack of emotional engagement and inconsistent or irrational discipline practices take a devastating toll. The child grows up suffering feelings of alienation, confusion, helplessness, and anger without having any idea why.

Many stressors have their negative impact by reducing the parent's capacity or willingness to provide unconditional love and attention. In a sense, all of the following sources of stress on children are related to loss of relationship with significant adults.

Work Stress on One or Both Parents or Caretakers. A 1999 article in *Modern Maturity* by Mark Hunter started with the headline: "Work work work work!—It's taking over our lives—invading our homes, haunting our holidays, showing up for dinner. Should we care?"

Americans are now working longer and harder just to keep up. In many cases, both parents are working. Hunter points out that the average time spent on the job has risen from 43.6 to 47.1 hours per week. For many, commuter time and stress have also increased. But that's hardly the end of it. Lunch hours often disappear, sick leave is down, and vacation time is more limited than it used to be. More than one third of workers surveyed by the Families and Work Institute said they "often or very often feel used up at the end of the workday."

The sense of job security originally offered by corporate giants like IBM no longer exists. No one's job is guaranteed in this era of mergers, acquisitions, and downsizing. An employee must struggle to keep up with constantly evolving knowledge, expertise, and technology. Many stay in unsatisfactory jobs simply to keep their health insurance.

Though Hunter describes the downside of this growing work compulsion, ironically the article includes a large three-quarter-page box, "Six Survival Tips," by a different writer, which urges midcareer people to work harder to keep up with their jobs and technology.[6] One piece of advice for survival: "Do something to make yourself invaluable?" But to whom? the writer doesn't say. Certainly not to your spouse or children. As much as anything, stress, exhaustion, and preoccupation with work keep parents from giving children what they need in the way of genuine relationship.

Parents need to make hard decisions about what's important in their lives. Most American families would probably benefit from a new balance with lots more genuine relating with their children.

Discord, Conflict, Separation, or Divorce of the Parents. Today's families often undergo drastic changes while children are in the home. These changes not only cause losses, they introduce new people and new stresses. A loving stepfather or stepmother is, of course, a great advantage, but even the best will also cause distress in a child by re-stimulating the suffering caused by the loss of the original parent.

Separation or divorce is the single most traumatic event in the lives of many children because it causes the most abrupt and severe loss of a significant person—one of the parents. Unfortunately, it is all too common. In 1970, 90 percent of children lived with both parents. By 1997, the figure had dropped to 64 percent.[7]

Being in a single-parent family is stressful on the parent and children alike. "Family-friendly" corporate programs could especially lighten the load on single working parents through on-site child care, job sharing, and more flexibility in hours, but corporate America has not been supporting these parents.[8]

As a parent who has subjected his children to divorce, I wanted to believe that I could more than compensate for the pain of divorce by giving my children quality time when they were living with me or with their mother. Of course, it's more complicated than that. Children suffer from living in conflicted families, but they also suffer from being separated from either parent.

Whether or not a parent stays in a marriage in order to meet the needs of the children is a very difficult, complex, and personal decision. Parents who live outside their children's home must be prepared to maintain relationships with their children and the residential parent despite the conflicts and frustrations entailed in separation and divorce. Because it's so easy to ignore children when they're not in the same house, and because it can be so difficult to maintain a relationship with them, to be a good nonresidential parent requires an extra measure of devotion.

Death or Relative Absence of a Parent or Parent Figure. When a parent dies, children are at least as vulnerable to bereavement as the surviving parent, and often more so, in part, because we don't always take their grief with sufficient seriousness. Also, a lost parent is often far more difficult, if not impossible, to replace than a lost wife or husband. The death of a spouse also renders the surviving parent less able to meet the needs of children, at least for a time, and sometimes throughout the dependency of the children. Parents going through bereavement must keep in mind the needs of their children. By looking to the needs of their children they can anchor themselves once again in important relationships, rediscover their value to others, and thereby help themselves recover more readily from their bereavement.

Even in the absence of an outright bereavement from death, today's families too often suffer from absent or neglectful fathers and overworked mothers. Among the poor, fathers are often entirely absent from a child's life. Among the more affluent, the father may be in the home or may live nearby, but may be "too busy" to spend much time with his children. Nothing would help America's children more than a nationwide rededication of men to fathering and to being big brothers. Fortunately, this need is being recognized by a number of churches, volunteer movements, and even the federal government, leading to advertising campaigns and other attempts to inspire men to devote themselves to their wives and children.

Sickness or Death of a Sibling or Friend. Once again, it is important to understand the extent to which children suffer from losses.

The lives of many children are impaired for years, or a lifetime, by sickness and death among their brothers and sisters, or friends. In therapy with adults it often turns out that these childhood events continue to exert their effects long into adulthood.

Death or Departure of a Pet.   Animals are often a child's best friend. An embittered wife in my clinical practice commented to her withdrawn husband, "We'll have to get a dog so the kids can have some unconditional love." Unfortunately, it's true that pets often provide the child's best experience of love. I have known adults whose main role model in childhood was a loving dog. Too often parents get rid of a pet, or fail to replace a lost pet, without realizing the emotional cost to the child.

Domestic Violence.   More than one half of women will experience some form of violence from their husbands during their marriages and more than one third of these women will be repeatedly battered every year. Domestic brutality, which sometimes afflicts husbands as well, has multiple negative effects on children. It terrifies them, of course. Both the perpetrator and the victim provide their children with very negative role models. Both are unable to give children the security and love they need. In addition, children in homes with domestic violence are themselves abused at a rate fifteen times greater than the national average.[9]

Physical, Sexual, or Emotional Abuse of the Child by a Parent or Sibling.   Throughout society, extremes of abuse abound. The family has been called "the cradle of violence."[10] Surveys conducted in the late 1990s show that one quarter of infants have been struck by the age of six months and one half by the age of one. A whopping 80 percent of sibling relationships involve violence. The number of children identified as abused and neglected per year approaches 3 million. Rates of physical and sexual abuse are escalating. In 1997 nearly one thousand children were known by official agencies to have died as a result of physical abuse. Among adolescents, an estimated 8 percent have been seriously sexually assaulted, 17 percent have been physically assaulted, and 40 percent have witnessed violence.[11] As documented in Chapter 2, many women suffer sexual abuse in childhood, contributing to emotional problems in adulthood.

In my clinical practice and conversations with women friends and acquaintances over the years, I have paid special attention to issues of childhood abuse. What I have learned suggests that sexual molestation is inflicted on the vast majority of girls before they leave home. Fathers and older brothers are among the most common perpetrators. Sexism, or the delusion of male superiority, creates an environment in all modern societies that is conducive to the male abuse of women and children.[12] It also inspires men, as well as older boys, to inflate their feelings of superiority by abusing vulnerable boys. Overall, it's difficult to get through childhood without enduring physical and sexual abuse, and it is wholly impossible to get through it without enduring the more subtle effects of sexism and the myth of male superiority.[13]

Witnessing Someone Else's Suffering.   Witnessing violence to a loved one breeds feelings of helplessness, guilt, anxiety, and shame in a child, and can inspire violence. Although many grown-ups don't realize it, they themselves may have been emotionally harmed by watching a parent or less favored child being abused. "Witness trauma" can be as shocking as, or even more shocking than, enduring the trauma oneself. Witnessing chronic illness in a family member can also cause negative reactions.

Witness trauma can occur also from watching television news, movies, and other dramatizations of human tragedy. Nowadays, being bombarded with images such as those from the Littleton, Colorado, shootings or the mass starvation in Africa can rob a child of innocence and security. I have known people whose childhoods were deeply affected by watching Holocaust newsreels or footage of disasters, such as floods and fires. A child's impressionable mind can record, and sometimes lock in hiding, images that will continue to haunt them over a lifetime.

Childhood Illness.   Acute and chronic illnesses often frighten and isolate a child. Hospitalizations often leave children feeling abandoned. The trauma of illness often has much more to do with a child's feelings of abandonment than with physical suffering. To offset these negative experiences, parents should take advantage of modern hospital policies allowing them to sleep overnight in their child's hospital room. Once again, adult relationships are the key to the psychological and spiritual well-being of children.

Confused or Contradictory Parenting Practices.   Counselors and therapists can be particularly useful in helping parents overcome self-defeating, inconsistent parenting practices. In situations in which children are prescribed psychiatric drugs to control their behavior at home, adequate parent training or counseling would solve the problem in a much better fashion.

Well-motivated parents often make their own mistakes by going overboard as they try to overcome their own problems that resulted from the mistakes of their own parents. Counseling that helps parents see the roots of their problems can facilitate their ability to overcome them, and as a result help them to treat their children more fairly and lovingly.

Personality Clashes and Conflicts with a Parent.   As adults we can choose the kinds of people we want to associate with, but our children never come preselected for compatibility. Often our children have personalities that conflict with ours. These seeming incompatibilities are not the fault of the child—nor of the parent—but they do require extra work on the part of the parent to develop and improve the relationship. When parents determine to find ways to relate to children who seem incompatible with them, wonderful things can happen. As David Keirsey's work demonstrates, seemingly opposite or incompatible personalities can turn out to have much to offer each other.[14] Individuals often select each other to provide qualities such as stability or an even temperament that they find lacking in themselves.

Envy of Parents and Siblings.   It is usually assumed that an especially bright, creative, or energetic child will be joyfully welcomed into a family. Unfortunately, the special child is commonly viewed with a mixture of envy, fear, and resentment in his or her own family. As the child becomes successful in school, sports, the arts, or other endeavors, siblings and even parents may feel competitive and even shamed by the comparison.

The rejection of especially remarkable children is one reason why so many end up in psychiatric treatment. They are not only more sensitive and more responsive to the stress and suffering in their environment, they are more likely to be the butt of envy or the object of misunderstanding from parents, siblings, and adults outside the family.

New Neighborhoods and Schools.   The problems associated with geographical mobility used to be limited to "army brats," whose mil-

itary parents rotated on assignment. Nowadays many children suffer
frequent dislocations as their parents get divorced or remarried, or
seek educational opportunities and new jobs. It is difficult for a child
to reach out to teachers, coaches, ministers, neighbors, or peers when
there are frequent moves and there is no guarantee that relationships
can be maintained for any length of time.

Loss of Childhood.   We are bringing up children as if they were
young adults, often depriving them of the fun and playtime that they
need during the day at school and with their friends and family on
weekends. In the extreme, children suffer from what psychologists call
"parentification."[15] The children become saddled with running the
household, cooking meals, and even raising their brothers and sisters.
Often, a child serves as the protector and confidant of a parent. In
clinical practice, it is found that parentified children often become depressed, guilt-ridden, and unable to pursue their own interests and
happiness as adults.

Family Isolation.   Suburban houses, nestled comfortably on quiet
streets and in cul-de-sacs, tend to isolate children from each other.
Children become dependent on their parents to be driven by car to
meet their friends and to pursue extracurricular activities, and parents
in turn often feel harassed and resentful about spending so much time
chauffeuring their children around.

The journalist Christopher Caldwell vividly described the situation
in which "children grow up in almost hermetic seclusion—a newer
and more soul-destroying condition, with dismal implications for
democracy." According to Caldwell, "Large lots, dead-end streets,
and draconian zoning laws mean that there are vast distances to travel
to reach any kind of public space. . . . For children unlucky enough to
inhabit a dead-end that has no children on it, this means: No friends
for you."[16]

That hub of American materialism, the shopping mall, has replaced
the neighborhood street corner or playground. Our children, desperately missing us in their lives, look in the wrong places for solace and
support. Parents stand by helpless to do anything to help their children. Or, like the parents of Eric Harris, T.J. Solomon, and Kip
Kinkel, they take them to doctors for psychiatric diagnosis and drugs.

Meanwhile, children who live in the chaos and violence of urban neighborhoods often end up isolated for a different reason: Their parents are afraid to let them go outside.

Isolation Caused by Technology. The educator and counselor Jake Johnson, Ed.D., from Bowie State College in Maryland, pointed out to me that technology, regardless of its content, "has become an intervening factor between parents and children. Some parents buy technological gadgets as educational tools but they also buy them as baby-sitting tools. Then they don't relate to their children."

A few decades ago, a child might cuddle up in bed at night with a radio before falling asleep, but other than that there were few technological seductions to draw a child into complete isolation within the home. Back then, even television was sometimes a shared family event. Nowadays television shows that cater exclusively to young people, and telephones, pagers, video games, and computers can sometimes encourage communication among youngsters; but they almost always separate them from their parents and all other adults. Some technologies, such as Walkman headsets or Game Boy handheld computer games, totally isolate the youngster from the family even when they are traveling in the car or eating in a restaurant, times that once were opportunities for communication.

Dinner was once the center of family life, the time when everybody got together on a regular basis. With the demise of the family dinner, parents became lucky to catch a glimpse of their children passing through the kitchen to get snacks. That underscores the importance of a detail in the life of the Littleton school shooter Dylan Klebold: His parents had given him a small refrigerator to keep in his room.[17] It's a technological convenience—you can snack without bothering to go to the family kitchen. If a family is filled with conflict, never having to cross paths may reduce the friction. But when an adolescent boy is going through a lot of weirdness and doing a lot of freaky things, that kind of isolation becomes one more factor leading toward tragedy.

In August 1999 the American Academy of Pediatrics recommended that children under the age of two not watch TV and that older children not have a TV in their room. Even more harmful than exposure to TV violence, the pediatric group warned, is that television removes children from the most basic and necessary stimulant of the growth and development of their brains and minds: close-up interactions with adults.[18]

2. Stressors Outside the Family

Adding to stresses within the family, stressors originating outside the family are brought home by children and adults alike.

Institutionalization and Placement.   After experiencing the kinds of family stressors we have described, many children end up in psychiatric facilities and juvenile detention and foster homes that further traumatize them.[19]

Psychiatric Stigmatization.   Biological psychiatry and the drug companies have been conducting a campaign to "destigmatize mental illness," as demonstrated by the White House Conference on Mental Health. The aim, as described in Chapter 2, is to get more people to accept calling themselves mentally ill so that they will employ more mental health professionals and consume more drugs. The real stigma is caused by biological psychiatrists with their false accusations that emotional suffering is caused by some defect in the brain of the individual. Being psychiatrically diagnosed, medicated, or hospitalized gives a child a stigma that a lifetime will not overcome. It should be avoided at all costs.

Physical, Sexual, and Emotional Abuse at the Hands of Trusted Adults.   Parents often fail to grasp the frequency and severity with which children are abused by other adults and older children. In fact, the idea is so painful to contemplate that many well-meaning parents don't pay enough attention to the dangers. Parents will frighten their children with the extremely unlikely possibility that a stranger will snatch them off the street, while they themselves ignore the far more likely possibility of abuse by individuals well known to the parents, such as baby-sitters or relatives who provide caretaking.

I believe that parents should take great care in assessing and monitoring any adult or older child who spends time alone with their child in any capacity. The younger your child, the more important this becomes. As for teenage baby-sitters and tutors, it is important to get to know them and their parents. This confronts the youngsters with the reality of potential accountability to their own parents. A great deal of suffering seen in any clinical practice has been generated, in part at least, by sexual and physical abuse from someone the child was supposed to trust.[20]

Abuse by Peers.   Ridicule and rejection by classmates is a major problem in the life of almost every school-age youngster. All parents should assume that their children will be subjected to some degree of bullying, teasing, and ridicule. Even if the child tries to dismiss it, it is having a negative impact. Especially in today's school environment, almost every child will be traumatized to one degree or another by these experiences. It is one of the major issues that our schools need to address.

Stressful Academic Experiences.   Too many children have become "school slaves" whose daily life is burdened by competition for grades and hours of daily homework. We adults forget how much this burden can weigh on a child and we sometimes exacerbate the load with our own expectations for grades and other signs of school success.

Religious Terrors and Guilt.   From the existence of Santa Claus to the existence of hell, children take to heart and believe what they are told. Adults who tell children about "burning in hell" may not realize that many children will literally cower in fear and suffer from nightmares of being "swallowed up" and "burned alive" for eternity.

In my clinical work, I find that childhood religious terrors and guilt often crowd into the consciousness of adults throughout the remainder of their lives, causing them unnecessary emotional suffering. Instead of encouraging a love of God and their fellow human beings, these painful memories cause resentment and withdrawal from further religious experiences. These children when they grow up may refuse to embrace any kind of spiritual life because of the association with abusive childhood religious indoctrination.

Terrifying and Violent "Entertainment."   The most adored childhood movies, such as *Bambi*, *The Wizard of Oz*, or *E.T.*, can terrify children, actually causing a posttraumatic stress reaction with nightmares and anxiety that can last for months or years. Parents need to be very careful about the movies that their young children watch and should talk with children regularly about their responses to the movies they have seen.

Nowadays, of course, children and young adults are exposed to so much violence from so many entertainment sources—including television, movies, and video games—they cannot help but be negatively affected by them. Media violence has a mesmerizing, almost hypnotic quality that glues many viewers to the unfolding drama. Watching so much violence against human beings is bound to desensitize some young people to the horror of killing while encouraging them to think of violence as a viable option to deal with conflict.

In a survey conducted shortly *before* the Columbine High School shootings of May 1999, 81 percent of parents surveyed reported that movie and television violence was their first media-related concern, even ahead of explicit sex.[21] More than a thousand studies have been conducted on the association between watching violent television and the development of violent attitudes in young people, and most of the research has confirmed that there is a causal relationship.[22] Parents are justified in being vigilant about the exposure of their young children to violence on television, in movies, and from other sources.

Catastrophic Events and Accidents.   From car accidents in the United States to war elsewhere in the world, children are commonly exposed to catastrophic events. However, the physical trauma and fear a child undergoes from an accident or other catastrophe is often less devastating than the associated disruptions in the child's relationships or the failure of adults to respond to the child's distress. Under the worst stresses, a good relationship with an adult will help a child survive and recover, whereas a feeling of betrayal or abandonment in time of need tends to cause lasting emotional damage.

Unsafe Communities and Exposure to Violence.   Recently, school shootings have made suburban children and their families feel unsafe, whereas urban families and children have for years lived with a daily fear of violence. Small children in the inner cities often have known many other children and adults who have been murdered. Some city children learn to identify the sounds of different kinds of gunfire the way a country child might learn to identify different birdsongs. It's mainstream America that seems deaf to the sounds of violence among the urban poor.

Racism, Sexism, Religious Persecution, and Pedism (Prejudice Against Children). Prejudices of all kinds have an impact on our children, including the sexism that exposes girls to ridicule and humiliation from boys, and often from each other as well. Sexism, racism, religious persecution, and pedism not only affect children directly, they create a social structure that impedes the growth and the hopes of children.

As soon as children are old enough to be aware of experiencing these problems—which can mean as soon as they are old enough to talk—parents should begin to chat about issues of fairness and justice in the world. Children readily understand these kinds of issues. It can bolster their sense of worth, and their understanding of the equal worth of others, when parents bring up these subjects for discussion. I am not talking about overwhelming children with "all the problems of the world." Instead, I urge parents to readily acknowledge and to discuss the unfairness that children will already see for themselves— for example, the ways boys are treated differently than girls, or the ways that so many children suffer from racism and poverty. Children will feel validated and even relieved when adults confirm their perceptions of these injustices.

Poverty. Despite the great economic expansions of the 1990s and the wealth accumulated by stock market investors, there has been relatively little trickle-down to the children of America. According to the U.S. Census Bureau, approximately 13 percent of Americans, including 20 percent of children, live in poverty.[23] The poverty figure for children has hovered around 20 to 25 percent for about fifteen years. The rates for blacks and Hispanics are almost twice as high, 38 percent and 40 percent, respectively. In absolute numbers, however, there are more poor white American children than blacks or Hispanics. The rate of poverty in the suburbs, while still behind the that of the city, has surpassed that of rural areas.

Children suffer from the many harmful effects of poverty, including disempowered or absent fathers, stressed mothers, inadequate or ab-

sent health care, substandard diets, air pollution, violent neighborhoods, and reduced educational development prior to and during
school.

The large numbers of poor and marginalized children in America,
from African Americans to Native Americans to white children,
should long ago have warned America about the impending danger to
all of our children.

3. Lack of Meaning

I discuss lack of meaning in this separate section because this stressor
is so important and yet its significance is so little appreciated. The lack
of meaning in our children's lives results from failures in many institutions, including the family, schools, and churches, and in the wider
culture.

No society in the world has tried to raise children without providing them a moral and spiritual grounding in their culture, a worldview
usually including values about honesty, courage, and a belief in something greater than themselves. When life no longer has any meaning,
children and adults alike become severely demoralized and vulnerable
to emotional collapse. Lack of meaning is one of the greatest stressors
in the lives of our children.

All cultures use religion and spirituality to teach their children what
to believe and how to conduct themselves. Among the five hundred
Native American nations that existed in North America at the time
the Europeans arrived, it has been found (among those that have been
studied) that they taught their children about honesty, ethical human
relations, courage, community values, and spiritual values, often including belief in a Great Spirit not unlike the Judeo-Christian God.

Increasingly, in North America, our children are being raised without any substantial context in which they can be taught values. Parents too often have neither time nor interest. On occasion, they even
doubt their right to "impose their own values" on their children.
More often, they don't realize how important it is for them to con-
sciously teach principles of living to their children. Churches too
often fail to engage the minds of young people, and public schools feel
discouraged about trying to provide moral leadership.

Meanwhile, our children cannot thrive without meaningful moral
and spiritual concepts. They crave the satisfaction of exercising their
critical intelligence. They want to find enduring truths with which to

replace the superficial values they see all around them. Without adults who offer something better, our children are likely to end up filling their minds with readily available pop culture and peer values. With luck they might latch on to those rare artists and role models who stand for positive values, but they will have to fight their way through a much broader and insistent spectrum of values from the shallow and materialistic to the hateful and violent.

Doug Smith, a psychiatrist and a Christian, wrote to me that the root problem is "lack of faith in God." Dr. Smith also pointed out that all of the school shooters have come from affluent families, judging by worldwide standards. He suggested that "affluence itself is a stressor." He quoted from the Bible: "Give me neither poverty nor riches, but give me only my daily bread" (Proverbs 30:8). Poverty may not be preferable to wealth, but certainly our society has made materialism its god, and with that it has robbed our children of the inspiration for principled living.

We may differ among ourselves about the ultimate meaning of life, or about the nature or existence of God, but there seems little doubt that our society fails to provide many children with a coherent, life-affirming philosophy.

4. Legal and Illegal Drugs

Parents, in my opinion, should never allow anyone, not even medical doctors, to give their children psychoactive (mind-altering) drugs for the control of emotions or behavior. Our children are already way overexposed to illegal psychoactive agents. They don't need parents and teachers, as well as peers, pushing drugs on them. In the case of uppers and downers (stimulants and tranquilizers), the drugs obtained illegally are often identical to the medications prescribed by doctors.

Whenever a child's outlook or attitudes seem to abruptly worsen, consider the possibility that the child is being adversely affected by medically prescribed or street drugs. Even a youngster who is relatively free of severe emotional problems can be driven into withdrawal, depression, indifference, irritability, and anger or psychosis by almost any psychoactive agent, even drugs that are commonly used, such as marijuana, Ritalin, and Prozac.[24]

Joseph Califano, Jr., president of the National Center on Addiction and Substance Abuse at Columbia University, pointed out in late 1998, "For the first time, more than half of middle-schoolers (that includes sixth-graders) report that drugs are used, kept and sold at their schools."[25] Califano observed, "The good news is that parent power can make a big difference. Kids who do not smoke pot credit their parents with their decisions; kids who smoke pot credit their peers." Something as seemingly mundane as regularly eating dinner with their parents correlated with reduced marijuana use among children.

I support Califano's point about parental engagement as a "protective factor" against youth drug use, but I wish our society were more willing to call for parental involvement out of simple regard for our children. Even if our love doesn't totally protect them from drug abuse, our children need our love to be happy.

5. The Availability of Guns

A review of sixteen school shooters through May 1999 shows that eleven obtained their guns at home, and most had experience with the use of weapons.[26] The others seem to have had little or no difficulty obtaining guns. But the problem of gun availability extends far beyond the danger of arming a potential school shooter.

In a 1999 op-ed piece entitled "A Little Massacre Every Day," the *Washington Post* staff writer Fred Hiatt pointed out, "In 1996, 4,643 children and teenagers were killed with guns—2,866 murdered, 1,309 by suicide, 468 in unintentional shootings. That means 13 every day—a Littleton massacre every day." The United States leads the world in handgun deaths. In 1996, there were 15 in Japan, 30 in Great Britain, and 9,390 in the United States. Overall, gun-related deaths, including accidental deaths, are in the range of 30,000 per year in the United States.

Even when death does not result, fire-arms injuries are physically and emotionally painful, often permanently injurious, and extremely costly to society. According to 1994 data published in 1999, almost three fourths of the nation's estimated 134,445 gunshot medical cases were nonfatal. The total medical cost was $2.3 billion. Other costs resulting from these injuries, such as lost productivity and disrupted family life, are additional.[27]

A *Washington Post*–ABC News poll conducted nationwide a few days after the April 1999 Columbine High School shooting found that guns are readily available to most teenagers and are commonly carried to school. One fifth of teenagers personally know someone who had brought a gun to school, half were growing up in homes with guns, and more than half said it would be easy for them to lay their hands on guns.[28]

A 1999 Centers for Disease Control (CDC) survey before the shootings found that 5.9 percent of the nation's 15 million high school students had carried a gun to school in the previous thirty days. A larger percentage, 9 percent, admitted to carrying a gun, knife, or club to school in that time period. The percentage who reported carrying a weapon outside of school in the same time period was 18 percent.[29] These figures reflect a decline over the past several years, but they are still very high, and reflect the fear that large numbers of our children and teens live with.

Psychiatric drugs have also infiltrated our schools. Many students are prescribed them; others take them from friends or drug dealers without medical or parental supervision. Psychiatric drugs and guns can make a volatile combination that may explain the particularly bizarre and largely unprecedented quality of many of the school assaults.

If you are able to keep your children away from psychiatric drugs and guns, you will help to protect them from some of the worst hazards that can threaten them. However, making psychiatric drugs and guns unavailable to children will not do anything about their underlying unhappiness. It would simply make them less dangerous without making them essentially better off than before.

The larger question is: Why are we giving so many psychiatric drugs to children and why do we do so little to make guns unavailable to them? Once again, it is a matter of priorities. If there is a common theme that ties together gun availability and the prescription of drugs to children, it is this: We are placing adult "rights," needs, and conveniences ahead of our children's safety and well-being.

Even in the months following the school shootings, Congress failed to pass substantial gun control legislation. Even among the congressional representatives from Colorado, only the representative from Littleton, Tom Tancredo, voted for gun control in Congress. Tancredo did this despite his Republican, libertarian politics,[30] and explained, "I can't go home to them [friends and neighbors] and say we didn't do anything because guns aren't an issue. Guns are an issue. They did take children's lives."

The Demise of the Nuclear Family

Many (but not all) of the environmental stressors I've described here relate to the decline of the nuclear family. Many others relate to the decline of schools. Nearly all of them relate to the weakening of bonds between adults and children in our society.

The nuclear family in America in general suffers from well-known multiple afflictions: highly stressed working parents with too little time for each other or their children, single parenthood with its exhausting demands, absent or uninvolved fathers who leave mothers with the unenviable task of raising children on their own, and the demise of the extended family. The rising cost of higher education often seems to turn children into an economic burden rather than a source of joy for a hard-working couple.

Writing in the May 31, 1999, issue of *Time* magazine, the reporter John Cloud said it succinctly: "There is surely some connection between the fact that parents spend 40% less time with their kids now than 30 years ago, and the violence that some of them commit." Our children are lonely for us.

Stressed-out parents, as already emphasized, give their children leftover time. Parents who are motivated to do their best often don't know what to do. They try to provide "quality time" but end up spending money for entertainment without necessarily communicating with their children. They lack a guiding set of values or principles for loving, talking to, educating, disciplining, and playing with their children. They lack role models for themselves in the neighborhood and community. When they run into difficulties raising their children, they have nowhere to turn other than to medical specialists who will diagnose and drug them. They do not imagine that as parents they have the capacity to learn how to improve the lives of their children by learning new approaches to improving life within the family.

The collapse of family life in America has many causes, but the revival of the family requires one particular change in attitude. As parents and adults, we have time and again made choices that reflect our own materialistic compulsions, social pressures, and personal needs rather than the relationship needs of our children. We must rethink how to live with relationship at the center of our values and relationship with children as a high—even the highest—priority. This will require reallocations of time and energy toward identifying and meeting the needs of our individual children.

At present, the peer group often has far more influence than parents in the life of a child. Although many factors have caused this, there is one basic solution: reclaiming our children by putting sufficient time and energy into our relationships with them.

Alienation from Schools

While the nuclear family has been disintegrating, public schools have been unable to take up the moral and social slack. Industrial-sized schools with overcrowded classrooms have become too cumbersome and bureaucratic to provide children with the kind of inspiration and personal contact with teachers that they crave and need. As if on a factory assembly line, kids today are moved along from grade to grade with the aim of producing a polished academic achiever. If they show signs of wear and tear, psychiatric drugs are often pushed on them to make them conform to their studies and routines. The children who founder in this "mainstream" are disposed of by one means or another, from special classes to expulsion.

To those unfamiliar with the reality of today's schools, these observations may seem like an exaggeration. But to those who are familiar with our schools, they are not. Nowadays when a child deviates from expected norms of behavior in the classroom, the school—without further ado—is likely to encourage the parents to seek a medical evaluation. If drugging the child does not produce the required conformity, the child will be sent to alternative classes that often do little more than manage behavior without educating.

Schools present other problems to children. Many children experience persistent and often extreme peer humiliation in schools, and become "school scapegoats." To become more child-oriented, our schools need to relieve academic pressure on many of the students and find better ways to protect all of them from abuse. The school environment cannot be made safe without teachers, counselors, and administrators becoming much more involved in the daily lives of students. They must create genuine relationships with them. (Academic pressure and scapegoating are discussed in more detail in Chapters 8 and 9).

Searching for the Causes of Black Violence

Long before the isolated outbreaks of school shootings, black children and youths were killing each other on a regular basis. The nation feared blacks' entering their white communities to steal, rape, or murder, but we rarely showed a similar concern for the devastating black-on-black violence taking place down the street or across the tracks within segregated communities.

It should be no mystery that black men in America have been angry for a long time. Their anger began with capture and abduction in Africa. It caused suicide, violence, and rebellion in the slave ships. It was reinforced in slavery and then hammered home in segregation. Today black rage is fueled by white racism, social apartheid, lack of economic opportunity, and all the other factors that combine to frustrate and humiliate our African-American citizens.

Many causes of emotional distress and violence among black youngsters are related to living in poverty in America. Family dysfunction among the poor is associated with increased rates of alcoholism, drug addiction, and domestic violence. Schools fail to provide the tools that youngsters need to survive in the wider world and then unemployment breeds despair over the future. Drug dealing and turf wars develop in a population that has little hope of economic self-improvement by legitimate means. Drug dealing leads to the ready availability of guns. Gangs sprout up as youngsters attempt to protect and nurture each other; but the gangs in turn breed fear of other gangs and further violence.

The causes of black rage have been scientifically studied, described in psychology and sociology texts, and portrayed in novels.[31] But even without scientific and literary confirmation, informed Americans should be aware enough of conditions in our inner cities to feel empathy for any child living in urban poverty who struggles with feelings of personal frustration, humiliation, and anger.

Most individual expressions and outbursts of rage are driven by feelings of shame or humiliation. White America has been humiliating the African Americans within its borders since initially forcing them to come here as slaves, and it has been humiliating the Native Americans since exterminating their nations, seizing their land, and imposing an alien culture upon them.

From the degradation of our own principles of liberty and justice to the death toll of the Civil War to the continued cost of cultural alienation and conflict, our often unethical and violent conduct toward African Americans and Native Americans has done our nation and all its people more harm than mere words can ever express. Open acknowledgment of this tragic injustice would encourage the necessarily long and difficult process of healing our internal social wounds.

Valuing All Our Children

We should not become preoccupied with Littleton and other school shootings to the exclusion of the plight of all of our children. Dr. Ron Hopson, professor of psychology and divinity at Howard University, told me about "the extraordinary puzzlement that the black community is going through over all the media concern being shown over the school shootings." The white culture, he explained, expects black children to be violent, "so all the killing in the inner city doesn't pop up on the cultural screen." By contrast, when white children shoot one another, everything stops and members of the media ask in dismay, "How could this happen?"

The lives of black children have always been lived under the fear of death. Black children every day are dying violent deaths in far greater numbers than whites are being killed in schools.

Despite this, Dr. Hopson observes, "Black children are made to watch the white culture wringing its collective hands over murdered white children while totally ignoring them. What do the black children think when the culture broadcasts the funerals of the victims of Columbine while no one records their deaths and their parents can't even afford to bury them?"

Dr. Hopson believes that we live in a culture in which individualism has ruptured relationship: "From the children of other races to our own children, we are afraid to ask about our moral responsibility for others. That's what is impermissible in this culture—to admit our connectedness to others."

All of Us

Our basic social fabric in regard to children is coming apart. We suffer from high rates of child abuse, as well as domestic violence that also impacts on children. Our children often grow up amid pedism, poverty, racism, and sexism.

Even among the most affluent, many grow up as latchkey kids mostly raised by themselves or by hired help. We feel so pressed by our jobs, professions, businesses, and other obligations that we have too little time and energy left for our children. Too often, our children get the remainders—our leftover time and energy—after we've taken care of everything else.

Our schools are becoming more competitive and less child-friendly. We provide less of a support system for pregnant mothers and single parents, and less child health care, than any other Western nation. It's as if the nation is saying, "Too many children, too little time and money."

My psychiatric practice has increasingly confirmed for me how starved our nation's children are for significant adult relationships in their lives. As we'll see in the next chapter, children even love to go to the doctor when the doctor takes the time to show an interest in them.

4

Transforming Ourselves to Meet Our Children's Needs

———◦•◦———

As a parent and a psychiatrist, I have been impressed by the great differences in children from the same family, by the varied circumstances in which they grow up, and by the contrasting challenges they present to their parents.

One of your children needs firmness, another patience, the other a mixture of both. Your daughter loved learning from early on, but her brothers required constant help and motivating to get any schoolwork done. One child was easy until reaching adolescence, another was trouble from birth and the problems never seemed to end, and the third, after a rocky start, sailed through the teenage years without difficulty. Looking back, you see what different worlds they grew up in, the first when family life was new and blooming, the second when you and your spouse nearly divorced, the third when your marriage reached a new level of maturity.

Parents end up drawing on different aspects of themselves to relate to each one of their offspring. Sometimes, when we realize that one of our children needs a new approach, we have to change in midstream what we are doing. Parenting, it seems, requires us to continually transform ourselves to meet our children's changing needs and circumstances.

Most of us end up feeling in retrospect that we could have done a better job of parenting. If only we had had more wisdom at the time, or more maturity and experience, or simply more energy and dedication. It's as if the job of parenting cannot be done to anything close to perfection. In our modern circumstances, it often seems that we're hanging on by our teeth.

Yet parenting is also a wonderful and gratifying job, for many of us the best part of life. It can engage us to the utmost and bring out the very best we have to offer other human beings. For all of us, it's one of the most challenging, rewarding, and important jobs of our lives.

Well Prepared for Parenthood . . .

Am I exaggerating the demands of parenting?

David Cohen is a professor of social work at the University of Montreal who specialized in child psychology during his schooling. He was a mature man of thirty-eight in 1992 when the first of his two children was born. He grew up in a closely knit, loving Jewish family and was determined to offer the same values and advantages to his own children. If anyone was well prepared for parenthood, it was Dr. Cohen.

But recently Dr. Cohen confessed to me, "I thought I knew everything and then I had children."

I asked him, "What did you discover?"

"It's all about myself," Dr. Cohen explained. "All my habits that were set in stone had to change. You really learn to be selfless. There are things that you do for someone—for your child—that you just have to do. You just have to do them," he repeated. "You cannot think about it, you cannot debate it—a child needs something that you must absolutely fulfill at that very moment and you take care of it.

"I'm talking about the simplest things," he continued, "like changing their dirty diapers, which you don't feel like doing because you're in the middle of dinner. Once you decide to have children, it's a life of service. I think it's great. It can be fun. I'm constantly learning, doing things I wouldn't have done. I'm a better person for having given service to my children."

Dr. Cohen offered some examples.

"Sometimes I've been physically ill, I've had a bad flu, and I was weak, and my wife Carole was away on a business trip, and I had to put my kids to bed—but *I* wanted to be the one in bed. And then I tried as hard as I could to be present for my children, to be there for them at their bedtime, and I ended up feeling better myself. I felt physically healthier from giving to them. And their response to my service is so wonderful that there's no words for it. You have to see their faces."

What did he mean about changing his habits for their benefit?

Dr. Cohen replied, "If my kid's nose is running, even in public, I'll do what it takes to clear it, whereas if it was my own nose, I'd be so much more careful and mannered. I don't want them to suffer and their needs simply come ahead of my shyness in public."

For Dr. Cohen, having children was a conscious decision. That made it easier to "serve" them. "I'm a slave to my kids, yet it's a choice and it's so wonderful."

He sounded very happy.

Visits to a Village Elder in Bethesda

It's so complex and stressful raising children in today's world, it's no wonder that increasing numbers of parents find themselves seeking help from books, parenting groups, workshops, therapists, and other sources. Too often, however, the focus is on "What's the matter with your child?" when the most useful focus is "How can I transform myself to meet my child's needs?"

Mark in the Lion's Den

Mark was only three and a half years old when his parents phoned me. At the urging of Mark's preschool teachers, who were concerned about his outbursts of violence (he had hurt two other children), his parents had sought psychiatric consultations.

"Mark stuck a child with a scissors?" I showed concern to his mother and father within the first few minutes of their initial session.

"It drew blood," his mother said with understandable concern.

"It wasn't that bad," Mark's father suggested. "They were just being kids, fighting over who would get the scissors."

"The teacher said he raised it up like this," she put her hand over her head, "and stuck him in the shoulder."

Mark's father, a high-ranking government official, was impassive. Experience had taught me that a father's silence—as insensitive or even hostile as it might seem—usually reflects insecurity and uncertainty. He probably was at a loss for what to do about his son, so he withdrew into the common male posture of poker-faced observer.

We were only ten minutes into the initial interview. I had asked them to come to the first session without their child to emphasize, as I put it on the phone, "We're the adults; we ought to be able to figure out what a three-and-a-half-year-old needs." His mother, who made the initial call, was struck by the difference in my approach. She and her husband had already consulted a doctor at NIMH—the National Institute of Mental Health—a scant few blocks away from my office. That doctor wanted to put Mark into a clinical trial for stimulant drugs. Now they had come to me, knowing that I do not start children on psychiatric drugs.[1]

The first fifteen minutes of the interview already indicated to me a great disparity in how seriously each of them took Mark's aggressive behavior. Mark had not only stuck a child with a sharp scissors, he had banged another child's head against a locker, causing a large bruise. I observed, "You two have a different take on your son's situation."

Mark's mother nodded strongly; his father shrugged.

Mark's mother informed me, "He thinks his son is a 'chip off the old block.'"

"You don't think that your son's conduct is such a serious problem?" I asked.

"No, I don't," he said defensively.

"Do you really think Mark's a chip off the old block?" I asked.

Mark's father looked unsure.

I took a guess and offered, "I doubt that you were an aggressive child. My guess is, you were anything but a difficult child. Mostly you did what you were told, got good grades, didn't make any trouble."

He smiled, "You got it."

"Maybe you don't want Mark to be as suppressed or overcontrolled as you were as a child?"

I don't usually raise such a "psychological" issue so quickly in a session; but I felt that this father, beneath the facade of indifference, was trying to figure things out. I wasn't sure that my intuition was correct, but I hoped it would open up the conversation.

"Maybe you are right," Mark's father said hesitantly. "But the doctor at NIMH never said a word about how we parent Mark. He said Mark had a 'brain disease.'"

I was not surprised by that. Steven Hyman, the director of NIMH, had taken the same position at the White House Conference on Mental Health, held in June 1999. The belief that unruly or upset children have brain diseases was a policy at NIMH.[2]

"Does he have tantrums at home?" I asked.

"No," his mother said. "But he did have one with my husband when I left them alone for a couple of hours last weekend."

His father brushed it off.

"If it were a 'brain disease,' I think the symptoms would show up with Mom, too," I suggested. "She spends more time with him than anyone else."

"Aren't kids allowed to throw tantrums once in a while?" Mark's father asked.

"Mark's behavior is serious if he's hurting other children. It's not good for him, either. A child gets very frightened over being out of control," I explained.

"I've seen it," his mother confirmed. "Mark was still upset when I got home after his tantrum with you," she told his father. "But the main problem isn't with us. It's at school," she said.

"So what am I supposed to do?" his father asked almost defiantly. "Beat him when I get home from work?"

"Do you beat him sometimes?" I asked.

"No," they both agreed. Mark's father didn't intend this as a threat; he was expressing his sense of futility.

"Usually, my husband's so tired at night, he just needs to relax when he gets home," his wife said, defending him. "People think government executives don't work hard but my husband works himself to death."

"I've had a number of government execs in my practice," I agreed. "You do work hard." I reassured him that I was sympathetic.

"I don't want to make excuses," Mark's dad broke in. "Working hard is no excuse. My son deserves more than that."

"Right. Now your real challenge will be to take his behavior more seriously. In fact, I'll give you a guarantee. If, in this session, you come to agree with me and with your wife that *you* need to take Mark's behavior more seriously, your son's behavior will improve in a few days or weeks at the most. It's almost always that simple with children before they become adolescents—they respond almost immediately to changes in their parents, especially if their parents figure out how to approach them better."

"But what am I supposed to *do*?" He begged for more of a plan.

"Do you have a relationship with your son?"

"Of course I do," he said, showing some pride for the first time.

His wife confirmed, "He's very good with Mark as long as he doesn't have to discipline him. They play a lot together. They always do something together on the weekends."

"Then you're already much more caring and involved than most of the fathers I see in my practice," I said. "You've got a real relationship with Mark. He'll be so eager to please you, any changes you make will have an immediate impact on him."

"But what am I supposed to do?"

"Before I get more specific, I want you to think about this: *If you have a relationship with your son at such a young age, he will take seriously anything that you take seriously.* If you want him to be aggressive, he will become more aggressive, at least for a while, even if it's not in his nature. If you don't want him to be aggressive—really don't!—he'll get that message, too, and he'll give up a lot of his aggression. Mark's control over his aggression will begin when you take his aggression seriously as a problem."

Mark's father was silent for a while, as his mother's face showed many things: relief, hope, even a touch of happiness.

"You're right," he admitted. "I guess I've been rationalizing." He went on to talk about his desire for Mark to be tougher than he himself had been as a child. He didn't want his son being relentlessly picked on in school the way he was. "But there's something more important," he added. "I haven't known what to do. My dad beat me. I promised myself never to lay a hand on Mark and I haven't. But what you're saying makes sense. I used to watch my own father's every change of expression in order to avoid disappointing him."

"Mark's the same way with you, just because he loves you," his mother reassured him.

Very often well-meaning parents try to avoid exposing their children to the abuse they endured as children; but in the process, they can overdo it. In deciding to avoid their parents mistakes, they overcompensate and end up making mistakes of an opposite kind. Having been beaten by his own father, Mark's father became so restrained he could not effectively discipline his son.

"You need to *talk* to Mark about it," his mother emphasized for her husband. Then she explained to me: "My husband comes home at night, I tell him the latest problem with Mark at school, and he just brushes it off."

"He's only three and a half," Mark's father explained, again expressing a sense of futility. "What good does it do for me to bring up something twelve hours later?"

"It will do a lot of good—even days later," I emphasized. "When you go out with him this weekend, tell him the truth—that you've decided to be more serious with him about his hitting other children. Tell him that he must stop hitting or any way hurting other children. Tell him that it's time for him to be more grown-up. Tell him you'll be asking him about it every day."

"He hates to get angry at Mark," Mark's mother said.

"Don't get angry at your son," I explained. "Just get serious! Your boy will catch on."

We reviewed some of the ways to talk to a small child, including making up stories together that involve a young boy who hits and a young boy who doesn't. At the end of the session, I suggested that Mark's father come in with his son for the next session.

Mark's father brought his son by with him one week later. He had been talking "seriously" with Mark about his behavior and there had been no incidents at home or in school during the past week.

Mark was a very active little boy who took a lively interest in my office. When new clients, young or old, walk into the office, their faces often soften with relief. This isn't going to be one of those stuffy, authoritarian places. Then their eyes light up with delight as they look about at the array of eye-catching items.

My office is full of the kinds of doodads people give to a father, husband, or friend. There are all kinds of things for children and adults to play or fiddle with around the room. Among my favorites: the large Canadian goose decoy made of plastic that peeks out from behind the couch, a flock of wooden and ceramic ducks, a bronze kaleidoscope, and a Mexican ceramic puppy that barks when slapped on the rear end.

A hanging wooden planter—a gift that my father-in-law made for me—has become a floating platform for three stuffed animals. One is a large white teddy bear and others are a brown river otter and her baby. I don't do "play therapy" with elaborate games or art supplies; but I do like to use stuffed animals to help children to express their feelings, and to teach them moral and psychological lessons about how to conduct themselves. Sometimes I'll talk about how happily my animals have learned to settle conflicts and to live together in my office.

After Mark felt comfortable in the new room, I took the stuffed animals from the hanging planter. Mark watched with great interest as I sat the two larger animals in my lap and let them bump together.

"Oops! What happened?" I asked Mark.

"Fighting!" he cried out, grabbed the animals, and began to tumble around the floor with them with the abandon of a professional wrestler.

"Wait! Wait!" I cried out in distress. "The animals in this room never fight. They take care of each other."

I asked him to give me back the two stuffed animals for a moment, gently petted them, and had them hug each other.

"Do you know the story of Daniel in the lion's den?" I asked Mark. "It's from the Bible."

Mark shook his head.

"It's about being gentle," I explained. "You're a big strong boy like Daniel and gentleness is your real strength. When you're as strong as you, Mark, gentleness is how you show your strength."

Mark wasn't talking much, but clearly he was listening. Not yet four years old, perhaps he couldn't fully get my meaning, but he was trying.

I got down on the floor beside a hassock that's positioned between my chair and the couch to be shared by me and my clients. Mark came over and stood at the other side of the hassock. It came up to his waist. "You be Daniel and I'll be the lion," I said.

He watched without responding.

"People wanted to hurt Daniel so they put him into the lion's cage. They wanted the lion to bite him."

The idea clearly made Mark nervous and I tried not to overdue the fear part.

"I'm the lion," I said, limping on all fours around the hassock. "Look," I showed him, "I'm limping. The lion has something stuck in his paw. It's a thorn. A sharp sticker. Like a splinter. It's hurting his paw."

As I sat on the floor, I lay the palm of my hand on the hassock in front of Mark. Mark, his face a couple of feet from mine, seemed mesmerized by my hand.

"Being gentle is the way you show how strong you are. Gentleness is your strength. You can help the lion by taking the splinter from his paw."

For many seconds Mark eyed the palm of my hand. He reached toward it and then drew away as if it were dangerously hot.

"It's a make-believe splinter," I reassured him. "And remember, your strength is being gentle. You can take the thorn from the lion's paw."

At last Mark reached over and took out the imaginary thorn from my palm.

"You see," I explained, "your gentleness helped the lion and he never tried to hurt you. Gentleness is your strength."

Then, still without a word, Mark climbed up onto the hassock, lay down, and rolled into my arms.

Mark's father said, "I wish his mother were here to see this." Then he said to his son, "We have a Bible at home. I could read you the story before bed tonight."

Mark smiled broadly.

When the session was over, Mark refused to leave. At the door to the office, he grabbed my leg with both arms and held on with a giant hug.

His father started to raise his voice, "Mark!"

I smiled and said, "Here, take my hand, Mark, we'll walk out together," and without hesitation he marched out hand in hand with me. "We can even feed the fish in my pond," I suggested, to his glee.

I talked with Mark's teacher by phone a few days later. She was delighted with the astonishing change in the little boy's demeanor and conduct in the classroom. At first she thought his doctor must have put him on drugs, but he wasn't glassy-eyed like the other children on stimulants.

What helped Mark so quickly?

Mostly, it was the change in his father. Mark had already become a much less angry and violent child before he saw me. His father was eager to change—to be more involved in being a moral leader for his son—and Mark's mother completely backed her husband up. The little drama of Daniel in the lion's den also helped Mark and his father, but it probably wasn't critical in the short run. I suspect it became more important in the long run as a part of Mark's new folklore about how a boy should conduct himself. The story, now a part of his personal mythology, would give him encouragement in being gentle in the future.

Our Personal Mythology

The drama about Daniel in the lion's den gave Mark a new story about himself—that his strength and his safety lay in being gentle with his power. I acknowledged his power and showed him a different way to express it. Although the hug Mark gave me showed that he'd been moved, it is of course hard to know exactly how the story did affect Mark because he did not verbalize much during the session. Before going to school the next morning, he did tell his parents that he was going to be "gentle—like the doctor said."

Saved from the Streets

If raising a child under relatively ideal circumstances is difficult, it becomes even harder when parents adopt a child who has already been traumatized by months or years of abuse and neglect. Even though the adoptive mothers and fathers are often experienced and well motivated, their patience and parenting skills can be sorely tested by these distressed children.

When a previously traumatized child inevitably displays emotional problems after adoption, it's easy to conclude that there's little or nothing the parents can do about it. Since they didn't cause the initial problem, it's tempting for them to assume they can have nothing to do with perpetuating it or with healing it. Certainly, a child who brings a troubled past into a family will stress the family; in addition, though, parents can contribute to the problem, or they can help to ameliorate it. The healing process remains the same—effective adult relationships. The parents of children who arrive in a stressed condition have to reach more deeply into their own resources, as well as into the resources of their community.

Tomas was a five-year-old abandoned street urchin in a South American city when he was rescued by a Christian mission and quickly was adopted by a religious family in America. Now ten, he was "out of control" at home. Four or five different psychiatric drugs had been tried, but it was becoming apparent that they made him more grossly disturbed. So his parents brought him to me for prescription-free help.

There was no question that these parents were not the cause of Tomas's problems. To the contrary, they had rescued him—literally saved his life—and now they had to deal with consequences of his early years on the streets. They loved him and were devoted to him.

Despite counseling and then psychiatric evaluation and drugs, the conflicts at home had escalated to the point that the parents, in frustration, were isolating him for hours at a time and inflicting hard spankings on a regular basis. They had lost control of the situation and now were losing control of themselves.

Within the first counseling session with Tomas and his parents, it was apparent that his mother and father had lost their moral authority. They were becoming engaged in combat that periodically escalated into somewhat brutal confrontations. I watched, for example, as Tomas—disdaining a simple request from his father—stuck his finger into his father's ribs. Tomas's father failed to react with appropriate moral indignation to signal that this conduct was wholly unacceptable from anyone. Instead, his father in turn grabbed Tomas's hand and turned it with enough of a twist to hurt him slightly. Tomas stoically refused to wince. A few minutes later, Tomas stuck his finger in his father's face and wagged it in a disrespectful fashion. His father reacted by wagging his finger back in Tomas's face, declaring, "See how you like it!"

Even their verbal encounters displayed this out-of-control mutual intrusiveness. Tomas's father would demand acquiescent answers: "You heard the doctor, didn't you? Didn't you?" Tomas in turn would jabber, make faces, squirm around, and generally behave like an obstreperous five-year-old rather than a ten-year- old who was—with the proper guidance—capable of controlling himself.

In the first few minutes of the first session, I began to intervene by saying, "Tomas, you can't stick your father in the ribs. You absolutely cannot do it. It's not allowed for people to treat each other like that."

Tomas grimaced.

"Tomas, I know you're thinking"—I indicated his father—"you're thinking, 'He does it, too.'"

Tomas's face lit up. Without saying a word, he let me know he was quite aware of that.

"Dad, you've got to stop trying to control this child by doing the kinds of things he does—like wagging a finger in his face—or by spanking him. This family has to start using their hands to show love and nothing else."

Dad looked awkward but said nothing.

"This is embarrassing," said Tomas, who promptly hid his face in his mother's shoulders. As so often happens, the child was responding so much more directly and even sincerely to what was happening than the parents.

Within minutes, Tomas began to respond to my moral presence as something real and meaningful. When I made suggestions, he listened and tried to go along with them. Before the session was over, he had learned—in the session, at least—to stop his habitual reactions of trying to poke or push his father. He would start to go after his father, then freeze his hand in the air as he realized what he was doing, smile knowingly at me that he'd caught himself, and then put his hand back in his lap. Within that same brief time, when I pointed out his behavior to him, Tomas was able to stop acting in such an infantile fashion. He was behaving in a much more mature way by the end of the session.

Tomas's father, as often happens, had more trouble correcting his more deeply ingrained, lifelong habits. He could hardly keep his hands off Tomas. At one point he said, "I touch him affectionately, too," and without waiting for an invitation from his son, he abruptly and somewhat roughly patted Tomas on the head. Tomas shook off the touch to show he felt intruded upon.

Despite Tomas's quick response to my firm but affectionate and sometimes humorous insistence on his behaving himself, his father continued to wonder if "it would work." He doubted that he could have any impact on Tomas by assuming a firm, moral, loving authority which prohibited anyone in the family from using their hands or physical threats to control each other.

By the end of the session, Tomas was cuddled up with his mom, while Dad struggled with the old behaviors of intruding physically. I noticed that Tomas's mother had a much more intuitive sense of setting limits and communicating love, and I began to encourage her to play a bigger role in setting the tone of the family interactions.

Was there something "wrong" with this child? Was there something "wrong" with his father?

Clearly, Tomas had been abandoned and abused, and hence emotionally injured, long before he came under the care of his adoptive parents. Tomas was reacting *normally* to abuse and abandonment, but a child's normal reactions to trauma can make the child very difficult to raise. Meanwhile, his father, too, was reacting to the stress—the stress of a very difficult child. Frustration of his own continued inability to deal with Tomas was bringing out his worst tendencies.

No one had given Tomas's father the tools to cope with a traumatized, rebellious child. Instead, the professionals had misled him into thinking that drugs were the answer. Events in this family would have unfolded from the start in a much more positive fashion if the professionals had taught the parents more effective ways of loving and disciplining an injured child.

As increasing numbers of children are being adopted from agencies in other countries, and from deprived families in this country as well, many are showing up in the offices of psychiatrists and other health professionals. Instead of psychiatrically diagnosing them, it's far more productive to say of these children, "These are special children who need redoubled efforts from us as parents, teachers, and counselors to use our spiritual resources to reach out and to guide them."

Getting Younger All the Time

Although I am a general psychiatrist who works with adults more frequently than children, I have been treating increasing numbers of youngsters in my practice. Perhaps because schools increasingly tend to encourage parents to seek psychiatric consultations for their children, I am seeing younger and younger children, including three- and four-year-olds like Mark. With so many parents bringing their young children for help, I'm developing a new identity for myself. The little ones seem to respond to me as if I'm the village elder. They hang on my every word, listen to the moral lessons I evolve while chatting or playing with them, and seem to remember them for weeks afterward. They even want to come back to "see the doctor," to feed his fish, pet his dogs, and maybe draw him a picture. I think it would even better if I were their real "grandpa"—but grandpas seem mostly to live elsewhere nowadays.

Despite the children's eagerness to relate to me as a grandfather, my major impact comes from helping their parents and teachers relate to them. Often it's not even necessary to see a child in order to be useful. When I'm working with adults individually or in couples, they commonly bring up problems about children or grandchildren I haven't met. The great majority of the time, I work to empower the adults to deal with the problems without any need to see the children.

The frequency with which younger children are being brought for help has a positive aspect to it in the greater readiness of parents to identify problems and to look for solutions. But it also reflects some negative trends. Our schools are increasingly using referral to pediatricians, family doctors, and psychiatrists as a means of dealing with behavior problems that ought to be handled by improved classroom management and educational techniques. The numbers of young children being brought to doctors also indicates that adult relationships with children are growing so strained that the cracks are showing at an earlier age.

There's a huge downside to the tendency for teachers and parents to seek help from medical professionals. Sending children to medical doctors for behavior problems—conflicts with parents or teachers—almost guarantees that they will treated with psychiatric drugs. Like the psychiatrist who evaluated Mark at NIMH—as well as Steven Hyman, the director of NIMH, or Harold Koplewicz, both of whom addressed the White House Conference—most physicians nowadays will blame the child's brain and prescribe drugs for the youngster. Stigmatizing children with psychiatric diagnoses and subduing them with drugs is not the answer. We need to transform ourselves as parents, teachers, caregivers, and citizens.

I do think it's a good idea for all children to have regular medical checkups and for children with persistent behavior problems to be seen for genuine medical evaluation. For example, some time after Mark saw me, his behavior briefly got worse again, but it turned out that he was upset from the pain of an ear infection. Fortunately, his pediatrician examined him instead of simply recommending psychiatric drugs.

Many doctors, once they knew that Mark had a past history of behavior problems, would not even have taken Mark's temperature or checked his ears. Instead, they would have assumed that he had a persistent "biochemical imbalance" and prescribed drugs. Medical problems can contribute to behavioral problems, but they are easily overlooked by physicians too eager to diagnose "attention deficit / hyperactivity disorder" or some other mythical "illness."[3]

Can We Generalize from Experience?

Do experiences in a doctor's office permit us to generalize about what our children need? I think they do—not because the office is so special, but because from the classroom to the living room to the Scout meeting or church activity, almost *any* experiences with our children permit us to generalize about their unmet needs for relationship and for meaning.

Pedism, or prejudice against children, is at its moral core a failure to take responsibility for our children. The psychiatrist Doug Smith wrote to me from Juneau, Alaska: "We have completely institutionalized pedism as the American way of life. We have absolved ourselves of the sacred responsibility to make sacrifices for our children. Instead of seeing the sacrifice as a holy trust and privilege, we see children as inconvenient nuisances."

Everywhere we find children, we are likely to find the same thing: that children are not a high enough priority of the adults who are caring for them and that, in particular, children are not being sufficiently engaged in meaningful relationships with adults. Everywhere we will also find that when children are young, they respond overnight to improvements in the way they are treated by the adults in their lives.

From the earliest years of life children respond in an instant to a loving, safe, and mature presence, and as soon as they are able to understand language, they begin to respond to meaningful guidance. That's why I have used the term "meaningful relationship" to sum up what children most need—and what children are most lacking from us Relationship and meaning are the two human ingredients that children most hunger for and most need for healthy maturation.

From the home to the neighborhood and church to the workplace, adults can create meaningful relationships with children in whatever context they meet them. The first step is to take every child seriously. As a part of that, we can greet the essential goodness or even the divine spark that we meet in each child. Children will respond in startling and gratifying ways when we greet them as people to be treasured in our lives.

The next chapter will examine a more subtle aspect of meaningful relationship: our children's need to express their critical intelligence.

5

Making Peace with
Our Warrior Children

———◆———

Many children become warriors in their own lives, struggling even to the death against the adults in their families and schools. Cornered and overwhelmed, some children will spit defiantly in the face of abusive adults, even as the escalating assaults threaten their lives.

Often these child warriors are especially energetic, brave, and honest youngsters. Out of pride, they won't "give in." Even against the combined forces of parents, teachers, and doctors—even after they have been threatened, beaten, or drugged—they continue to fight back. Instead of battering these defiant souls into submission, we need to win them over—to teach them peace. The process can only begin through the adults in their lives' learning to be peacemakers with children.

This drive to protect one's sense of worth and fairness is inherent in human nature. It's one of our most praiseworthy human qualities, but it can get children into dreadfully dangerous conflicts with their peers and with adults. And it is easily twisted in self-defeating, harmful directions.

None of the school shootings mentioned in this book is remotely comprehensible without grasping the importance of pride and justice in motivating young people. Anyone old enough to talk is old enough to have a sense of pride and concerns about justice. In adolescence

85

these issues take center stage. It is an aspect of the human search for meaningful relationship. In family and school conflicts, teenage resentment and rebellion are often driven by a sense of being unfairly treated. These feelings can prime teenagers for explosions of anger, outrage, and even violence. Many of our most unhappy, disturbed, and rebellious children are especially preoccupied with these issues.

Talking Intelligently with Children

More than sixty-five years ago, the psychologist Alfred Adler described how children are able to carry out useful, thoughtful conversations with a therapist about their conduct, what motivates it, and why it needs to be changed. Adler observed:

> I have never known a child who could not understand his difficulties when they were set before him. If I find a child who fails to follow me as I trace the roots of his mistakes, I can always be sure that I have blundered either in interpreting his situation or in describing it to him. Every normal [that is, not feeble-minded] child is capable of fathoming the springs of his own actions and reaching a true understanding of his own life.[1]

Notice that Adler assumes that any failure to communicate with the child reflects on him as a therapist rather than on the child. Unfortunately, in psychiatry and "mental health" today, eternal truths are commonly neglected, repressed, or forgotten. Modern psychiatrists usually have no idea that they can have—or could learn to have—serious, productive conversations with children who are brought to their offices. They don't even know that children carefully observe their worlds and make decisions—for better or worse—about how to react to what they see and experience.

In my own experience as a parent and a psychiatrist, talking rationally and honestly with children about their actions is not only possible, it is the best way to learn from them and to teach them. This approach requires and further enhances mutually respectful relationships.

Critical Intelligence in Adolescence

Teenagers often display an especially keen critical intelligence—independent thinking that cuts through the superficiality, hypocrisy, and contradictions of the world around them in search of more enduring truths. Critical intelligence challenges orthodoxy and indoctrination. It often leads to a heightened sense of justice, and a desire to make the world a better place, not only for themselves but for others. Though they frequently focus on themselves, demanding to be treated more fairly by their peers and by adults, young people can also become involved in political and religious activities that have inspired them. When there are no adults available to motivate and to guide them, their critical intelligence can become perverted into destructive rebellion against their families, schools, and communities.

The Courage to Think

Researchers who study and write about intelligence almost invariably describe it in terms more appropriate to machines than to human beings. Even when analyzing innovative expressions of intelligence such as critical thinking, insight, or creativity, scientists tend to describe these phenomena in terms of computer-like models.[2] Research in intelligence is vastly hampered by this failure to understand the moral and psychological core of genuinely insightful thinking. The human faculty that I am calling critical intelligence cannot be separated from the virtues of courage and determination.

It takes courage to be intelligent about life—to face the truth despite its consequences. It requires the placement of a high value on autonomy and independence, the right to think for oneself.

When children are chastised or made fun of for expressing their critical intelligence, they quickly learn self-censorship, first in regard to what they say, and then in regard to what they think. Self-censorship destroys critical intelligence.

In most families and schools, and in all peer groups, a child's ability to think critically must overcome many negative reactions. By the time most of us reach adulthood, we no longer dare to think independently about the authorities, dogmas, traditions, customs, and political ideologies that surround us. The price of critical awareness seems too high. Our forbidden faculty of critical intelligence has been effectively suppressed. Critical intelligence—piercing through what we are *supposed* to see in order to find and to confirm what we *really* see—poses dangers to us. Typically, we can anticipate the dangers so well that we suppress the thoughts before they become fully formed.

Even when people are heroic in other areas of life, they often choose to inhibit their own critical intelligence to avoid suffering a loss of status and power among peers. The courageous signers of the Declaration of Independence, some of the most critically intelligent men in history, were unwilling to draw obvious conclusions in domains that would have threatened their status among their peers. While risking their lives in defiance of King George, none of them risked their status—or the approval of the Declaration of Independence—by insisting on an end to slavery or by promoting the equality of women.

Men like Jefferson and Adams cannot be excused on the grounds that no one else in the eighteenth century had confronted these issues. Slavery was a subject of controversy at the Second Continental Congress in Philadelphia, but Jefferson compromised his original draft, which was critical of slavery, in order to get the Declaration of Independence approved by delegates from the Southern states. Of course, Jefferson was himself a slaveholder. Similarly, women's issues were not unknown in their era. In 1782 Abigail Adams, the wife of John Adams, wrote her husband a letter reminding him that women were "excluded from honours and from offices" in the government and that "even in the freest countrys our property is subject to the controul and disposal of our partners, to whom the Laws have given a soverign Authority."[3] She wanted women to be given credit for maintaining their patriotism in the face of such gender injustice. Jefferson and Adams did not lack the knowledge or awareness to make similar observations of their own on the oppression of women.

Children do not easily give up their critical intelligence. All healthy children at times express themselves like warriors fighting for a cause, however personal. They adopt this role with their first nonverbal refusal to cooperate. They express it with one of the first words all children learn to speak: "No." It quickly develops into those familiar complaints, "I don't want to. You can't make me. It's not fair."

In the late twentieth century children have become increasingly sophisticated in their perception of their personal rights. Unlike generations that grew up in the 1940s and 1950s, today's children are much more aware of emotional and physical abuse, marital problems, alcohol abuse, and almost any other problem displayed by the adults in their lives. They learn about these phenomena from television dramas, public service ads, and the movies, and sometimes they are taught about them in the classroom. Much more than earlier generations, they talk about their own family lives with other children. Often they are ahead of adults in demanding better treatment for themselves.

Self-Respect and Justice Combined

A healthy self-respect becomes distorted into a dangerously compulsive pride in reaction to repeated humiliations. Pride becomes a statement of identity—the refusal no matter what to give in to being rejected, dismissed, ridiculed, shamed, or humiliated. Pride and a sense of justice declare: "I will resist at any cost anything that threatens my self-respect or dignity."

Feelings of injustice and pride can arise for children in the same situation. At home, a child feels unfairly criticized or punished, as well as rejected or misunderstood; justice and pride are both offended. In school, a bigger boy ridicules a smaller one, offending the victim's sense of justice and feelings of pride. When the victimized child begins to feel helpless and overwhelmed, healthy feelings of self-respect can be transformed into vengeful, violent pride.

Self-Respect, Justice, and Critical Intelligence

Motivated by self-respect and a sense of fairness, children naturally try to see through what is said to them in order to discover what's really going on. They know they aren't always told the truth—that things are presented in a way to make them go along without resisting or complaining.

Out of self-respect and a sense of justice, children ask themselves: "Is this what I really want or is Mom making believe it is?" "Is this really fair to me or am I being jerked around?" "Will Dad keep his promise or is he just trying to get me go along with something I won't like?" "Is it really fair for my sister to get the best seat in the car?" "Is it fair for Dad to yell or hit me when I'm not allowed to do the same things to him or anybody else?"

These questions represent the beginning of what I call critical intelligence—the willingness and ability to see through hypocrisy and manipulation to find out what's really going on in human relationships. As the child grows older, critical intelligence sees through the customs, dogma, or prejudices of the surrounding culture in order to find underlying or universal truths.

Unlike mechanical kinds of intelligence, such as mathematical or technical abilities, critical intelligence requires courage and determination. Some children, when they perceive authority to be unjust, will defy it with such bravery and determination that they end up paying dearly for their actions. Others cave in under pressure. They suppress their own critical intelligence in the interest of "getting along" or avoiding punishment and rejection.

As adolescence approaches, many youngsters elaborate complex theories of justice or borrow them from other sources. Early childhood protests against "unfairness" now become genuine and sometimes highly motivated concerns with "larger issues." Unfortunately, if the youngsters endure unrelenting feelings of shame, rejection, and abandonment, the "larger issues" may never get addressed. Instead of becoming moral warriors in the service of higher causes, they remain driven by feelings of humiliation and compulsive, self-defending pride.

Stuck in personal injuries, some young people will seek vindication through violence against real or imagined enemies.

Sandy's Story

Because Sandy died in an accident after our therapy was largely over, I can tell her story exactly as it occurred. Only her name has been changed.

A week before she came to my office for the first time, Sandy had been taken by her parents to another psychiatrist. Sandy was feeling so depressed she was practically bedridden, rarely spoke anymore, had stopped eating, and would lie awake at night. She couldn't imagine returning to her second year of college in the next few weeks.

The doctor interviewed her matter-of-factly for twenty minutes and diagnosed her as suffering from "severe clinical depression." A "major depression" like Sandy's, he explained, is caused by a "biochemical imbalance." He wanted to prescribe an antidepressant for her.

When Sandy balked at taking drugs, the psychiatrist informed her parents that hospitalization—even against Sandy's will—was the only other safe option. Most families would have felt obliged to follow the doctor's advice and direction, even against their daughter's wishes. But Sandy's parents decided to do it the hard way—to rely on Sandy's wishes and their own assessment of her real needs. Sandy's parents phoned me on an emergency basis, asking whether I would see their daughter to give them a second opinion.

When I met her, Sandy was eighteen years old, and at least a year ahead of herself in school. I always thought of her as a precocious young kid—slight in build, bright-eyed, with a trademark mischievous grin, always dressing down in jeans and a shirt, wise and innocent all at once, shy and daring at the same time. If she'd been a few years younger, she would have been labeled noncompliant, oppositional, or defiant.

Already feeling misunderstood and even betrayed by the first psychiatrist, who wanted to force her into a mental hospital, and distrusting of authority in general, Sandy resented seeing yet another "shrink." She expected nothing useful from me—until the ambience of my office caught her attention.

More than twenty-five years ago I decided to build my psychiatric office onto my home so that I could spend more time with my family and see my clients in a more natural and comfortable setting. I designed a twenty-four-foot-long room with a twelve-foot picture window with a southern exposure that looks out on the backyard and goldfish pond. A window box stretches along the inside of the window and tropical plants try to reach the sun through the glass. The asparagus plant has been with me since I first opened my practice in 1968.

The ceiling is high, rising up three more feet in a gentle slope toward the back of the room, and it is beamed. Plants, colorful models of birds, and chimes hang from the ceiling.

Much of the available wall space is occupied by bookcases that are crammed with many hundreds of volumes that span the therapy arena from psychopharmacology to spirituality. There're a couple of bookshelves of my own publications as well. The remaining wall space is covered with large nature photographs, some of them award-winning, by my wife, Ginger. From a distance they look like oil paintings. Boxes of legal cases are strewn about. One quarter of the room is taken up by my desk, computer, and files.

"You actually live and work in here," Sandy observed. "You've got pictures of your family . . . even your dogs. Hey, a psychiatrist with a life," she said wryly. Her sense of humor revealed to me a genuine spirit peeking through the darkness of her suffering.

I asked Sandy to begin her story wherever she wanted. This is what she told me:

A few weeks earlier she had returned to this country after taking a semester off from college. She had been in Ecuador and Peru as a volunteer representing a private human rights group. In Ecuador she would interview families who reported missing members, take photographs at morgues, and help families identify their dead. She held women who wept on her narrow shoulders after their husbands' tortured bodies had been deposited on their wives' doorsteps.

Sandy herself had been seized on the street and whisked off in a death squad car—only to be released an hour later after flashing her incredible humor and magical wit. Even these violent men, it seemed, couldn't stand to torture or to kill such a radiant youngster, and before reaching their dread destination, they dropped her off, physically unhurt, on the side of the road.

"Those guys in the death squad had more empathy for me than that shrink my parents took me to."

My expression showed that I had trouble reaching her conclusion.

"The death squad guys were political enemies," Sandy explained to me. "They were taught to hate me. They could have justified to themselves doing anything to me—anything as horrible as they could think of—and instead they responded to me as a person and let me go. That psychiatrist had no reason to hate me, but I couldn't get through to him. He still wanted to lock me up and drug me, and to me, that's like death and torture."

Within half an hour, Sandy and I were developing an empathic connection, a genuine bond of mutual respect and affection. Three decades older than Sandy, I would have been proud to be her father.

I didn't think of Sandy as having "clinical depression"—I thought of her as a miraculously spirited, critically intelligent young woman who had survived stresses and conflicts that would have destroyed almost anyone else, including me. The first psychiatrist she saw seemingly had no idea he was dealing with a young woman of enormous critical intelligence who, because of her sense of justice, had exposed herself to trauma that would have shaken anyone to the core of their being. Sandy's withdrawal into herself, her long silences, fasting, insomnia, and refusal to return to college were all the product of severe stress and conflict.

"If you do have a biochemical imbalance," I teased her, "then you're imbalanced toward too much empathy for your fellow human beings, complicated by too fine a sense of justice. You've also got too much courage hormone."

A little smile broke through her glum expression, but she quickly lapsed into blaming herself for doing so little, being so weak . . .

"Sandy, when I was eighteen, I thought it was heroic of me to spend a day volunteering on the back wards of a mental hospital. You've been confronting the worst that this world has to offer—political oppression, death squads, and torture."

At the end of her first session with me, Sandy stood up and announced, "You take it." She swept her hands from her abdomen to her mouth as if disgorging something gruesome. "It's my 'clinical depression.' It belongs in a shrink's office. It can stay here as long as you two can stand each other," she joked. "Just don't try to pet it; it'll take your fingers off." I patted the imaginary monster to show her I wasn't intimidated.

Within a week her parents phoned to let me know that Sandy was already seeming like herself again. Sandy and I would have a few more weeks of intense work to do before she returned to school but we both knew she could do it if she wanted. It was now more a matter of deciding what she wanted to do.

A therapeutic miracle? No, although it feels like a miracle when it happens. But lifting a person out of severe doldrums is part of the anticipated work for therapists who genuinely engage their patients. If the individual is young, and the parents are wholly supportive of empowering the youngster, the task is infinitely easier. Since "depression" is essentially profound hopelessness, hopefulness can banish it. Often in our lives, one person can renew our hope. Young people need relationships with mature adults who can be compassionate toward their frustration and suffering while also communicating an enthusiasm for life.

The Trauma Beneath the Surface

Of course, many youngsters become depressed without the kind of extreme life-threatening stress that Sandy underwent. But in my experience, all "depressed people" are struggling with conflicts and trauma, past and present, that largely account for their despair and hopelessness. When dealing with young people, the stresses are usually grossly apparent. Often youngsters have perceived the nature of the family conflicts and tried to voice their views to their parents and previous doctors, only to be dismissed for "blaming their parents." Yet as soon as the family members get together with a therapist, their conflicts typically leap out into the room to perform like real-life actors and actresses.

Political Awareness and Despair

Sandy's anguish was more than the product of witnessing and facing torture and death, and more than the result of her own past history of family stresses and conflicts. She was also profoundly disillusioned by her failure to get U.S. officials at the American embassy to acknowledge that anything dreadful was going on in the country of their Latin ally, Ecuador. Death squads? Torture squads? They never heard of such things. Sandy, so personally involved in confronting evil, was shaken by her country's willingness to sacrifice defenseless people in the name of "national interest."

Any child growing up in the modern era of television must face these same issues. How can our country, how can anyone, live comfortably in the knowledge of so much universal suffering? Questions like this must be answered, one way or another, by our children as they grow up. Too often, the answers they find leave them feeling alienated and resentful. Too often they feel driven to seek self-destructive or violent outlets for the frustration born of critical insights into injustices that no one lets them talk about and seek to understand.

Sandy hated oppression and hypocrisy, whether it was personal or political, aimed at her, aimed at a friend, or aimed at another group of people. Yet this young woman barely out of childhood didn't hate oppressors as individual people. This made her most remarkable for an eighteen-year-old—or for anyone of any age so devoted to human freedom and political reform. She might get angry at perpetrators, but she understood that they had been victims themselves, and she wished them no harm. She only wished them to stop their perpetrations.

In our initial sessions, Sandy would ask in anguish, "How can people torture other people? How can they do it?" And then she'd answer herself, "Because they're dead inside from what's been done to them." She'd weep for victim and torturer alike. And she would demand to know, "How can people make believe it isn't going on?" That was tougher to answer.

Sandy's experience with the previous psychiatrist is an indication of how quickly psychiatry tries to move to take over the lives of critically intelligent young people by diagnosing and drugging them. With help from her parents, Sandy escaped from enforced psychiatric conformity. She found someone who was more interested in listening to her story than in making up a diagnosis aimed at justifying drugs and involuntary hospitalization. She obtained the kind of help she needed to empower her own unique expression of herself—to write her own story and to begin to live it. All of our young people deserve this opportunity.

The Critical Intelligence of Marginalized Groups

Girls are more likely than boys to understand sexism; African Americans and Native Americans more likely to understand racism than European Americans; religious minorities are more likely to recognize the intolerant aspects of majority religions; and, as we've seen, children are more likely than adults to understand abuses of authority in their family and school. Members of a marginalized or minority group often are more able to exercise critical intelligence about the nature of authority in the society. Even when groups as a whole tend to internalize or accept their oppressed status, some individuals among them are likely to grasp the injustice.

Cultivating critical intelligence in part requires becoming more empathic toward minorities and oppressed groups. Listening to them can teach us more about ourselves than we have dared to think about on our own or among ourselves.

While it has been remarked on frequently enough to be a cliché, I am constantly reminded that the cabdrivers who take me to the TV studio or an academic debate commonly have a more informed and sophisticated analysis of socioeconomic forces at work in America than the media representatives or scholars that I will be encountering at the end of the ride. Not only do they often have a better intuitive sense of what's going on, but a surprising number also have read more extensively than I or the people I'd be debating on the relevant subject.

Cabdrivers as individuals have often been disappointed in fulfilling their aspirations and have been unable to overcome obstacles placed in their way by society. They are working class when often they wanted to be more. Those who have their own cabs are small business owners in competition with larger businesses. In the case of immigrants, many held more respected and remunerative positions in their own countries and also have a more cross-cultural perspective than Americans.

Although minorities have a tendency toward greater critical intelligence concerning the society in which they live, many inner-city black children and young people are so traumatized and so limited in their experience that they may have little sense of the origins of their despair in a racist society. It is lifesaving for young black boys and girls to develop and to express their critical intelligence, even though their doing so may be threatening to blacks and whites who have risen in the educational hierarchy.[4]

Critical insights into the history and contemporary expression of oppression can, instead of fostering violence, provide survival tools that enable oppressed minorities to make more informed decisions on how to direct their lives. Dr. Clemmont Vontress, professor emeritus of counseling at George Washington University, points out that understanding racism is an example of the truth setting a person free— in this instance, free of unconsciously imprinted racism.[5] The same of course can be said of any oppressed group, from women and children to Native Americans and ultimately to every American who has too little voice in the conduct of our society.

When Children Withdraw

Most perpetrators of sudden outbursts of violence turn out to be shy, withdrawn people who have for many years been harboring overwhelming feelings of hurt pride and injustice. This observation is confirmed by the lives of most serial murderers and political assassins. Nearly all of the school shooters described earlier have also been described as shy and somewhat withdrawn. Shame and humiliation destroy a person's self-respect and motivate a lust for revenge. This is the psychological dynamic that drives almost all children who become violent.

For self-protection, children will withdraw from devastating feelings of injustice and humiliation. Having made a judgment that a head-on conflict cannot be won, they make a strategic retreat. But withdrawn children do not stop feeling outraged. They are expressing a more extreme version of "I don't care; I hate you; I'll go off by myself." Meanwhile, feelings of hurt pride and injustice simmer inside, ready to boil over, sometimes in a violent fashion.

When Children Give In

Few young people have Sandy's vitality and determination. Most children eventually surrender—they "adjust" to the conditions of their lives. They become adults who, unknowingly, are alienated from their own childhood feelings.

Most adults seem unable to recall the intensity with which they wanted as children to stand up for themselves and their causes. As a result, we become so alienated from our viewpoint as children that we cannot identify with children who are struggling to stand up for themselves and what they believe.

Fighting to the Death

In childhood, the rebellion against authority in the form of parents and teachers often becomes do-or-die. Under more extreme conditions, the child may perceive no hope of victory. Do-or-die is replaced by a do-*and*-die philosophy such as that expressed by some of the school shooters described in this book.

Do-or-die as an attitude is common in childhood. Most children and adolescents who end up in a psychiatrist's office have, to some degree, adopted it. These hurt, angry children, convinced that justice is on their side, will often fight to the bitter end against the combined might of parents, teachers, and doctors, even in the face of being psychiatrically diagnosed and having drugs prescribed for them. Like genuine warriors, they die without compromising themselves.

In my practice I see this all too often: a child is brought into my office for an initial interview drugged into a near stupor by several psychiatric medications. Yet he manages to arouse himself for a fight the moment his parents say something that seems offensive or unfair.

Little boys and girls like this, often labeled "hyperactive" or "oppositional," won't give up fighting any perceived insult. But their rebelliousness only convinces their parents, teachers, and doctors that there is "something wrong with them."

There is nothing physically wrong with these children. There is no scientific evidence that they have "crossed wires," a biochemical imbalance, or an genetic flaw in temperament. Usually, they are wonderfully energetic, intelligent youngsters with whom an equally energetic therapist can easily establish a rapport.

Like a Dangerous Criminal

Andrea was brought into my office by her two parents, each on one of her arms, the way police escort a dangerous criminal into custody. They sat down with her, one on either side, as if to prevent her from breaking loose. She was only nine years old and probably weighed all of sixty pounds.

She glowered at me.

"She's on how much medication?" I asked.

They rattled off the names of an antidepressant, a tranquilizer, and a sleeping pill.

"She's impossible to control!" her mother explained defensively.

"Wow," I declared with enthusiasm, "you must have incredible energy, Andrea! That combo of drugs would zonk me out."

Andrea looked interested.

"She's a terror," her father asserted. "We've tried behavioral programs, medications, parent training . . . Nothing works with her."

"Ha!" Andrea shot back.

" 'Ha'?" I asked. " 'Ha'?"

"Yeah, ha!" she defied me.

"I like your spirit," I declared.

"Yeah, sure," she said.

"You're used to being bullshitted," I said, and then covered my mouth.

She grinned, "Yeah."

"Tell me, who doesn't tell you the truth."

"Everybody."

"Really, Andrea," her mother protested.

"I want to hear what she thinks," I explained.

"Everybody," she repeated pointedly in the direction of her mother and then her father.

"You're parents lie to you?"

"All the time."

They were both shaking their heads.

"Tell me . . . "

"They said we were going out for ice cream tonight. Some ice cream parlor," she added, glancing around the room.

I laughed at her cutting humor.

"We will go out for ice cream," her mother said.

I waited but Andrea did not respond. Often children simply cannot debate an adult, even when the adult is obviously in the wrong.

"Andrea means that you told her about the ice cream to get her to come here," I explained. "So it doesn't matter if you're going to take her out afterward."

"Exactly," Andrea confirmed.

"It's true," her father said. "We've had so much trouble handling her, we've taken to telling her whatever will work."

"Well it's not working!" Andrea stood up and started for the door.

Her father grabbed her arm.

"Wait!" I said. "Please, let her go, Dad."

The instant her father released her, Andrea jumped two steps toward the door—but did not try to leave.

"Andrea," I said firmly. "I get what you're saying. Your dad has admitted that he lied. I want to help you and your parents get along without anymore lying."

"Yeah, right. Why should I believe you?"

"Because you can see I'm being honest with you. You can see I'm on your side. You're the kid—you need someone on your side."

She nodded.

"I'm on your side, Andrea. That's the first thing. And I want to help your parents to be on your side, too. The three of you are just very confused about what to do. I promise you, I'm going to be honest with you."

I saw her visibly relax.

"Right now you think you've got to fight for everything—and I want to make it different for you."

She sat down on the floor.

"Andrea, get off the floor," her mother said.

"It's okay. I'm glad she has decided to stay. Andrea, I'm very glad you're staying. I would have been very frightened if you'd run out of the office."

"Why?"

"Your parents would have been mad at me."

She laughed at the truth of it.

Her father nodded and laughed.

"I can take care of myself," she said.

"Andrea, no one's as tough as you're trying to act. I mean, I admire your spirit, but I know you're scared underneath."

"Yeah, how do you know that?" she asked defiantly.

"Because I feel scared right now and I'm"—I counted—"I'm eight or nine times older than you. I know your parents are scared, too. We're scared because it's so hard to know what to do when a little girl is so defiant and angry."

She looked at her mother and father. They nodded. Her mother began crying.

Andrea wiggled over to the couch and leaned against her mother's legs while her mother cried and patted Andrea's hair.

Soon Andrea and her parents were able to exchange promises. Andrea would try very hard to stop herself from fighting against everything they said and did, and they would work hard on never lying to her. In my experience, every time parents have devoted themselves to changing their own behavior, children have quickly changed as well. This proved to be true with Andrea and her parents.

Children are usually very aware of being patronized and lied to by adults. A psychiatrist who diagnoses and drugs them is quickly put into that category of adults who cannot be trusted. On the other hand, anyone who approaches them with more dignity and honesty will be quickly recognized as "something different." When an adult empowers their sense of pride and justice, and shows an interest in their critical intelligence, and believes them when they say they are being misled and lied to, they usually become eager to talk.

Youngsters readily understand that they are in rebellion rather than suffering from a "mental illness." A compassionate discussion with a child usually discloses that the child's problems are rooted in do-or-die conflicts with adults and peers in the family or school. Meanwhile, their parents may have grave difficulty seeing beyond their child's distressing or "bad" behavior.

Even when a child has been severely traumatized by an accident, by emotional or physical abuse, or by the loss of a loved one, issues of pride and justice arise: "Why me?" "Why did this happen to me?" "Did I deserve this—what did I do wrong?" "Can I ever trust anyone again?" "Did God let me down?"

Similar issues arise when a child witnesses the suffering of others. Seeking answers about the unfairness of life, he or she raises questions: "Why was I the one who didn't get hurt?" "Why did my friend die instead of me?" "Why do they always pick on Sarah?" "Why doesn't my friend have enough money for lunch?" "Why am I so much better off?"

By the time a child becomes "a problem," he or she is enmeshed in conflicts involving pride and justice. Often the child has drawn a line in the sand and refuses to give in, "no matter what."

All too often, mental health professionals fail to fully appreciate the internal moral and psychological struggles that are always going on inside their young patients' minds. As a result, these therapists and doctors fail to connect with children on a genuine basis. Without realizing what they are doing, the professionals end up siding with the parents in conflicts over pride and justice. In the end, the child gets diagnosed and prescribed a drug, which guarantees there will be no positive resolution to the conflict.

Even well-intentioned parents are likely to go along with the doctor's simplistic diagnoses and mind-numbing drugs, because they distrust their own natural understanding of what is going on in their child's heart and mind. Often, however, when another professional suggests that drugs are not the answer, these same parents will quickly remember, "Yes, I always thought the drug approach was wrong." They may quickly grasp that their struggles with their child are better understood as conflicts that they haven't learned to resolve.

Leonard and His Mother

The little boy was only ten years old. His mother had an M.B.A. and a Ph.D. in economics. But as so often happens, it was easier to talk about the root causes of things with Leonard than with his mother. Leonard, meanwhile, was being given enormous doses of the stimulant drug Ritalin in order to make him more manageable at home and in the classroom. Especially at home he would frequently become defiant in response to anything his mother requested of him, and the two of them would become embroiled in bitter struggles.

Leonard's mother was very busy working for a Washington, D.C., think tank that frequently required her to make instant responses to breaking news. Often she would get home late at night. Sometimes she had to travel and leave Leonard in the care of a nanny. On top of that, his father had left the family when little Leonard was only six and had never been heard from again. Leonard spent most of his time at home with baby-sitters, never knowing when his mom would show up. When she was home, she and her son were, in her words, "at each other's throats."

Probably owing to the large doses of Ritalin, Leonard was frail and small, had trouble sleeping at night, and was often jittery. He also had bouts of headache and nausea within an hour of taking the first dose each morning. His mother wanted Leonard taken off the drug but she feared it would become even more difficult to manage Leonard's obstreperous and rebellious actions. At home or at school, he was a handful. His way of talking back to his mother or his teachers often incited them to anger.

Leonard was diagnosed with attention deficit/hyperactivity disorder because he was often too agitated to sit still. In addition, he was diagnosed with oppositional defiant disorder because he was so often angry at the adults in his life. He had physically attacked his last psychiatrist—the one who assigned him his diagnoses and prescribed him the drugs. A mere eighty pounds, Leonard was easily controlled before he could inflict bodily harm, but the outburst resulted in a medication increase.

Leonard's mother was obviously nervous as they sat down in my office. Leonard looked around the room as if casing the joint for future demolition.

"You collect stuff?" he asked me.

"They say three of anything is a collection," I agreed. "I've got three of a lot of things."

Leonard surveyed the room and recited, "Ducks . . . turtles . . . frogs . . . fish."

"I like models of little creatures," I explained.

"Are they expensive?" he asked, picking up a small elephant carved from white jade.

"Just that one—" I started to say.

"Leonard!" his mother interrupted with horror at his impertinence. "Put that down."

"It's fine," I said. "I don't leave things in easy reach that kids cannot touch." I made a joke: "I won't balk until he demands to know my gross annual income."

Leonard looked at me impishly as if about to ask about my income. I in turn burst into laughter. "He's going to ask my income," I declared. "No one has ever dared ask me that!" I said with genuine admiration of his chutzpah.

That defused the tension and Leonard began grinning.

His mother looked mystified.

"I hear you attacked your psychiatrist."

"Mom told you? Well, he's a jerk," Leonard observed. "All he wants is to give me drugs."

"You don't respect him?"

"Would you?"

"No, I probably wouldn't—not if he's the one who put you on such a big dose of drugs."

Leonard cocked his head. Then without his usual bravado, he asked, "Are you for real?"

"Yeah," I said matter-of-factly. "Too real for some people."

"I'll bet the other shrinks hate you."

"Leonard! Dr. Breggin is a very respected doctor."

I gave a big sigh. Leonard, whatever his faults, was not lacking in critical intelligence.

"Leonard, you're right about some of them."

Leonard got the point: "Depends on what kind of shrink it is—if they hate you or not?"

"Exactly."

"My doctor would hate you!"

His mother stifled a laugh.

"I want to hear what you and your mom are always fighting about," I began.

"I don't listen good," he said without hesitation. "It makes her mad. So she hits me and threatens me."

"Leonard, I never threaten you."

So she wasn't denying hitting him.

"You do hit him?"

"I know I shouldn't," she admitted. "That's one reason I'm here. I'm at the end of my rope. But I never *threaten* him."

"Why don't you ask Leonard what he's referring to," I suggested.

"Leonard, I never threaten you, do I?"

"Today, on the way here," he said.

"What?"

"You said if I didn't shut up and calm down, you wouldn't play chess with me when we get home after seeing the doctor."

"I just didn't know what else to do," she confessed with embarrassment.

At ten years old, Leonard was a master at seeing through hypocrisy. He also had a good grasp on the way people relate to each other. Evaluating people and situations was much more of a struggle for his mother.

We talked for a while longer. Leonard asked if I could be his doctor and I deferred to his mother. She said she'd try it for a while.

"You've got to give it a chance, Mom," he said like a parent talking to a child. As an aside, he explained to me, "She's pretty frustrated with doctors right now."

"It's fine with me if you take your time deciding," I said to Leonard's mother and then added, "but if you do make up your mind, Leonard's right about giving it a chance. He needs to know that you'll stick to your decision unless you have a good reason to change your mind. His time with you is so unpredictable, but he needs to know you'll come here with him. Otherwise, he won't feel safe about relating to me."

"He's right, Mom," Leonard said.

Toward the end of the session, I asked if I could make some suggestions, and they both agreed.

"First, Leonard, I want you to agree to work very hard on not fighting back every time your mother asks you to do something, like helping with dinner, or going to bed on time. She's your mom, you need to respect her and to let her give most of the directions. You should only take a stand if you think it's something very important to you. And then, ask your mom nicely to listen to you."

He started to protest and I interrupted. "No, wait, let me get all of my recommendations out at once. Who knows, maybe you can both agree to the whole bunch of them. If not, we'll keep working at it, until we find something we can agree on."

"Okay," he said.

"So, Leonard, you'll try your best not to talk back, and when you do disagree with something, you'll be respectful. And when you don't agree about something important, you'll ask your mom if you can discuss it with her."

As with so many children, when an adult appeals to their reason, Leonard was already nodding, even though I hadn't yet asked anything of his mother. Leonard was even aware of the kinds of decisions he had made—for example, to fight back at every opportunity—that were exacerbating his conflicts with his mother.

After I gave Leonard my suggestions, I turned to his mother.

"Now, Mom, no more hitting, ever. Okay? Never touch Leonard except to be sweet to him. Hands are for gentle pats, not for hitting."

"No more hitting, I promise," she said to Leonard.

"Ever?" Leonard emphasized.

"Never, ever," she agreed.

Leonard shook his head in wonderment.

"The next one is a little more complicated," I said to his mother. "When you're mad at Leonard, or when you want to punish him, *never* threaten to take away anything that you enjoy together like playing chess. Don't ever take away any of your precious time together, whether it's going out to dinner, seeing a movie, taking a walk, or just hanging around in the same room together. When you're angry, don't even hint at doing anything that further disrupts your relationship. See what I mean? Always treat your relationship like a treasure that can't be broken or manipulated, no matter what."

"What's 'manipulated' mean?" Leonard asked.

" 'Jerked around,' " I answered. "When you manipulate someone, you jerk them around emotionally instead of being straight with them. Like, you try to make them feel bad, so they'll do what you want. The two of you should stop jerking each other around. I want to see you treat each other as if you're special."

They were both silent and almost expressionless.

"So what do you two think?" I asked.

Leonard, the ten-year-old, looked me in the eye and said, "I think you're amazing."

"You are, too, Leonard," I said from the heart.

"You are amazing, Leonard," his mother confirmed.

It was the first positive thing she had said to Leonard since arriving. He grinned and gave her a big kiss. She let him lean against her, and they hugged.

Over a period of several weeks, Leonard's mother and I worked on lowering his medication. The gradual reductions weren't meant as a reward for good behavior, but Leonard treated them that way. His behavior—and his mother's—consistently improved from week to week as they learned to treat each other according to principles that recognized each other's sense of worth and justice. Within a few months, Leonard was no longer a serious "behavior problem" at home.

The vignette about Leonard and his mother illustrates important points about what I call "critical intelligence" in children. As in so many of the families I work with, the child who's been psychiatrically diagnosed and drugged displays more critical intelligence than his parents. In this case, Leonard knew that he was being unfairly treated by his first psychiatrist. But he didn't have the skills, maturity, or opportunity to express his insights without empathic help from an adult. In do-and-die frustration, he attacked the doctor.

By contrast, when given the opportunity to reason together about family conflicts, and to have his own dignity and sense of fairness confirmed, he became eager to cooperate. Surprisingly, he initially became more willing than his mother to accept responsibility and to try to change. He even took a parental role by reassuring and encouraging his mother to give the therapy a genuine effort. He was also willing to let go of past grievances in order to smooth things out with his parent. Young children often tend to be more genuinely forgiving than their parents. Life has not yet so deeply embittered them.

The Genetics of Critical Intelligence

The capacity for language is built into human biology. It is so much a part of the fabric of the brain that given the slightest opportunity children will quickly learn to talk. Critical intelligence, which is necessary for survival, seems to be built into the brain so that given the slightest opportunity children will display an inquiring mind.

In *The Wild Child*, the former psychoanalyst Jeffrey Moussaieff Masson, Ph.D., documents the explosive mental growth of a sixteen-year-old boy, Kaspar Hauser, who was discovered wandering the streets of Nuremberg, Germany, in 1828.[6] He had been imprisoned since early childhood in an unlit cellar room until his escape. As he learned to talk, he expressed surprise at how little he was aware of the possibility that other human beings like himself lived outside the dark room. He showed concern over the anxiety that his unknown jailer must have felt while keeping him confined.

Kaspar challenged conventional views presented to him about God and religion, so that his biographer, Anselm von Feurbach, described him as possessing an "inborn Pyrrho." Pyrrho of Elis was the original skeptical philosopher of Greek antiquity and, perhaps, the father of the concept of critical intelligence.

The teenager Kaspar made astute observations on the motives and hypocrisy of the adults who tried to civilize him. Kaspar himself later described the experience of being questioned by four priests shortly after he was found. The priests insisted that he accept a theological interpretation of creation that made no sense to him, and in response he asked for time to read and think, presumably to make up his own mind: "When I said to them that I don't yet understand any of that, that I had to learn to read and write first, they replied that these other things have to be learned first. They did not go away until I let them know I wanted them to leave me alone." By contrast, when a more thoughtful professor showed Kaspar how his own "invisible thinking and desire, that is, your spirit" could move his limbs, Kaspar was able to grasp the existence of a greater spirit, God. The realization made him joyful.

Thus, in this adolescent boy who had been utterly isolated from human contact and even from life itself, a basic critical capacity quickly flowered. A basic human faculty came bursting forth without the encumbrances of society and culture. His rapid maturation also confirms the close connection between language and critical thought: both develop quickly at the slightest nurturing. Any parent who has grown tired of a two-year-old's asking questions can attest to the close connection between the development of language and a child's demand for "answers."

I asked Jeffrey Masson, whose books on animal life and spirit are widely read,[7] what he had concluded about critical intelligence from his extensive studies of people and creatures. Dr. Masson replied,

> Living in a way consistent with one's own nature is the greatest source of happiness, and animals or humans who are deprived of that do not thrive. Critical intelligence is a part of living in accord with one's nature as a human being and anything that interferes with that—imprisonment or a drug imposed on the natural human capacity for joy—is a form of abuse. To put children into confinement or to drug them is to distort their human nature and impede the development of their intelligence. Critical intelligence requires freedom, a lack of confinement, a lack of interference with the human brain. Schools unfortunately are a form of confinement. It is not where most children want to be—confined to a classroom all day. Drugging them to make them stay compounds the harm.

The Special Awareness of Children

Why do children often display more critical intelligence than their parents, teachers, and doctors? For one thing, children today are much more sophisticated than in previous generations. From *Zena* to *The X Files*, they are constantly exposed to movies and videos with stories built around defending truth and justice. Often their parents are less sophisticated than they are in these matters.

However, even without contemporary sophistication, children in general see more readily through hypocrisy to the underlying truths about what's going on in relationships. Their critical intelligence usually flourishes until they get a bit older and grow more hopeless about implementing their viewpoint in the real world.

Parents in my practice will often confirm that their especially troubled or troublesome child was "different" from an early age. The diagnosed child will be described as "more sensitive," "always questioning," "never taking anything for granted," "always wanting everything his own way," "always challenging everything," "always ready to complain," and "always thinking about everything."

In my personal and clinical experience, our best and most wonderful children are the ones who cannot or will not hide what they are really thinking and feeling. They are irrepressible. But their expression of critical intelligence exposes them to grave risks. Doctors, for example, will tell parents, "Your child has problems with impulse control." Instead, the doctors should explain, "Your child is more vital, energetic, courageous, determined, and potentially more powerful than other children. Sure, right now your child seems willful and disobedient, but it's a mark of his special sense of independence and autonomy. We need to work together to guide all this energy without suppressing or invalidating it."

As seen in the stories in the clinical vignettes earlier in this chapter, children with a higher sensitivity and critical intelligence respond dramatically to anyone who welcomes their special qualities. When these children meet an adult who respects and empowers them for their unique qualities, they blossom with gratitude and joy, and do everything possible to make the relationship work. In my own practice, these children enjoy coming for therapy, and try their best to make it work.

Empathy and Critical Intelligence

As a Harvard College student I volunteered at a Massachusetts state mental hospital, and my empathy for the "mental patients" I encountered there made clear to me that I would never want a lobotomy or electroshock. I knew I would never want to be treated like a "mental patient." As I describe in *Toxic Psychiatry*, my unwillingness to see myself as inherently superior to "mental patients" started me on a career of reform work that eventually was aimed at enlightening my own profession through the International Center for the Study of Psychiatry and Psychology (see Appendix B).

Genuine critical intelligence depends on recognition of the common human nature that we share. An empathic connection with human beings in general rips away the sham and hypocrisy that encourages us to feel superior. Generational, gender, racial, and cultural barriers melt before the insight that we are made of the same essential human stuff.

Recalling Our Own Childhood Experiences

To be critically intelligent about children, we must be willing to accept their shared humanity with us. To accomplish this, we must empathize with our own experiences as children. If we allow ourselves to remember and to understand some of our own frustration and suffering when we were children, we will be far more able to understand the needs of all children for rational discipline, justice, unconditional love, engaging education, and lots of play.

As children, we suffered every time we were exposed to irrational discipline, every time we failed to receive unconditional love, every time we were bored in school, and every time we didn't get to play enough. We suffered as well whenever we were hurt, threatened, treated unfairly, or otherwise made to feel unsafe. To understand what every child needs, we need only remember what we needed—and often didn't get.

Unfortunately, most people cannot recall childhood with any accuracy. Sometimes major traumas are remembered, such as sexual abuse, the death of family member, or a serious accident or illness; but if they are surrounded with guilt, shame, and other intolerable emotions, even major events are often entirely forgotten.

More subtle conflicts between children and their parents are almost always forgotten by children after they grow up, in part because their childhood perceptions were always being undermined at the time. Few adults are able to recall or to recount the kinds of conflicts described between children and their parents in this chapter. If they hadn't been dealt with in our therapy sessions, Andrea as an adult would probably not be able to recall her outrage at being lied to by her parents, and Leonard might not even remember attacking his psychiatrist. Even with the emphasis placed on these experiences in therapy during their childhood, they might not be remembered in later years.

Often we distort what actually happened, usually to protect ourselves from painful memories, sometimes to side with one parent against another, sometimes to remain loyal to family myths and lies. We tend to forget that healthy impulse to be a warrior in the service of justice. To fully understand ourselves as children we must dare to lift the veil of amnesia in order to reach some of our own suffering and childhood aspirations for a principled life. Despite great effort in therapy, most people end up recovering only a very partial picture of their childhood experiences, but it is often enough to inspire courage and empathy for oneself and others.

If recalling childhood emotions and experiences proves too difficult—as it often does—we can do the next best thing: We can *assume* that our childhood was filled with unbearable confusion, unfairness, conflict, and suffering, and then resolve to treat children as treasures to be loved and protected to the fullest extent of our ability as caregivers.

If you assume that every child is sensitive, vulnerable, readily injured, and easily broken, then you will never be far from the truth. If you assume that all children are motivated by pride and justice, you will be able to communicate with them. If you assume that all children should be treated as sacred trusts who deserve your full measure of devotion, you will be on the right path. If you seek to find the vulnerable, precious child in yourself and in all other adults at all times in your dealings with yourself and others, you will have achieved enlightenment. You will become a gift to the children in your life to whatever degree that you remain enlightened in your dealings with them.

In our families and schools, we need more open discussion of the limitations and flaws of our society, including our families and schools. Instead of leaving our children to turn to destructive sources of guidance on the Internet or on television, we will be able to inspire them to make their own contributions to society. Above all else, we must recognize that children have a finely tuned sense of pride and justice to which we must appeal in building relationships with them.

Demands for More Conformity

In the wake of the violence unleashed at Littleton, Colorado, and Conyers, Georgia, there has been a tendency to demand more conformity among our children. In a county not far from here, the school board unanimously prohibited students from wearing "long trench coats" or "bulky, oversized coats" in school buildings.[8] A fourteen-year-old girl in Harrisburg, Pennsylvania, was strip-searched and suspended for two weeks because, during a class discussion about the Littleton tragedy, she said she could understand how unpopular students might lash out violently if pushed too far.[9]

The writer Jon Katz, in his article "Report from Hell High," describes the nightmare created for "goths" and other seeming misfits by the Littleton tragedy. He describes the hostile reaction by schools to any student expressions of critical intelligence concerning these tragedies. Katz received what he called a "powerful and painful" e-mail from an Illinois high school student:

> My social studies teacher asked if we wanted to talk about Littleton. I said I had some sense of how those kids might have been driven crazy by cruel students, since it happens to me. I said I had thought of taking my father's gun to school when I was in the ninth grade and was so angry. I was sent home. When I got there, three detectives were going through my room.

Another student wrote to Katz, "We were all called into an assembly and asked to turn in our friends who were moody, emotional, angry at the way they were treated in school. That's everybody I know." Katz observed, "Overnight, the geeks and misfits and oddballs became instant suspects in a kind of 'geek profiling,' a national hunt for the strange."

Many students around the country seemed to sympathize with the actions of Eric and Dylan as an expression of their own angry feelings. A teenage boy in my practice told me, "I identify with Eric Harris. Completely." He himself was the constant butt of ridicule at his highly regarded private school. Meanwhile, he was a model student whom no one would have suspected of harboring violent resentments. Later I encouraged him to share these feelings with his family, not to alert them to a danger, but to gain their attention to how desperate he was feeling about the abuse he was taking in his private school. His parents, fortunately, began a search for a school that would put a higher premium on mutually respectful relationships among the students.

When adults do show respect and understanding for a child's pride and sense of justice, they create the basis for a healing and creative relationship.

6

Child Monsters? Or Hurt Children with Stories to Tell?

———•✦•———

If you were to come upon a bedraggled little boy trudging along the road amid refugees escaping from a war-torn region, you would quickly try to locate his family. In the interim, you would offer food and water, and provide for any other immediate needs. If he remained sad and tearful, and sat in stony silence, you would want to hug and to reassure him, and to encourage him to talk.

You would hope, perhaps above all else, that the little boy would begin to speak. You would be sure that he had a tragic story to tell, and that the telling might give him some relief, help to build a relationship with you, and provide information on how to find his family. Given his desperate condition, you could anticipate that the rest of his family would need help as well.

Suppose, after a short time with you, the boy started to act frightened and angry? Suppose he began to push you away and to hit you when you came close? You would assume he'd been badly hurt by his recent experiences. You would reassure him that you were a very safe person who would never harm him. You would make clear that you would protect him. You would try to help him to recover and to regain his trust of adults. You would continue to make every effort to get him to talk and to locate his family.

Every day children as bedraggled and sad as the little refugee boy are brought to mental health professionals and no one is listening to their story. Typically, they are alienated from their parents but no one focuses on helping them reconnect in a loving way.

Parents who bring their child for help these days all too often believe that the child has no story to tell the psychiatrist. They have no explanation for their child's dejection and unwillingness to talk. The psychiatrist also often doesn't press for any details about the family's history and current functioning as it affects the child. Instead, the doctor diagnoses the child with "clinical depression" or some similar disorder, and prescribes drugs.

If the little boy, like our refugee, began to show a great deal of fear and anger, he might be given a second diagnosis, such as oppositional defiant disorder. Little or no effort would be made to discover the source of his anger and conflict with his family. Instead, he would be prescribed more drugs. If he continued to refuse to communicate, he might be diagnosed with autism or schizophrenia, and be given the most toxic agents of all, the adult antipsychotic drugs such as Haldol, Risperdal, and Zyprexa.

Instead of discovering the child's story, the biologically oriented psychiatrist might inform the little boy's parents that their son suffered from a brain disease or a biochemical imbalance. The doctor, exactly like the psychiatrists who spoke at the White House Conference on Mental Health, might become emphatic about it: Nothing in the boy's life could have caused his sadness and withdrawal. In keeping with this foregone conclusion, psychiatrists with this viewpoint would make no detailed inquiry into physical, emotional, or sexual abuse in the home or elsewhere. Any attempts to talk with the child would focus on disclosing serious "symptoms," such as hearing voices or wanting to kill himself.

Doctors nowadays often assume that children have no story to tell, but like the refugee child encountered on the road, they often have tragic stories to tell—if only we would listen. Through our listening the children might find some relief, we would engage them in healing relationships, and we would discover better ways to help, if only to remove some of them from an abusive home or hurtful situation.

Harm Caused by Psychiatrically Labeling Children

What happens when we tell parents and teachers that the children in their care are "at risk" of becoming violent because they seem nervous, tense, anxious, depressed, sad, secretive, withdrawn, angry, or friendless? What is the result of encouraging parents or teachers to "identify" children from a "mental health" viewpoint? What consequences follow from encouraging parents and teachers to think like psychiatric diagnosticians?

When parents, teachers, or other caretaking adults are taught to believe that they are dealing with "an ADD child" or a "child with clinical depression," they are less likely to view themselves as having anything substantial to do with causing or with healing the child's problems. Instead of viewing themselves as enmeshed in conflict with the child, they view the child as the sole cause of the problem. Diagnosing the child in effect divorces the parent or teacher from the child's problem by declaring, "I'm okay; you're not."

Our Contradictory Attitudes Toward Children

America has always held ambivalent attitudes toward children who are difficult, maladjusted, upset, or angry. On the one hand, we preach the message, "There's no such thing as a bad child, there's just bad behavior." We believe that any child can be reached with the right effort. This hope motivates most attempts to improve the conditions of children's lives, whether the children are in their own homes, in foster placements, or in institutions.

On the other hand, our society also holds with the contrasting "bad seed," or "monster," myth that difficult children are genetically predetermined to cause trouble. Thinly disguised in scientific lingo, this theme runs through biological psychiatry, and has been heavily marketed to the public. It surfaced once again at the White House Conference in June 1999 as the basic explanation for the emotional distress and anger of our children.

The Bad Seed Tradition

The psychiatrist Paul Wender, a pioneer decades ago in promoting the psychiatric diagnosing and drugging of "hyperactive children," has compared badly behaved children to "infant King Kongs."[1] Turning common sense on its head, he has argued that a child's behavior causes any inconsistencies or problems seen in the parent's behavior.[2] In 1973, he declared that physicians who "rarely used medicine, or feel that it is rarely needed . . . should not treat a hyperactive child."[3] He now believes that attention deficit / hyperactivity disorder (ADHD) is "genetically transmitted and biologically mediated" by hundreds of different genes, to account for the hundreds of variations that he sees.[4]

Another longtime proponent of the ADHD viewpoint, the psychologist Russell Barkley, put it most simply: "There is, in fact, something 'wrong' with these children."[5] There is nothing wrong, Barkley says, with the mothers and fathers—leading to his great popularity among certain groups of parents. Over the years he has emphasized using stimulants to enforce "compliance," a euphemism for blind submission to authority. Like Wender, he concludes that the child's problem is "primarily biological."[6]

Men like Paul Wender and Barkley—and Dr. Harold Koplewicz, from the White House Conference on Mental Health[7]—dominate current child psychiatry. They misinform parents, teachers, and health professionals that the emotional problems and conflicts faced by children have nothing to do with upbringing, schooling, or any other environmental or human factor. Even child abuse—which is epidemic in our society—is left out of the equation of what makes children upset or difficult to manage.[8] They ignore the genuine needs of children while vigorously pushing an antichild stance, instead of a child-oriented one.

The bad seed myth sprouted once again in the popular press after the rash of school shootings in 1998–99. Two weeks after the tragedy at Columbine High School, the May 3 *Time* magazine displayed pictures of Eric Harris and Dylan Klebold above a giant headline that read THE MONSTERS NEXT DOOR. By loudly proclaiming violent children to be monsters, the cover served to distance us from them. Where previously they had seemed in many ways to be "the kids next door," now they became "the monsters next door."

After yet another school shooting, this time at Heritage High School in Georgia, *Time*'s managing editor tried to soften the monster metaphor by warning, "But it feels important to see how 'normal' these kids can look and to worry a bit more whether they could be the kids next door, or even our own."[9] Nonetheless, that same May 31 issue marshaled the most powerful tool of all when it comes to distancing ourselves from our children: psychiatric diagnosis. It informed readers on how to identify depressed children rather than how to identify and to ameliorate the kinds of negative or absent family and school relationships that can make children feel desperate.[10]

Diagnosing "Behavior"

The most common childhood diagnoses—attention deficit/hyperactivity disorder, oppositional defiant disorder, and conduct disorder—describe *behaviors* that annoy, frustrate, or threaten us as adults, such as inattention to schoolwork, disobedience, rebellion, and anger. The diagnoses categorize these behaviors without in any way explaining their origin. They don't encourage us to feel empathy for the child or to explore the sources of the child's distress. Instead, they put the child in a category that requires no further exploration or understanding on our part. It's as if the children have no story to their lives.

In the past, these diagnoses were lumped under the category disruptive behavior disorders, or the DBDs. In reality, they are not "disorders" at all but manifestations of conflict between children and adults, but the diagnostic sleight of hand blames the source of the conflict on the child.

Alan Among the Doctors:
The Story of an Oppositional Little Boy

Alan was ten years old when his mother and father brought him for a mental health evaluation. They had been separated for six months and though they knew they would never get back together, they cared so much about Alan that they tried to put aside their differences to seek help for him. He had become a severe behavior problem in his mother's home and in school.

Now they sat in the child psychologist's office. Alan was standing defiantly by himself while his mother and father sat angled away from each other in the two chairs in front of the doctor's desk.

"Alan," the psychologist asked, "do you know why you're here?"

"Yeah, I know why I'm here," the ten-year-old shot back. "They made me come."

"Do you know why they wanted you to come?"

"They think I'm crazy."

"No," his parents said in unison.

"Then why am I seeing a shrink?"

"Alan, don't be disrespectful," his father said.

His mother apologized to the psychologist: "It's not you. He's always like this with strangers."

"Strangers?" his father said. "He blows off teachers, too."

"So? So what? There's nothing you or anybody else can do about it," Alan said scornfully toward the psychologist.

"Alan," the doctor said, "would you mind sitting in the waiting room for a while. There're some toys and books to keep you busy while I talk to your parents alone."

"I'm out of here," Alan said as he marched from the office.

Mom followed him out to settle him down and then returned.

"Alan's been like this ever since *he* left." Mom pointed angrily at her husband. "He's putting himself and that *girl* ahead of everyone, including his own son." That "girl" was the woman her estranged husband was dating.

The psychologist began taking notes.

"It's not about that girl," Alan's dad said, "it's about us. We were fighting for years."

"It's because you drink!" she said.

"I haven't had a drop since I left *you*," he spat back.

The psychologist stopped taking notes. He was not oriented to families or to conflict resolution. His specialty was disorders of children.

"So, how long did you say Alan has been having difficulties?"

"Six months, a year."

He wrote that down and underlined it. Unlike many professionals, he was aware of the actual criteria for the diagnosis of oppositional defiant disorder. It required that the symptoms be apparent for six months or more.

"What changes have you noticed?" the psychologist asked.

"He's so angry and resentful," Alan's mom explained. "He defies me all the time—won't give in to anything I ask."

"Noncompliant." The doctor wrote down the technical name.

"He doesn't respect you," her husband broke in. "You give in too often."

"Should I hit him like you do?"

"I know that was wrong. I don't hit Alan anymore."

"Oh, sure, you're a saint since leaving me. You know, doc, Alan has started doing the same things his father always did." She gestured angrily. "You always blame everyone else for your problems and Alan is doing the same thing."

The psychologist was now so busy taking notes that he hardly looked up.

"So all of Alan's problems are from me?" Dad complained. "What about your mother! She's spiteful. She's vindictive toward me! You know what Alan asked me last week? 'Daddy, why does Grandma hate you so much?' "

"Maybe you could have told him, 'Because I'm screwing a girl who's young enough to be your big sister.' "

That led to silence.

The psychologist asked, "Is Alan like that—very spiteful?"

Mom nodded.

He wrote another note.

She added, "It's been like that for months. I think it started the first time he heard his father threatening to leave me. He's been giving his little sister a hard time, too. He *deliberately* annoys her until she starts crying. Then he starts arguing with me that it's not his fault."

"Does he lose his temper easily?" the psychologist asked.

"Yes . . ." Mom said.

"Not with me!" his father declared.

"He's afraid of you!" she shot back.

The psychologist moved his pencil down a printed list, making check marks. "Eight out of eight," he said mostly to himself.

"Eight what?" father asked.

"You two really need to understand something," the psychologist said.

They both grew silent. They felt sure that the psychologist was about to come down on them as rotten parents.

Instead, the psychologist said, "You need to stop blaming each other. It's neither of your fault. Alan has oppositional defiant disorder. He has all eight traits on the list when it only requires four to make the diagnosis. With a child like Alan, parents can end up at each other's throats."

Alan's parents looked at each other with mixed disbelief and relief.

Mom murmured, "I was always afraid that the divorce and all the fighting caused Alan's problems."

"Parents always blame themselves. We know differently now. Children like Alan cause the family problems. I've seen them cause divorce."

The estranged husband and wife looked at each other. A wisp of hope crossed between them but Dad shook his head. "We were fighting before he was born," he explained.

"We were fighting before we were married," Mom added.

"So what do we do about Alan?" Dad asked.

"He has a chemical imbalance that makes it hard for him to control his impulses. There are a number of drugs that can help children like him. Individual counseling might help him, too. First I want you to bring back Alan a few more times for psychological testing. I believe he may also have attention deficit/hyperactivity disorder. Then we'll refer him to a psychiatrist with whom I work closely. He can prescribe the medication, probably lithium. We've had a lot of success with lithium in cases like this."

Alan's parents set up a series of appointments to have Alan tested by the psychologist to confirm the diagnoses. They were not told much about the tests and were dismayed when I later explained the methods to them. For example, Alan was put in a room by himself to do very simple math problems while he was watched through a one-way mirror by an assistant who counted the number of times Alan looked up from his paper. Alan looked up a lot and that was one of the main criteria for confirming that he had ADHD.

Bear in mind that Alan didn't know he was being watched, that he was alone in the room and therefore could have assumed it was okay to let his attention wander, that he had no idea that the number of times he looked up was of any importance, that the math problems were very simple, and that—despite looking up frequently—he got them 100 percent correct in a short time. The child thought he'd "done great" on the test that was used to give him a psychiatric label for the rest of his life.

Alan's mother and father were told they didn't even have to wait around the office while the testing was done; just drop him off and pick him up. They were also given a card with the psychiatrist's name and phone number. Alan's father asked if he had to go to any of the additional meetings and the psychologist reassured him that it was unnecessary. Alan had a disorder that could be directly treated without involving him.

Unfortunately and perhaps unbelievably, Alan's story is not exaggerated or even unusual. Instead, it is typical. Nowadays, if an upset child is taken to a health professional, in most instances the child will be given a psychiatric diagnosis and prescribed a medication. If counseling is offered, it will more often be given to the child than to the parents. The sources of the problem in the family, school, or elsewhere in the child's life will be ignored. Instead, the grateful parents will be told that they are not responsible for their child's distress and that they cannot help their child change.

It is of course absurd to hold Alan's brain—or, for that matter, Alan himself—responsible for feeling angry and upset about his obviously conflicted, even tragic family situation. As unfounded as it is, the biological viewpoint nonetheless provides the theoretical basis for the widespread diagnosing and drugging of millions of children throughout the United States.

Diagnosing Alan

Alan's diagnosis of oppositional defiant disorder is defined in the 1994 *Diagnostic and Statistical Manual of Mental Disorders, 4th Edition (DSM-IV)*, the "bible" of psychiatric diagnosis created by committees of the American Psychiatric Association, an organization heavily supported by the pharmaceutical industry.[11] Although enmeshed in dreadful family conflict, Alan clearly fits the official diagnosis, which focuses exclusively on the child's behavior.

Here in its entirety is the section describing the criteria for making a diagnosis of oppositional defiant disorder in the *DSM-IV*:

A pattern of negativistic, hostile, and defiant behavior lasting at least 6 months, during which four (or more) of the following are present:
   (1) often loses temper
   (2) often argues with adults
   (3) often actively defies or refuses to comply with adult requests or rules
   (4) often deliberately annoys people
   (5) often blames others for his or her mistakes or misbehaviors
   (6) is often touchy or easily annoyed by others
   (7) is often angry and resentful
   (8) is often spiteful or vindictive

How many children has each of us known who could be described in this way? In fact, almost any child going through a difficult time would fit these criteria.[12] The list of criteria for oppositional defiant disorder is simply eight ways to say a child is angry. One could replace the diagnosis with a finger-waving accusation at the child, "Angry child, angry child! You're an angry child!"

But what is an angry child? An angry child is a hurt child. How do children get so hurt that they become "angry, angry, angry"? There is an infinite number of ways, all of them relating to the child's relationships. They could only be understood by learning the story of the child's life. But by labeling the child as the source of the problem, we stop focusing on how and why the child gets so angry, and in doing so we lose sight of how to help by improving his life.

Of course, these angry behaviors are typical of almost any child at one time or another. To handle this drastic flaw in the diagnostic process, the manual adds a "note" stating: "Consider criterion met only if the behavior occurs more frequently than is typically observed in individuals of comparable age and developmental level." The caveat is meaningless because there are no standards for "typical" when it comes to anger in a child. The *DSM-IV* makes no attempt to help the practitioner decide what is typical and what is not. Indeed, there is no way to establish standards for "typical" anger, since every child faces varied and different circumstances that could provoke or suppress anger. The same child will display very different behaviors depending entirely on the circumstances. For example, Alan still behaved very well when spending time with his father, and before his parents separated, he had gotten along with everyone.

The Big Unanswered Question

Unfortunately for children and anyone who wants to help them, the *DSM-IV* fails to deal with the most important question, "Why is this child so angry?" Instead, the diagnosis implies that the anger is generated from within the child without outside cause. The diagnostic manual has no set of criteria for evaluating a family in conflict or for describing a family situation that would distress a child.

By default, the diagnostic manual allows the adults in the child's life to remain outside the diagnostic loop. The manual offers no checklists for all the angry, confused, frightened, and conflicted attitudes that Alan's separated parents were bringing into their child's world. Nor does the manual's definition of oppositional defiant disorder mention anything about the child's suffering. The focus is entirely on listing the angry behaviors that would make life difficult for adults.

In Alan's case, the further evaluation by the psychologist confirmed that the boy also had attention deficit/hyperactivity disorder in addition to his oppositional defiant disorder. Alan's mother and father felt deeply concerned and quickly took Alan to a psychiatrist, as instructed.

Drugging Alan

As predicted by the psychologist, the psychiatrist put Alan on lithium. In fact, only fifteen minutes passed from the moment mother and son walked into the office until the moment they walked out with the prescription.

Within a few days of starting lithium, Alan's mother noticed a glaze over her son's eyes. That weekend his father noticed his son had lost the sparkle in his eyes. An Internet search under "lithium" revealed to Alan's parents that this toxic metal can cause kidney and thyroid disease in adults, as well as many mental problems, including memory dysfunction. To his dismay, Alan's father discovered that lithium is not approved for children by the Food and Drug Administration (FDA), and there were few studies of its safety or efficacy in children.

Alan's father called the psychiatrist to explain that his son looked like he was in a fog since starting on the lithium. The psychiatrist said the medicine would have to be taken for years, maybe even for all of Alan's life. He said the negative effect would wear off and then he added, "But if it doesn't, we can add a stimulant like Ritalin or Dexedrine to give him more energy. It will also take care of his attention deficit."

A cold shudder went through Alan's father's body. His son on medication for the rest of his life? With more and more medicines to counteract each other's effects? "Not my son," he said and hung up the phone.

Rewriting the Ending to Alan's Story

When Alan's parents reached my office after having been referred to me by a holistic physician, they looked uncomfortable, even apprehensive, about starting a whole new therapeutic approach. Unlike the other two doctors, I had suggested they leave Alan home for their initial session. Within a very short time it became apparent to me that both parents were aware that fighting between themselves was causing a great deal of their son's distress. It further became apparent that they continued to care for each other great deal. We spent most of the first session working on their communication problems rather than on Alan's angry behavior. By the end of the ninety minutes, they had decided to give their marriage another try. Alan's father moved back into the house and Alan's angry behavior improved dramatically within days. I saw Alan once to confirm that all he needed was an end to the conflict between his parents, and a unified, rational program of discipline and unconditional love.

Typically a couple like Alan's parents will work for a year or two in weekly couples therapy to learn how to resolve long-standing conflicts while nurturing a more loving relationship. Many of the principles for resolving their own conflicts with each other would be readily applicable to dealing with their children as well.

In the end, my job wasn't to "treat" Alan but to work with his parents to improve the life of the whole family. Sometimes it is also very useful to involve the children as well, but once Alan's father returned home, my job was to empower him and his wife to be better parents, not to take over the parenting job from them.

Who's in Charge, Children or Adults?

When children are having difficulties, adults in their lives should begin by examining themselves for the sources of the problem. If they can find the source within themselves, it's good news; that puts the adults in an ideal position to change their own behavior to improve the children's lives.

Very often, but not always, the problem lies at least partly within the home. At other times, the child may be reacting negatively to humiliation, bullying, or other stressors outside the home, such as those described in Chapter 3. However, blaming one or another party for the conflict is not nearly as useful as identifying the problem and enlisting everyone's support in providing loving, rational solutions.

Even when children's problems lie in the peer group, school, or other source outside the home, parents are best positioned to find out about the problem, to work on correcting it, and to help their child overcome the effects. Even if we cannot figure out the source of our children's negative behavior, as parents it remains within our power to help to heal our child's confusion, misconduct, or suffering through a caring relationship.

Most children don't need a "psychiatric evaluation" or a "therapist"—they need loving, skilled parents more able to handle conflict between themselves and with them. They need teachers, and other adults as well, to make beneficial, meaningful relationships with them. For the vast majority of children who are diagnosed and treated by health professionals, it would be far more honest and effective to direct the help toward the parents and other adults in the children's lives.

7

Are Psychiatric Drugs Making Our Children Psychotic and Violent?

———◆———

In the aftermath of the 1999 school shootings, we discovered that at least some of the boys involved had been taking psychiatric drugs. As the June 1999 White House Conference on Mental Health exemplified, these disclosures did not discourage psychiatrists from advocating the more widespread medicating of children to *prevent* violence.

When asked by members of the media to comment on the potential for psychiatric drugs to *cause* violence, experts usually dismissed the danger as highly unlikely or even impossible.[1] Nonetheless, the history of school shooters who have been taking prescribed stimulants and antidepressants should raise concerns.

Many media representatives have themselves acquiesced to these experts' agendas by not even mentioning any potential connection between psychiatric drugs and violence. For example, on July 30, 1999, long after all the data were available, MSNBC cable TV probed the causes of school violence by examining the lives of several of the shooters without mentioning that any of them had been taking psychiatric drugs.[2]

Eric Harris was on a Prozac-like drug, Luvox, on April 20, 1999, when he assaulted Columbine High School in Colorado. When his body was autopsied after the shooting, he was found to have what was reported as a "therapeutic" (clinically effective) blood level of the drug.[3] He was reported to be seeing a therapist by that time, although his visits had been reduced to one per month at the time of the killings. At about the time he started on medication and therapy, Eric also began writing a journal filled with hate and violent plans.[4]

As mentioned earlier, four days before the Columbine tragedy, Shawn Cooper, a fifteen-year-old high school sophomore in Notus, Idaho, was on Ritalin when he twice fired a shotgun at students and school staff, narrowly missing them.[5] T.J. Solomon was taking the amphetamine-like stimulant Ritalin for depression at the time he shot at his classmates at Heritage High School in Georgia. Kip Kinkel, who killed his parents and shot his schoolmates at Thurston High School in Oregon in 1998, was reportedly taking Prozac some-time before the shooting and Ritalin at the time of the assault, but the information has not been fully confirmed.[6] Thirteen-year-old Mitchell Johnson and eleven-year-old Andrew Golden may have been taking psychiatric drugs when they fired on their classmates in Jonesboro, Arkansas.[7]

Before you decide to take your children for psychiatric evaluation for possible medication, you need to know whether or not the drugs can make children worse, and even psychotic and violent.[8]

Making Children Psychotic with Prozac-like Drugs

Children who are put on antidepressants, especially Prozac-like drugs—Prozac, Luvox, Zoloft, Paxil, and Celexa—*frequently* have a manic reaction. (Mania is a severe mental disturbance in which an in-dividual typically feels omnipotent, grandiose, godlike, and invincible, and sometimes becomes violent.)[9] During a short-term controlled clinical trial, Prozac caused a 6 percent rate of mania in children treated for depression.[10] This means that for every 100,000 depressed children given Prozac, about 6,000 will develop mania in the first few weeks.[11] The Prozac-like drug Luvox caused a 4 percent rate of mania in young people treated for obsessive-compulsive disorder during clinical trials conducted as part of the process of getting FDA ap-proval.[12]

These are extraordinarily high rates of drug-induced psychosis. Unavoidably, they will rise even higher in routine clinical practice, where the children are less rigorously monitored and where the drugs are given for much longer than in typical clinical trials, which last only four to eight weeks.[13]

When asked about the dangers of Luvox following the disclosure that Eric Harris was taking the drug, some drug experts dismissed the problem, stating the drug could not cause aggressive behavior. One expert quoted in the media cited a 1 percent rate for Luvox-induced mania in children, which is too low. He further claimed that only children predisposed to bipolar disorder (manic-depressive disorder) would develop mania in response to the drug.[14] But in the studies for FDA approval that demonstrated a 4 percent mania rate for Luvox, the children did not even suffer from depression, let alone bipolar disorder. They had obsessive-compulsive disorder. In short, there is no scientific support for the concept that only children "genetically predisposed" to mania will become manic on psychiatric drugs. In fact, there's no convincing evidence that mania is genetic.[15] However, even if some of the youngsters were especially vulnerable to becoming manic, it would still be tragic to tip them over the edge into this destructive psychosis by giving them drugs.

The pharmaceutical companies that distribute Luvox have participated in suppressing knowledge about the dangers of the drug. The Upjohn Company jointly markets Luvox in the United States by special arrangement with Solvay Pharmaceuticals, Inc., the drug's manufacturer. In their initial joint press release about Luvox, Solvay and the Upjohn Company mention a variety of relatively minor side effects, such as dry mouth and constipation, that were reported to occur only 4 and 2 percent, respectively, more frequently with the drug than with placebo.[16] But the drug companies utterly failed to mention the 4 percent manic reaction rate in children.

Not That Biochemical

Within days after the Columbine High School shootings, biopsychiatry advocates began to display multicolor brain scans in the media to promote the wholly unsubstantiated claim that they could see "differences" between the brains of violent and nonviolent people. At that time it was thought that neither Harris nor Klebold had been taking any drugs, and so it was in the interest of drug advocates to link the boys' violence to a biological cause.[17]

For example, the headline of an an April 1999 *USA Today* article, CHEMISTRY OF A KILLER: IS IT THE BRAIN?, referred to speculations about as yet undetected biochemical imbalances in the human brain.[18] The report showed two brain scans supposedly from violent and non-violent persons, but the different rates of metabolic activity recorded in the scans could represent anything, including normal metabolic changes during different kinds of routine mental activities.

USA Today quoted one longtime advocate of the biology of violence, the psychologist Adrian Raine, as saying that there may be something wrong in the prefrontal cortex—the anterior surface of the brain—of violent people. Actually, the prefrontal cortex is involved in all higher human activities and, in a metaphorical sense at least, anything and everything "wrong" in the thinking, feeling, or actions of a human being would emanate from that region. Everything and anything "right" would also have to emanate from that same region.

Not long after this, on May 3, 1999, *Newsweek* published a story entitled "WHY THE YOUNG KILL" with a subhead that asked, "Are certain young brains predisposed to violence?"[19] The article displayed the obligatory brain scans, this time purporting to show a huge area of violence-related hyperactivity spanning about one half the frontal region of a sixteen-year-old boy. It included not only the prefrontal region but the *whole* frontal region as well as some associated areas that lie farther back and deeper in the brain. Even more than the prefrontal region, this large portion of frontal brain would have been involved in *all* of the boy's general mental or emotional activity, from abstract reasoning to judgment and empathy. If the scan did detect an abnormality, as claimed, it would have to be a massive defect that would compromise a broad range of mental functions with no selectivity for violence. The claim was as meaningful as declaring "there's something wrong inside the head in violent people." It was pseudoscience, developed to sell a bill of goods—a biological myth—to the media and public.

It became widely known in May 1999 that Harris was taking Luvox at the time of his outburst of violence. Luvox is a Prozac-like drug that produces biochemical imbalances, and Prozac-like drugs have been implicated in many acts of violence.[20] It now became threatening to biological psychiatry and drug advocates to focus on biochemical abnormalities as a potential cause of violence. Media coverage of the biology of school shootings died down.

Nonetheless, speculations about the biological causes for violence were resurrected at the White House Conference on Mental Health in June. In order to claim that psychoactive drugs could cure violence by fixing brain disorders, the speakers at the White House Conference completely skipped over the facts about several shooters taking psychiatric drugs, which clearly would have undermined claims for the efficacy of drugs in preventing violence and indeed would have raised the opposite possibility: that drug-induced abnormalities might exacerbate or cause violence.

How Dangerous Is Drug-Induced Mania?

As mentioned previously, mania is a severe mental disturbance in which an individual typically feels omnipotent, grandiose, godlike, and invulnerable, and sometimes becomes violent. During mania, people often experience extremely high energy with little need for sleep. Their minds seem to race, their thoughts and words may ramble, and their judgment deteriorates. During mania, impulse control weakens, and a person can be easily angered, and may react with aggressive or violent behavior.[21]

Though it may seem unlikely that a disturbed person could do so, during mania individuals frequently make elaborate plans that are carried out with varying degrees of success. Commonly the plans end in disaster—for example, when they lead to wasteful spending sprees for high-cost items such as multiple automobiles or unrealistic investments. These wayward plans can stir up angry and even violent confrontations with family members or police who oppose the grandiose and sometimes life-endangering ventures.

However, individuals who fit the criteria for mania can successfully carry out complex goal-directed activities. The capacity for mania to fuel extraordinary, elaborately planned accomplishments has led some biological psychiatrists to claim that men like Abraham Lincoln, Theodore Roosevelt, and Winston Churchill were suffering from alternating moods of depression and mania.[22] Though I consider it absurd to reduce the accomplishments of great individuals to biopsychiatric explanations, the attempt to diagnose these men does confirm that psychiatrists find an association between mania and elaborate and even successful planning. This is critical to understanding how a drug-induced manic psychosis could underlie an elaborately developed violent scheme such as a school shooting.

Eric Harris's ravings on the Internet, quoted in Chapter 2, indicate feelings of grandiosity, omnipotence, and invulnerability. For example, he stated, "I am the law" and rambled about taking God-like retaliation against other people. District Attorney Dave Thomas reviewed some of the quotes in the diary found in Harris's home. Thomas described the diary as "disjointed" and "rambling," a condition that is consistent with manic psychosis. The journal detailed year-long plans for the school shooting, which Harris hoped would kill 500 people, as well as plans to hijack an airplane to crash into New York City, all of which is consistent with grandiose manic ambitions to make a big, violent impression on the world.[23]

The American Psychiatric Association's 1994 *Diagnostic and Statistical Manual of Mental Disorders, 4th Edition (DSM-IV)* is a conservative text that rarely highlights harm done by psychiatric treatments. Yet the manual repeatedly confirms that both antidepressants and stimulants cause mania or mania-like reactions. It states, for example, "Symptoms like those seen in a Manic Episode may be due to the direct effects of antidepressant medication."[24]

The manual also confirms that manic reactions can include aggressive behaviors that lead to jail or involuntary confinement to a mental hospital.[25] It specifically mentions increased "goal-directed activities"—that is, compulsive planning—as a specific symptom of mania.[26]

Children who become manic from taking psychiatric drugs are often mistakenly diagnosed as manic-depressive (bipolar). Instead of being taken off the offending drug, they are given an additional one for the control of "mania."[27]

Reports to the FDA About Luvox

As a part of their effort to keep an eye on drugs that are already on the market, the Food and Drug Administration welcomes and collects reports from consumers and professionals concerning adverse drug effects.[28] A single report cannot usually confirm a causal relationship without more evidence than provided in an isolated summary. However, a series of related reports that are consistent with the drug's pharmacological effects can confirm a pattern of adverse reactions. Thus the FDA often relies on data from spontaneous reports when it decides to take major actions such as adding an adverse effect to a drug label or even withdrawing a drug from the market.[29]

Between November 1, 1997, and July 2, 1999, more than fifty reports of adverse mental and behavioral reactions to Luvox were sent to the FDA. There were more than twenty reports of stimulant-like reactions such as aggression, mania, agitation, anxiety, and nervousness, often in combination. There were also about a dozen reports of drug-induced depression and suicidality.

In the first five months of 1999, before the Columbine High School shootings raised professional awareness, the FDA received numerous reports that named Luvox as the "primary suspect" in causing dramatic reactions including mania and aggression. Some of the reports were made by health professionals and some by consumers (usually the person who was prescribed the drug). On January 2 a consumer reported that a thirty-five-year-old man experienced aggression, mania, paranoia, and "thinking abnormal" while taking Luvox and no other drug.[30] On February 5, 1999, a health professional reported a case of drug-induced anxiety, depression, and mania in a thirty-nine-year-old man who required hospitalization. On February 19, 1999, a research "study" sent in a report of "abnormal behavior, aggression, agitation, anger, mania aggravated, mutism" in a forty-eight-year-old man whose only drug was Luvox. On April 16, 1999, a consumer reported abnormal behavior, catatonia, and suicidal ideation while taking only Luvox. On May 21, 1999, a professional reported that a ten-year-old boy had developed drug-induced "aggression, agitation, physical abuse, suicidal ideation, violence-related syndrome" requiring hospitalization. On May 28 the FDA itself reported a life-threatening case from the scientific literature involving a toxic drug reaction with Luvox as the primary suspect. The symptoms included aggression, agitation, and cognitive disorder in association with other severe physiological impairments.[31]

Only a small percentage of adverse reactions—probably a fraction of 1 percent—actually get reported to the FDA;[32] the reports of reactions to Luvox that were sent in are but the small tip of a much larger iceberg.

Prozac and Littleton: Not the First Time

A tragedy remarkably similar to the Columbine High School shooting occurred in November 1989 in Louisville, Kentucky, when Joseph Wesbecker, heavily armed, assaulted coworkers at his former place of work. Like Harris and Klebold in Colorado, he walked systematically through the building, shooting some of his peers and bosses and sparing others. Before the rampage was over, he had shot twenty people, killing eight. Like the boys at Columbine High School, he then killed himself.

Joseph Wesbecker felt humiliated and outraged by some of his coworkers and bosses at work, which is similar to what Eric Harris felt about school. Earlier Wesbecker had threatened retaliation, but like Eric Harris he was not an actively violent person and his threats were largely ignored.

Prozac had been added to Wesbecker's drug regimen about five weeks prior to the assaults. Wesbecker's doctor suspected that Prozac was making him delusional and irrationally angry toward the people at his former place of work, and told him to stop taking the drug. Wesbecker followed his doctor's instructions, but Prozac is long-acting, and at the time of the murders a few days later, the drug was still active in Wesbecker's system.[33]

Criminal Cases of Drug-Induced Violence in Young People

As a medical expert I have testified several times that Prozac and Prozac-like drugs such as Zoloft have caused or contributed to violence committed by teenagers with no prior history of harming anyone through physical violence. In one case, a sixteen-year-old boy, while taking Zoloft, beat an elderly neighborhood woman to death after she criticized the loudness of his music boom box as they passed on the street. In another, a fourteen-year-old girl who was taking Prozac for depression fired her parent's pistol point-blank at a neighborhood boy. Fortunately the gun jammed.

The third case especially resembles some aspects of the Columbine High School shooting. A sixteen-year-old boy with a history of suicide attempts but no violence against others received Prozac and other drugs while residing in a cottage on the grounds of a mental hospital. Over a period of several months he became increasingly irrational. Then, seemingly without a rational motive, he began making bombs and collecting incendiary materials to burn and blow up the cottage. He knifed to death a female attendant and then tried, and failed, to destroy the building with a bizarre array of mostly ineffective devices. Like the shooters at Columbine, he had given warnings that he was planning violence, including to hospital staff, who apparently did not take him seriously.

Nightmares of Being a School Shooter

The scientific literature confirms that Prozac can make children psychotic, suicidal, and violent. Frank was a twelve-year-old boy in the seventh grade who suffered "long-standing obsessions and compulsions that included compulsive checking, washing, and arranging of his room and obsessional preoccupations with germs, dirt, and video games."[34] He was successful in school but was isolated. He was somewhat depressed with "nonspecific suicidal thoughts," but mostly he suffered from anxiety. He had never been actively suicidal or in any way violent.

Frank was entered into a controlled clinical trial at a Yale University research clinic. Some of the subjects were given Prozac and others, for comparison, were given a placebo (an inactive sugar pill). The study was double-blind, meaning that no one was informed as to whether Frank was receiving Prozac or the sugar pill. Soon after starting to take the pills Frank was described as improved by the clinicians but he reported feeling high, a sign of artificial euphoria or hypomania. Then, thirty-eight days into the drug trial, the young boy became desperately worse: "[Frank] experienced a violent nightmare about killing his classmates until he himself was shot. He was awakened from it only with difficulty, and the dream continued to feel 'very real.' "

Frank was not a copy cat. The study was published in 1991, long before high school mass murders became so much a part of our landscape.

The report continues: "[Frank] reported having had several days of increasingly vivid 'bad dreams' before this episode; these included images of killing himself and his parents dying. When he was seen later that day he was agitated and anxious, refused to go to school, and reported marked suicidal ideation [thoughts] that made him feel unsafe at home." When the double blind was broken, the researchers discovered that Frank was taking Prozac.

Although Frank had never undergone a psychiatric crisis before taking Prozac, he now required several weeks of intensive treatment on a locked hospital ward. Approximately two months after the Prozac was stopped, it was restarted—this time as part of his treatment, not a research study. When the dose was increased, he again developed suicidal feelings. Finally the doctors realized that Prozac was probably causing his emotional crises, and they stopped giving it to him.

Frank's violent and suicidal turmoil is written up in the journal as a probable adverse reaction to Prozac. From the evidence in Frank's story, including his relapse after restarting the Prozac, and his recovery on two occasions when it was stopped, there seems little doubt that his violence toward himself and others was caused by the Prozac.

Driven Crazy by Prozac

The same 1991 Yale study described a young girl who was transported into a violent state while taking Prozac. Susie was a fourteen-year-old in the eighth grade when, much like Frank, she was given Prozac for the treatment of "long-standing obsessive-compulsive symptoms and perfectionistic tendencies."[35] A "model student and musician," she had begun "compulsively rereading homework, with the constant feeling she had not mastered it." She would stay up all night studying. She was an extreme example of the kind of slavish preoccupation with school that afflicts many of today's students. Like Frank, Susie had no history of violent or suicidal activities.

About three weeks after starting Prozac, Susie scratched her wrists with a knife, and began ruminating about how to kill herself "by cutting, shooting, or hurling herself downstairs." When her Prozac was increased, she worsened.

Susie's Prozac was stopped, but she continued to become more emotionally disturbed and violent.[36] She had to be restrained to prevent her from banging her head, scalding herself, or mutilating herself. She frequently insisted, "I just want the opportunity to kill myself." Entirely out of character, she chanted, "Kill, kill, kill; die, die, die; pain, pain, pain" over and over again.

Doubting that Prozac had caused her problems, Susie's doctor's resumed the drug after several weeks. Now Susie became "increasingly bizarre" and also violent: "She choked and stamped on her teddy bear and cried out, 'Bear wants to die with me, don't you?' " She was once again taken off Prozac but did not improve. Seclusion and restraint were frequently required. Nine months later she remained profoundly disturbed, was hospitalized, and was subdued with powerful psychiatric drugs.

Like Frank's story, Susie's was published as a probable example of an adverse reaction to Prozac. From the report, it seems that Prozac made this youngster irreversibly psychotic.

Further Confirmation of Prozac-Induced Mania and Violence

Frank and Susie were not the only children to become disturbed while taking Prozac in this Yale report. Self-injurious and violent behavior developed in six (or 14 percent) of the forty-two children aged ten to seventeen who received Prozac at the research clinic. Nearly 10 percent had to be hospitalized for treatment of their adverse reactions to Prozac.

Another Yale study dated 1990–91[37] resulted in an extraordinary finding: 50 percent of children age eight to sixteen developed two or more behavioral abnormalities while taking Prozac. Stimulation or agitation were the most common adverse drug reactions, including excitation, restlessness, insomnia, and social inhibition, with increased "impulsivity." The effects tended to last as long as the drug was taken.

A team from the University of Pittsburgh reviewed the hospital charts of children and adolescents (age 9–18) who had been prescribed Prozac. They found "manic-like symptoms" in an extraordinary 23 percent of the young people and "irritability" in another 19 percent.[38] Many of the children developed drug-induced hostility or anger: "The irritability had a quality of a *grinding anger* with short temper and increasing oppositionalism."

Overall, it seems unlikely that parents aware of this data about drug-induced mental disturbances and violence would want to put their children at risk by going along with medicating them. In my several decades of clinical and forensic work, where I often have the opportunity to talk with patients and their families about previous treatment experiences, I have never heard of parents' being informed of these facts by doctors who prescribe the drugs. Most parents would refuse to give these substances to their children if they knew the truth about their harmful effects, and when they do learn the facts from books or other sources, they often try to withdraw their children from the drugs.

Antidepressant-Induced Depression

Prozac not only causes mania, it can also cause depression. During the testing of Prozac for FDA approval, depression or a worsening of depression was so often reported as an adverse effect of Prozac that depression was originally listed as a *frequent* Prozac side effect in the official FDA-approved label. However, this adverse effect was edited out at the last minute.[39]

Banning Prozac-like Drugs for Children

Not only do Prozac and related drugs very commonly cause serious adverse reactions, but also there is no consistent evidence indicating that they are helpful to depressed children. As a result, a number of researchers have raised scientific and ethical issues about continuing to prescribe antidepressants to children.[40]

If the medicating of children were subject to rational ethics, the studies cited in this chapter would in themselves completely rule out the prescription of Prozac and Prozac-like drugs to children. Only outright ignorance or a compulsive determination to prescribe drugs combined with a callous disregard for the well-being of children could allow informed doctors to continue prescribing Prozac or Luvox for children. Prudent medical practice would also prohibit prescribing other Prozac-like drugs, such as Celexa, Paxil, and Zoloft, to children.

At present, no drugs have been FDA-approved for treating depression in children. This doesn't prevent doctors from prescribing drugs as they wish, but it has, in the past at least, prohibited drug companies from advertising and promoting their drugs as useful for purposes that the FDA has not approved. For example, the drug companies have not been allowed to tout antidepressants for children in ads meant for the public or in promotional materials for doctors.

These protections for children were potentially obliterated on July 29, 1999, when U.S. District Court Judge Royce C. Lamberth ruled that it was unconstitutional for the FDA to infringe on the free speech rights of drug companies to make any claims they saw fit for their products.[41] If the ruling stands, it will vastly inflate the already enormous power and riches of the drug companies, and it will add fuel to the disaster of child drugging.

Making Children Psychotic and Violent with Stimulant Drugs

T. J. Solomon was taking the stimulant Ritalin when he shot at his fellow students at his Georgia high school and then placed a pistol in his mouth. Kip Kinkel, the Oregon shooter, was probably taking Ritalin around the time of the shooting. Can Ritalin cause abnormal behavior and psychosis with violence and suicide? As in the case of Prozac-like drugs, there is powerful, convincing evidence that stimulants, including Ritalin, can cause mania and violence. The same effects are also produced by the other stimulants given to children: amphetamine (Dexedrine, Adderall), methamphetamine (Desoxyn, Gradumet), and pemoline (Cylert). Results of clinical trials indicate that the rates of drug-induced mania in children are probably lower with the stimulants than with the Prozac-like antidepressants.

Stimulant-Induced Mania

The *DSM-IV* confirms that stimulants, like antidepressants, can cause "manic-like mood disturbances."[42] The psychosis can have manic qualities or it can look more like schizophrenia, with delusional and paranoid features.

I have obtained a complete summary of reports made to the FDA concerning the adverse effects of Ritalin, spanning a period from 1985 through early 1997.[43] Culling this data, I counted hundreds of reports about Ritalin use resulting in psychiatric disorders, including agitation (55 reports), hostility (50), depression (48), psychotic depression (11), abnormal thinking (44), hallucinations (43), psychosis (38), and emotional lability (instability) (33).

A review of the literature also confirms that Ritalin and amphetamine stimulants such as Dexedrine and Adderall very commonly cause depression, sadness, lethargy, and crying among children.[44] In addition, these drugs induce obsessions and compulsions, overfocusing, abnormal movements including tics, growth suppression, brain and cardiac abnormalities, and a variety of other problems.[45]

The "Biochemical Imbalance" Speculation

There is no evidence that any psychiatric or psychological disorder is caused by a biochemical imbalance. The current most popular theory among doctors and laypersons is that depression is caused by too little activity of the neurotransmitter serotonin. These opinions are driven by a very successful public relations campaign initiated by the drug company Eli Lilly & Co. The purpose of the campaign is to sell Prozac, which is tailored to affect serotonin levels in the brain.[46]

Antidepressants vary in the number and kind of neurotransmitters that they impact on, so each drug company tries to create the impression that depression might be caused by the particular neurotransmitters that are affected by its drug. A new antidepressant for which its manufacturer was seeking FDA approval was laboratory-tailored to selectively affect the neurotransmitter norepinephrine. As a result of the drug company's premarketing public relationships campaign, the media are already ballyhooing the norepinephrine neurotransmitter system as a potential cause of depression.[47]

In reality, there are *hundreds* of biochemicals actively involved in neurotransmission in the brain, many of them newly discovered. Additional active substances will no doubt be identified in the future. In regard to the ones we know about, in most cases we have little knowledge about their most basic neurochemistry, and we have no idea how they integrate with each other or with the function of the mind. There's no evidence that any of their balances or levels are abnormal in the brains of children or adults who suffer from depression, anxiety, attentional or behavioral problems, or any psychiatric problem.

It is not a speculation but a fact demonstrated in thousands of laboratory studies in normal animals: All psychiatric drugs produce severe biochemical imbalances and related abnormalities by interfering with the normal brain function.[48]

Does the Brain Recover?

Since all psychiatric drugs create abnormalities in brain function, it is crucial to ask, "Does the brain recover from these drug-induced distortions?" The research is most extensive in regard to the oldest of the drugs, the amphetamines such as Adderall, Dexedrine, Desoxyn, and Gradumet. Short-term exposure to amphetamines can produce long-term and even permanent damage, including lasting neurotoxic changes and cell death.[49]

Writing in *Meyler's Side Effects of Drugs: An Encyclopedia of Adverse Reactions and Interactions*, two well-known medication experts, Everett Ellinwood and Tong Lee concluded: "Drug levels in children on a mg/kg basis are sometimes as high as those reported to produce chronic central nervous system changes in animal studies."[50] Dr. Ellinwood is professor of psychiatry and pharmacology at the Duke University Medical Center. Tragically, very few doctors realize or seem to care that these drugs are so destructive, and most parents are left uninformed.

Similar research on Ritalin is relatively sparse and inconclusive. Meanwhile, there are other sources of evidence for the probability that Ritalin causes permanent damage, including brain shrinkage measured by brain scans of adults who were given Ritalin as children.[51]

Long-term follow-up studies by Nadine Lambert from the University of California at Berkeley have shown that Ritalin given to children predisposes them to later cocaine abuse as adults.[52] This confirms that taking Ritalin as a youngster permanently changes the brain, creating a later craving for more stimulants.

There are no studies on the brain's ability to recover from the malfunctions caused by Prozac and its knockoffs, such as Zoloft, Paxil, Luvox, and Celexa. In legal cases against Eli Lilly, the drug company that makes Prozac, the head of research has admitted under oath, in a deposition, that no attempt has been made to test whether the brain can recover from Prozac-induced abnormalities.[53] These abnormalities develop within the first few doses given to animals and it would be relatively easy and inexpensive to determine whether their brains recover, if the drug company wanted to get at the truth.

Put simply, we know that *some* of the drugs given to children are killing their brain cells, and it's reasonable to fear that others may do the same thing. Whether or not they help on occasion is a moot point; psychoactive drugs should never be given to children. Their dangers are too great. As we shall see in the next section, even when they seem to work, they are actually harming the child.

A Special Warning to Parents

Parents and others concerned about children need to be warned that increasing numbers of youngsters are being placed on especially dangerous antipsychotic (neuroleptic) drugs. There are many drugs in this class, including older drugs such as Haldol, Mellaril, Thorazine, Navane, Trilafon, Prolixin, and Clozaril,[54] and newer ones such as Risperdal, Zyprexa, and Seroquel.

Removing children from antipsychotic drugs as rapidly as medically possible can save them from a lifetime of permanent neurological disease.[55] These agents commonly cause an irreversible neurological disorder called tardive dyskinesia, with involuntary movements that can become disfiguring, painful, and disabling. Some children will begin to develop permanent tics, muscle spasms, and distortions of their posture and gait after only a few months of neuroleptic treatment. By the time they have been exposed for five years, one third or more children will develop the drug-induced, permanent disease.[56] Especially in children, tardive dyskinesia is often associated with an irreversible deterioration of mental processes and behavior.[57]

Furthermore, neuroleptics cannot bring about a real healing. Instead they produce a chemical lobotomy by suppressing all emotions, painful or not, without improving the child's mental or spiritual condition. In my opinion there is no justification in rational medical practice for ever giving these drugs to children.

Suppressing Our Children's Signals

Suppose a group of children is standing on the shore of an island waving their arms crisscross above their heads in the universal distress signal. Now imagine that a "hospital ship" spots the children and comes ashore. Suppose further that the doctor orders the nurses to give the children Prozac or Ritalin to abort their signals of distress. Now suppose the ship departs without finding out why the children are alone on the island, where their parents are, what dangers are surrounding them, or even whether they want to be rescued.

That of course sounds ridiculous. Yet in ways small and large this is happening throughout the nation. Millions of children are desperately signaling distress and doctors are sending them home with drugs that suppress their ability to communicate their distress.

Making Good Caged Children

The suppressive or subduing effects of psychiatric drugs have been especially studied in regard to Ritalin and the other stimulants.[58] These drugs have the same effects on normal animals, normal children, and disturbed children. Their suppressive mental effects can even be seen in animals from rats to chimpanzees. Stimulants eliminate spontaneous behavior such as escape attempts, exploration, mutual grooming, curiosity about their surroundings, and the desire to socialize with other animals. Normal behaviors not only are crushed, they are replaced by compulsive, narrowly focused solitary behaviors, such as playing with pebbles aimlessly, pacing a narrow corner of the area, or picking at one's own skin.

In effect, stimulant drugs turn normal animals into good caged animals. These drugs have the same effect on children, making them easy to manage in our schools and families by suppressing their spontaneity and enforcing obsessive compliance.

Suppressing Relationship

Making relationships requires many highly evolved human attributes such as social awareness, empathy, and the ability to feel and to express feelings. All psychoactive drugs impair these abilities. Alcohol, for example, may blunt anxiety, produce a shallow conviviality, and convince the mildly intoxicated individual that he or she can relate better than ever. Nonetheless, the alcohol is actually impairing the ability for genuine engagement. Stimulants and antidepressants may make children more docile, less spontaneous, and easier to manage, creating an illusion of improved relating, but the child is less engaged than ever.

As Frank experienced in the Yale study, antidepressants and stimulants sometimes cause an artificial euphoria that is also mistaken for an improvement. It's actually a toxic reaction along the continuum that leads to mania.

Turning Schools into Mental Hospitals:
The "Mental Health" Response
to the School Shootings

So Many Children Already on Drugs

When I was a young doctor in the 1960s, there were mental hospitals for children that administered less psychiatric medication than many of today's public schools. There was no lack of potent drugs in the psychiatric arsenal. The basic stimulants—Ritalin and the amphetamines—were FDA-approved for children in the 1950s, and many other powerful drugs, such as the original tranquilizers, antipsychotics, and antidepressants, were also readily available. But there was a different attitude in medicine: Doctors were reluctant to give potentially toxic agents to children.

Now, however, throughout the nation schoolchildren are being watched like hawks by teachers, school counselors, and psychologists who are quick to recommend medical and psychiatric evaluation. They can be virtually certain that in almost every case the doctor will prescribe drugs, especially stimulants like Ritalin, Dexedrine, and Adderall that subdue behavior.

The International Narcotics Control Board, an agency of the United Nations, acts as the umbrella organization for national drug enforcement agencies, such as the U.S. Drug Enforcement Administration (DEA). In February 1995, the International Narcotics Control Board deplored that "10–12 percent of all boys between the ages of 6 and 14 in the United States have been diagnosed as having ADD and are being treated with methylphenidate [Ritalin]."[59] According to the board, the United States "accounts for approximately 90% of the total world manufacture and consumption" of Ritalin. The board raised concerns about doctors' seeking "easy" solutions to "behavioral problems which may have complex causes." It also repeated earlier concerns about "promotional practices" that were leading to overprescription in the United States.

The International Narcotics Control Board has continued to express very strong concerns about the widespread prescription of stimulants in America. In February 1999 it warned that treatment rates with stimulants "in some American schools are as high as 30 to 40 percent of a class and children as young as age one year are treated with methylphenidate [Ritalin]."[60] It again cited "aggressive advertising by certain pharmaceutical firms." It stated, again, "Treatment with drugs may often just be the easy way out, rather than dealing with the cause of the problem." Meanwhile, the DEA has been voicing similar concerns and documenting the grave dangers associated with prescribing stimulants to children.[61]

No official statistics are available, but it has been estimated that probably 4 million to 5 million children are on stimulants, and many more are taking a variety of other psychiatric drugs. A recent estimate that nearly 6 million children aged six to eighteen are on psychiatric drugs in the United States is probably accurate.[62] The rate of drugging children continues to escalate, especially with other stimulants besides Ritalin, such as Adderall, as well as Prozac and related drugs.

In many schools, so many children receive medications that they must line up at the nursing station for their afternoon dose. Indeed, some schools have more stimulant drugs in their nursing office cabinet than pharmacies have in their inventories.

In public and private school settings that specialize in emotional and behavioral problems, most or all of the students are likely to be enmeshed in the mental health system and receiving drugs. In effect, our children are attending mental hospitals disguised as schools. What they really need are safe havens—learning centers where individuality and community are both respected, so that no one feels driven to extremes of despair and violence. Nonetheless, as described in Chapter 2, President Clinton's response to Littleton was to propose a massive increase in psychiatric interventions in the schools.

An End to the Suppression

America's schools are selectively suppressing our most critically intelligent, brave, energetic, and creative children. I bear witness to this tragedy on a daily basis in my clinical practice as well as among my friends' and neighbors' families. There's a war against children going on in our schools and the most outstanding of our children are the first to be targeted for control by drugs. We're using drugs the way gardeners use herbicides to destroy weeds—except these toxins are aimed at the flowering of our children.

Schools are not the only institutions that encourage the drugging of children. Controlling children with psychiatric medications is rampant in foster homes and in any institutional setting, such as juvenile detention centers and prisons, where docility is valued.[63]

Who are the children who cannot or will not keep their heads down, out of the line of fire? Not the most docile but often the most rebellious. Not the most ordinary but often the brightest, most energetic, most courageous, and most critically intelligent. The youngsters brought to my office with psychiatric labels should instead be labeled "best and most beautiful." It's almost always easy to engage these children in a lively, thoughtful, insightful conversation about themselves, their families, and their schools. Frequently they are more able to do so than their parents.

If a child is quiet, well behaved, submissive, dutiful, the child will not get diagnosed and drugged. But children with any spunk are likely at times to frustrate, offend, or make trouble for the adults in their lives. It's up to the adults to channel that energy into creative outlets, not to snuff it out with drugs. In my psychiatric practice, it's a joy to interact with the children who are brought to me.

The drugging of our most energetic and rebellious individuals not only crushes them with drugs, it sends a frightening message to all schoolchildren. It warns, "If you do not quietly conform, you're in danger of getting diagnosed and drugged, so sit down and shut up, or else." The drugging of the most energetic children deprives the school of its most exciting, invigorating souls. They may seem more disturbing than inspiring, but that's largely because our schools aim more at conformity than at empowering our children.

People, Not Pills

By rendering children less able to demand meaningful, engaging, satisfying relationships, psychiatric drugs cement into place their lack of relationship with us. In the extreme, this disruption of relationship becomes expressed as drug-induced psychosis and violence.

As long as we send millions of children to psychiatrists for psychoactive drugs, we are not going to address the real problems that our children face growing up in America. Furthermore, being psychiatrically diagnosed and medicated will make many of our children worse off than before they got into the mental health system.

Children as a whole would be better off if psychoactive drugs were never used to control their emotions or behavior. Physicians can practice ethically and effectively without ever starting a child on psychiatric drugs. Parents and teachers can learn better approaches to the children in their care. In every case, the suffering and misbehavior of our children can and should be handled through improved relationships with adults.

8

Putting an End to School Slavery

———◆———

Nothing exemplifies the increased burdens we place on our children better than the backpacks we require them to carry to and from school. These packs are literally deforming the backs of some of our children, causing spinal and shoulder problems that require medical treatment. When I recently tried to help a ten-year-old in my office pick up his backpack, I strained my shoulder under its weight.

For many young students the burdensome backpack has become the symbol of all they hate about school, especially the boring books and never-ending hours of homework. As obtrusive as they are, students still "forget" to bring their backpacks home from school.

School assignments and notes for their parents somehow fail to find their way into the backpack, or else disappear like into a black hole from which they cannot be retrieved. "I put it in here, I put it in here, I'm sure I did," the beleaguered eleven-year-old protests as she searches through endless papers and books looking for that paper her mother is supposed to sign.

For too many teachers, the "messy backpack" has become the symbol of disobedience and the cardinal symptom of "attention deficit/hyperactivity disorder." They bring up these messy packs in parent meetings and write about them in the comment sections on report cards.

I didn't have a backpack when I was in elementary or high school, or even in college. Nor did I endure the endless hours of homework that now gets toted back and forth in them. That homework, of course, is what makes the backpack such a hated symbol.

Could we could begin school reform by doing away with backpacks and never giving children more homework than they can fold up and put in their pocket? At the least, it would be a symbolic step toward liberating our children from academic indentured servitude. The real burden is in the minds and hearts of our children, whose lives have become dominated by rote work rather than by spontaneous play, and whose personal experience of "learning" entails subjugation to burdensome tasks.

School Slavery

I was talking in my practice with a fourteen-year-old patient who has little time for anything but studying. "You feel like a school slave," I observed.

"School slave . . . Yeah, I like the sound of it. Call me 'school slave.' That's just how I feel." He kicked his backpack so hard he stubbed his toe. "I hate that thing."

Parents throughout the country complain about the amount of homework being given to their children, sometimes starting in the first and second grades. They also worry about the competitive pressures placed on their children by schools. But do parents dare let up on their children? A father lamented to me that his son had extremely high SAT scores and was second in his class but couldn't get into any of his first three college choices. This kind of potential disappointment has ripple effects throughout family life, making parents stand over their children like homework slave drivers.

But competition for what? Often youngsters would much more enjoy and benefit from lesser-known, smaller, more student-centered schools. Instead students, their parents, and their school counselors become driven by the outward signs of achievement rather than by their genuine academic and social needs.

Like slaves, our children feel alienated from their "masters." Excessive work makes children resent their teachers and schools, as well as learning itself. It can put them into chronic, debilitating conflict with their parents, who feel they must compel their children to "keep up." Many parents end up bringing their children for psychiatric evaluation in large part because of the anger and even violence that is generated around getting homework done.

Many desperate parents end up asking doctors to prescribe stimulant drugs for their children in the hope of ending the struggle over homework and improving their grades. Outlawed as artifical enhancers of athletic performance in amateur and professional sports, stimulants are being routinely prescribed to enhance academic performance in elementary school. But as I have documented in *Talking Back to Ritalin*, there's more likelihood of the drug impairing learning than improving it. When children do get higher grades on stimulant drugs, it's due more to their increased conformity than to any real academic progress.

The Daydreamer

Mr. and Mrs. Mandel are family friends and so I've been able to follow their son's development over a period of more than a dozen years. Their story is one I hear repeated with slight variations everywhere I go in the country. It began in the late 1980s, when prescribing Ritalin was going through a period of escalating promotion.[1]

The Mandels were unaware that their son was having any problems in school, when his teacher called for a special meeting. The teacher began the meeting by explaining that Brian was a wonderful child but that he had some difficulties that needed attention if he was to make the most of school.

"Brian continually forgets to bring his pencils from class to class," the teacher explained. "All the children get reminded in homeroom to make sure they have their pencils for their other classes, but by the time your son gets to his second or third period, he has nothing to write with."

"Maybe Brian's having trouble getting used to switching from class to class," Mr. Mandel explained. "He's in five different rooms every day. When I was in fourth grade, we didn't have to switch from class to class."

The teacher explained that the school was not expecting anything of Brian that wasn't required of all the children.

Mrs. Mandel jumped in. "Oh, my husband isn't trying to be difficult."

The teacher continued, "Brian does get his homework done but it's unbelievably sloppy."

Mrs. Mandel suppressed a grin. Her husband's sloppiness and absent-mindedness were a constant source of mirth in the family. It had not, however, prevented him from becoming a successful journalist.

"From what we've seen in the report cards, he's not doing badly," Mrs. Mandel said.

"He could be doing better," the teacher said. "But he daydreams. He's so busy looking out the window—sometimes I have to stand right next to him to get his attention. It's like he doesn't even hear me," she complained.

At home, his parents called Brian "the dreamer."

"He has a problem being respectful," the teacher went on. "When asked to do something, he . . . well, how should I put it . . . he doesn't just do it."

"He *thinks* about it first," his father interjected.

Mr. Mandel was starting to look angry.

"Well, he certainly is bright," the teacher agreed. "But he's just not getting the grades he should get."

"He is extremely smart," his mother confirmed. "He should be getting A's in everything, but he just doesn't apply himself."

After a silence, Mr. Mandel asked, "What does this add up to?"

"We think he should be evaluated," the teacher said. "At the staff meeting, the school psychologist concluded that Brian may have A.D.D.—you know, attention deficit disorder."

"Ritalin?" Mr. Mandel asked. "You're suggesting medication?"

"Oh, we can't do that—we're teachers. But we can spot a child who needs a medical evaluation. I have another child in my class on Ritalin. His behavior is much improved and his grades have gone up."

To the Mandels, the unthinkable was happening: Their perfectly wonderful child was being described as defective.

The teacher went on: "The math teacher says Brian is so sloppy, she thinks its a coordination problem—that it's *neurological*."

At home that night, Mrs. Mandel told her husband that this felt worse than when they heard when Brian was two that he might have a heart murmur. It turned out to be a "functional murmur." Some kids have hearts that sound a little different. But now they were talking about his brain . . . his very self.

"Maybe we just love him too much," Mrs. Mandel cried, "but I don't think there's anything wrong with Brian."

"There isn't anything wrong with him. We've got to get him out of that school. Now," Mr. Mandel said.

"Now?"

"He's not going back tomorrow. I can work on my column at home and cancel my luncheon appointment. He's out of that school, as of now."

Within three days, they found a small private school that emphasized the "whole child." They sent over Brian's school records and then the principal met with Brian while a student proudly showed Mr. and Mrs. Mandel around the school.

Everywhere the Mandels went in the new school, children were busy at work by themselves or in small groups on projects. They looked interested, even fascinated with what they were doing. A few teachers wandered about as if unattached to any one group of children, giving a little advice here, a little encouragement there. A couple of classes were meeting, but they were so small— six and twelve students—and so active that they were more like workshops than lectures. In a cozy corner of the large lounge, three students were taking a break and having a soda, right in the middle of the school day. In another corner of the lounge, two students sitting together on a couch were working together on some puzzling aspect of their math work.

But it wasn't the activities that was most striking to behold—it was the children's faces. They looked as though they were having a good time.

When the Mandels got back to the principal's office, Brian had already left on his own tour of the school. He had been invited to spend the whole day. It looked like a good sign to the Mandels.

The atmosphere at the private school was so markedly different from the public school's it was difficult to think of them both as "schools." If this new place was a school—what kind of place had Brian been attending up to now? What was its function—its purpose?

Sensing their confusion, the principal explained, "We try to make it a learning center—a place where children are captured by learning. We try to make it safe and we try to make it fun. We want learning to be something wonderful."

But then came the hard part. Even though the principal had seen all of Brian's prior school records, Mrs. Mandel felt obliged to recite the teacher's critique to him. When she was done, the principal replied, "As I said, we have a different approach to children. I'm sure we'll enjoy having your son here and I think we can help him to enjoy learning."

When she could finally speak again, Mrs. Mandel blurted out, "You'll *enjoy* having our son? You want him to *enjoy* being here?" The principal smiled knowingly as if he'd heard this response before.

Brian Mandel never became a top performer, even in this child-oriented school. School remained just one of several different things he did. Mostly, he seemed to like looking around outdoors. His father would take him on trips to various parts of the city and out in the countryside, so that Brian could look around. Later Brian would go off by himself on his bike and then with the family car. Brian seemed especially entranced with buildings—old ones, new ones, ones under construction. Sometimes, just for the fun of it, he would sketch a building. He resisted taking art lessons, but he liked to practice drawing by himself for hours at a time. He had the time and energy to explore his own interests because the school gave no more than an hour of homework a night.

Sometimes the Mandels would meet other parents whose children were in the public school or in competitive private schools. Though many of them bragged about their kids, universally they worried about the stress that afflicted their children. Brian, by contrast, was relaxed and happy most of the time, and he got up in the morning with the expectation of having a nice day. The family life was free of the usual stresses generated by conflicts over grades and homework.

Brian seemed to find himself academically in college. It was as if he'd been waiting for the right moment. He fell in love with architecture and dove into his academic studies. He went to graduate school on a scholarship.

In retrospect, it was unbearable to the Mandels to imagine what would have happened to their son if the fourth-grade teacher's opinion had held that day and he had ended up drugged into conformity with the public school's expectations. Yet this is happening every day to *millions* of our children. The Mandels rejected medicating Brian, but few other parents would have the strength or self-confidence to take a stand. Few fathers would have been able to stay home with their child while another school was located.

Many parents do not have the resources to send a child to private school as an alternative. And too often, private schools match or outdo public schools in their compulsion to push stimulant drugs. Private schools that specialize in problem children may end up with nearly all of them on psychiatric drugs.

Obviously, something has to be done about our schools. They must become more child-friendly—more able to welcome and to nurture children with a broad spectrum of talents and academic strengths, and with a variety of attitudes toward school.

What's More Important Than Homework?

Charlene is a dignified, strong, resilient woman, a corporate executive in a world dominated by men, yet a woman with great feminine and creative resources. She came for a consultation about her eight-year-old daughter, Taura, with whom she was having severe conflicts.

Charlene explained to me, "I've told the baby-sitter a million times to have Taura finish her homework before I get home. So Taura lies to her. Then I get home and we find out there's more math to do, or something else to read. She says, 'Oh, Mom, I forgot' but I can tell she's lying."

"Does Taura like school?"

"We have her in one of the best private schools—costs a fortune," was her mother's answer.

"Why does she have to her finish her homework before you get home?"

"Because we don't have time to do it otherwise."

"Why not?"

"She and her little brother have to help with dinner as soon as I get home. My husband comes home an hour later and I want to have everything ready for dinner."

"When do you have fun with the kids?"

"Fun?" She looked at me like I was a madman.

"Tell me more about the homework."

"Oh, it's awful. It takes her forever to do it and then she makes such a mess of it."

"I never had homework in second grade. Did you?" I asked.

"No, of course not, but now all the schools give homework. Some in the first grade."

"Tell me what you say to her about homework."

"I tell her it's important. She's got to do it if she's going to—"

"To what?"

"It sounds a little odd," she admitted. "I tell her she's got to do her homework if she's going to get ahead in life. But she's eight years old." Taura's mother became visibly sad.

"I suppose some second-graders might settle down to homework on their own before their parents get home," I mused aloud, "but I think it's a lot to ask. I can see you really agree with me about that. Have you thought about doing it with her? Make it a kind of play time."

"Did I tell you I used to play jazz professionally?"

"No," I responded.

"I can't believe how I've lost that zest."

"You could 'jazz up' her homework—improvise, make fun things to do, have a snack, and show her how to do some of it."

She was dumbfounded. I could see her shaking her head to herself. She was seeing the truth: that being a mother had ceased being fun. It had become a duty to prepare her daughter to perform her best in life.

"Don't you think the private school will take care of putting academic pressure on your child? If I were you, I'd stopping taking a second-grader's homework so dreadfully seriously. Then she'll probably lighten up, too. You could even make a game out of it. If it's overwhelming her, I'd even do some of it with her, help her along, so you can get to other things she likes."

"She loves to read!"

"Well, that's wonderful. Reading is the single most important thing to learn in school. If you can read, you can learn anything on your own. Do you read much with her?"

She shook her head. "We're too busy and fed up fighting over homework."

"She's learning to hate schoolwork," I said.

"For sure," her mother agreed.

"Make it as much fun as possible. Schoolwork should be as much fun as possible."

"That's bizarre," she laughed.

"Is your work fun?"

"It used to be."

"What happened?"

"I'd rather be home with my children. They are so much more important to me than anything else."

"So?"

"So I work because otherwise we couldn't afford private school."

"You mean, you work at something you hate so you can force your child to do things she hates—and the two of you are fighting all the time instead of having fun and loving each other."

"It's true. I come home tired. I wish I weren't working. We could live off my husband's salary, but we have all these things we want for our kids."

"You've got a college degree, and an M.B.A., and you're a musician. You could home-school your children if it came down to that."

"I thought I was coming to consult with you about what's the matter with my daughter . . ." she said thoughtfully. "It's a vicious cycle. I'm pressured, working too hard, having too little time with them, and I'm doing it all 'for them.' "

"What do you think is the most important thing in their lives?" I asked.

"Being prepared for the future? I don't think that one is going to fly with you," she laughed. Beyond preparing for life, she had no other clear-cut priorities at her fingertips.

"It's important to have a central idea about what's important, something to return to when the going gets rough."

"Look, I just work. I work hard. I try hard. I guess that's my priority."

"Think about it—what matters the most to your daughter and your son?"

"Pizza and ice cream?" she quipped.

"Really," I encouraged her.

She seemed genuinely puzzled.

"When you started acting like homework isn't so important, I got lost. I've got to push the homework or they won't make anything of themselves. But I see what you're getting at. I've made homework one of the most important things in the world."

"You and millions of other frustrated Americans who are at war with their children."

"I've got an M.B.A.," she joked, "but I haven't the faintest idea what's the most important thing in the world to my daughter. I suppose, if I remember what I was taught in business school, it's relationship. I think we had a seminar in that once," she quipped.

"And what does Taura get most upset about?"

"I was going to say, 'Doing her homework makes her the most upset.' But it's not that. She gets most upset when I go to work, or worse, when I'm mad at her, or if her dad is mad at her, that's the worst thing for her. I see what you mean. My husband and I are the center of her life. Nothing else is even close. And we're the center of our son's life, too. Of course. Everything depends on us and how we relate to our children. If my husband looks even a little disappointed, it's enough to make the little guy burst into tears."

"That's what I want you to be thinking when you leave here tonight—that you and your husband are the most important factors in your child's life, that the *quality of your relationship with your children* is the most important gift you can give them. Nothing else is close, including doing their homework or pushing them to succeed in school. If they've got a good relationship with you, they will get the best of what you have to give—a feeling of being loved, of being worthwhile. And they'll also get a feeling of competence and ability from being able to be with you successfully, to talk with you, to share your interests, to learn from you and with you. Nothing, absolutely nothing—including homework—should ever come between you and your relationship with your children."

"You're sure?" she said, teasing me for my somewhat righteous enthusiasm.

"I've never seen a child say, 'Mom and Dad love me, I love them, and I think I'll let my life go to hell.'"

"Can I bring in my husband to talk about this. He needs to hear what you're saying, too, and to hear it from a man—that nothing is as important to his children as his relationship with them."

"I'd love to meet him," I replied.

Depressed All the Time

Philip is a ninth-grader who gets good grades. But he says he feels "stressed and depressed all the time."

Philip feels his entire future life hangs in the balance of the grades he gets. When he has a project due on a Monday, he doesn't leave his room the whole weekend. He gets mostly A's, but sometimes he hates his classes and his teachers so much that he feels physically ill when he tries to study.

His parents are both first-generation professionals and they want the best for their three children. They have "lost control" over the two younger ones, who to one degree or another have asserted their independence. Philip, as the oldest, has taken their desires most seriously; he tries to be a perfect schoolboy, but he's brimming with rage about it.

Philip's mom is a computer programmer and his dad is an accountant. They are in professions where there is little room for mistakes, and Philip is phobic about getting anything wrong. But no one would imagine that his parents were in any way abusive. Friends see them as very gentle and even inoffensive people—nerds in their own school days.

As I often do with parents, I asked Philip's parents initially to come in without him so that we could talk about his situation. Then I had a second meeting with Philip, his next-younger sister, and both his parents. Nothing very eventful surfaced. There seemed agreement that Philip took his studies too seriously. I saw Philip alone and he talked mostly about some of the tensions in the house surrounding so many children and so little time with two working professional parents. He also talked, as most children do, about the other boys who routinely picked on him. Feeling something was missing from the picture, I asked Philip to come in with his father the next time. It would be my fourth session with members of the family.

Philip sat on the couch next to his dad, who, unlike most fathers of an adolescent boy, would occasionally reach over and try to tussle his son's hair with apparent affection—except Philip winced.

"Does he ever hit you?" I asked Philip.

"No . . . of course not," his father answered for him in an entirely believable manner. I believed him—but at that moment Philip turned on the couch, cocked back his arm, and smashed his father against the side of the head. The blow was struck with an open palm but it snapped his father's head to the side.

Shocked, I braced to throw myself between the two, but Dad did nothing.

"He hits me just like that when he doesn't think I'm studying hard enough."

Philip's father looked almost bewildered. The combination of being hit, and being hit by his son in front of a psychiatrist, had to be discombobulating.

His father said in a faltering tone, "I . . . I just sometimes get impatient with him when I'm helping with a project, so I just give him a little tap to get his attention."

Wham! Philip slapped his father again on the side of the head.

"Like that!" he shouted at this father.

I waited. This was becoming more interesting than frightening.

"Do you really hit him like that?" I asked.

"Yes, I guess so," his father confessed.

His son gave a sigh of relief and physically sank back into the couch.

Philip's father was not a brutal man. He had been beaten brutally by his own father and, by his standards, an occasional "slap up side the head" wasn't much. Mainly, he was expressing his frustration. His father felt compelled to make his son "use his full potential" and in his frustration he did what he'd been taught to do. He hit.

It turned out to be relatively easy to get Philip's father to stop hitting. After it was out in the open, and after being told it couldn't be done ever again, he realized on the spot it was wrong to do. I don't believe he ever again raised his hand to his son.

But getting him to let up the pressure on his son's grades? That was far more difficult. For Philip's father, pushing Philip to be successful continued for a time to take precedence over the boy's psychological and spiritual condition.

By the time I met Philip, the compulsion to perform in school already outweighed everything else in his own mind. Even though he had *learned* the compulsion from a combination of school and family pressures and stresses, he would have difficulty easing up on himself.

Even when young people like Philip have internalized their problems—made them part of their own viewpoint—it's not helpful to accuse them of manufacturing the problems themselves. Though children do make decisions that direct the course of their lives, they always make them from among limited alternatives presented by their families, schools, and other sources of adult influence. It is far more beneficial to emphasize the responsibility of adults rather than children.

At the same time, children can be encouraged to take responsibility for changing their own self-defeating patterns of behavior. They are especially willing to assume this responsibility when they don't feel blamed for originally developing the problems. They also feel enabled to take charge when they are told that the patterns are not genetically coded into their brains.

Ending School Slavery

Our schools set strict standards for rote academic performance—doing it right rather than doing it with love or understanding. They set high standards for conformity in behavior—sitting down and shutting up for hours at a time.

Increasingly, most of our public and private schools seem unwilling to tolerate any signs that a child cannot or will not go along with the regimen. Daydreaming? If it's not a crime, it's a symptom of a disorder. Sloppiness? If not a crime, it's at least a sign of abnormal behavior.

The children who will not or cannot submit to this regimen are too often given labels like "learning-disabled" and ADHD. But there's not a stitch of scientific basis to any of it.

Learning-Disabled, or Flawed Slave

Consider the concept of learning disability or, as it's officially designated, learning disorder.[2] Usually, the disorders are designated according to the three R's: reading (previously called dyslexia), writing, and arithmetic disorders.

We have a lot of "LD" children in America. Parents hear the term "LD" and automatically think of children who see words in reverse, or read backward, or upside down, or not at all. What causes these "disorders"? Doctors are fond of giving parents a variety of genetic and mechanical explanations: crossed wires, biochemical imbalances, neurological deficits . . . the usual villains.

In the last chapter I debunked behavioral diagnoses such as ADHD and oppositional defiant disorder as utterly lacking scientific or rational justification. As easy as that was, demolishing the LD diagnosis is even easier. I only have to ask you to read the official definition of learning disorder from the American Psychiatric Association's 1994 *Diagnostic and Statistical Manual of Mental Disorders, 4th Edition (DSM-IV)*: "Learning Disorders are diagnosed when the individual's achievement on individually administered standardized tests in reading, mathematics, or written expression is substantially below that expected for age, schooling, and level of intelligence."

In other words, an "LD child" is nothing more nor less than an "underachiever." Furthermore, the underachievement is identified in a very simplistic fashion. An LD child is one who does substantially worse on a standardized test of math, or reading, or written expression than on a standardized test of general intelligence (IQ).

What about specific problems supposedly associated with so-called learning disorders, such as word reversals? What about having trouble "transferring information" from the board to a piece of paper? None of these problems qualifies as a disorder, disability, disease, or syndrome. They are simply developmental stages. Reversing is simply something some children do before they've learned to do it right. It has no correlation with any kind of disorder or even with delayed reading or other school problems. In any event, a search of the *DSM-IV* reveals no mention of reversals or similar "symptoms," and sophisticated researchers don't believe in them anymore. As we saw, the most up-to-date official definition of LD in the *DSM-IV* does not describe any symptoms or behaviors at all.

This is worth pondering: If your child did *above* average on a test of general IQ but average on a more specific reading test, your child would be labeled as having a reading disorder. But if your child did average on both the IQ and the reading tests, your child would simply be called average, and would receive no diagnostic label. In one sense, it's better to do average on both tests rather than to do much better on your IQ battery, because you'll be thought of as average rather than disordered.

What is the most common reason a child doesn't read, write, or do math up to the level of his or her general intelligence? Answer: The child hasn't been properly taught. Another reason? The child isn't as good at taking reading or math tests as at taking IQ tests.

Overall, the attempt to dissect our children's "learning disabilities" does them more harm than good. I urge parents not to have their children subjected to psychological tests aimed at measuring the subtleties and complexities of their learning processes. These expensive tests make fine employment for psychologists but make parents obsessive about the development of their children's abilities and cause children to feel abnormal or different.

The IQ Controversy

Controversy over the validity of tests for general intelligence has been raging for decades. The very existence of general intelligence, which is the core of the IQ concept, has been challenged. Instead of possessing a single unitary mental capacity called IQ, individuals always have a variety of strengths and weaknesses along the broad spectrum of intellectual functioning. In short, some people are good at some things, others at other things, and no one is good at everything. These variations in individual ability may result from a combination of natural endowment and life experience, but even the relative weight of genetics and environment continues to be a matter of heated debate. As the multiple-intelligence theorist Howard Gardner puts it, "Dissatisfaction with the concept of IQ and with unitary views of intelligence is fairly widespread." He continued, "The whole concept has to be challenged; in fact, it has to be replaced."[3]

Remember, the definition of LD depends on the validity of the IQ test. On the basis of one flawed concept, general intelligence, or IQ, we label our children with another flawed concept, LD. Once again, the question arises, "Whose disorder is this?"

The LD label should be viewed as nonsense. But it is powerful nonsense. The LD concept convinces parents to think there's something wrong with their children that requires sending them for professional help. The LD label was engineered, among other things, to create business for professionals. Otherwise, the professionals would have to say, "Your son or daughter is an underachiever." You'd say back, "I already knew that. Tell me something useful." But they have nothing useful to say because it wouldn't serve their interests to tell the truth: "No one taught your child how to read, or write, or do math."

But a more dreadful purpose lies behind the concept of LD. It lets schools off the hook for failing to teach our children. Instead of a school's having to admit, "We've failed to help this child learn reading, writing, and arithmetic," the school can say, "The child is LD." Not only has this harmed millions of individual children, it has also delayed school reform by blaming a generation of children instead of the learning environment.

We have so many "LD" kids because our schools are failing to teach the basics of reading, writing, and arithmetic. It's that simple.[4]

The LD concept bears part of the responsibility for making school slaves of our children. Calling a child LD is a way of blaming the already beaten-down school slave for not performing up to expectation.

We need, instead, to reform our schools to make them into better learning environments for all of our children by finding ways to inspire the love of learning that lies within every child.

Catching Up with Modern Life

A child does need to learn to read, and it's also important for a child to develop other basic abilities, such as math and writing. There are many reasons a child might fail to reach full potential in any of these areas.

A child whose older brother is a "math genius" might give up trying to compete. A girl who believes that math or science aren't "feminine" may find herself unable to concentrate on the subjects. Even more commonly, youngsters who have been taught that they are "stupid" will panic when they encounter tests. In my practice and among my friends, for example, I've known very good students and eventually competent lawyers who grew so frightened by the bar exam that they repeatedly failed to pass.

But there's another significant reason why some children don't seem to live up to their potential—it's not really *their* potential. It's not what they are especially able to do or desirous of doing.

There is among human beings an enormous diversity of ability. Evolution favors diversity because diversity makes groups of people more willing and able to handle all the tasks required in community living. Daydreamers become poets and keepers of the myths. Very active, energetic children grow up to be traders and explorers. Aggressive youngsters may defend or expand the tribe's territory. Sedentary people take up activities around the home and camp. Humanity thrives on diversity.

Ironically, the "sit down and shut up" mentality that dominates today's schools is not preparing children for doing anything useful or rewarding in contemporary society. In whatever capacity they work as adults, they will rarely if ever be asked to go through the kind of humdrum, rote, heavily controlled daily activities that we impose upon our children. Many adults will express their high energy levels by traveling. Others will spend hours by themselves "daydreaming" in front of computers as they create new programs. None will grow up to sit in classrooms of thirty listening to a teacher drone on.

Our schools need to catch up with the modern work world, which rewards successful people pursuing autonomous, creative activities, sometimes alone, often in teams, and almost never in a passive, wholly receptive, school-like manner. Among other things, transforming our schools requires breaking up the classroom into smaller learning centers and engaging children in interesting, creative activities. It also requires resisting the temptation to overburden children with homework that ultimately turns them off to learning.

Working Outside of School

Parents eager to encourage responsibility often require their teenage children to work while they go to high school. Teenagers themselves often want a job to earn money. Nearly half of twelfth-graders in the United States put in twenty hours per week working during the school year, often at minimum-wage jobs in restaurants, stores, and nursing homes.

In 1998 a panel of the National Research Council and the Institute of Medicine found that students who put in twenty or more hours a week working are more likely to get into trouble and to use alcohol, cigarettes, and drugs.[5] They are at risk for sacrificing sleep and exercise, family life, and schoolwork. For every additional hour worked, one study found, there is a corresponding likelihood of dropping out of school. Working high school students have twice the rate of work-related injuries of adults. Some work is good for young people, the study concluded, but a large number of hours has adverse effects.

Especially for middle- and upper-class children, working hard during the school year at an outside job is a relatively new phenomenon. When I went to a suburban high school in the early 1950s, none of my friends worked outside school except during the summer or on occasion for their parents. Beyond a modest amount of homework, it was assumed we would enjoy ourselves outside the regular school hours. Those of us who had special interests or were more ambitious could fill our time with organized sports, drama club, the newspaper, and similar activities. However, this was a matter of choice, and we were expected to enjoy what we were doing.

The current tendency to view a working teenager with approval is a part of the overall trend to see young people as small adults tooling up for the "real world." Unfortunately, they often end up working even harder than adults and with considerably greater stress.

Meanwhile, one quarter of American families with children live at or below the poverty line, requiring many teenagers to work in order to provide income for necessities. This is one more example of how overall conditions in our nation adversely affect the well-being of our children. The growing disparity in wealth between the lower and the upper classes most drastically impacts on the children of the poor. The extra burden of earning income while they go to high school makes it even harder for them to break out of the cycle of poverty.

———◆———

Parents often become obsessed with their children's progress through their developmental and academic stages. Not content to watch the children's natural abilities unfold in a spontaneous fashion, parents and teachers try to enforce precocious rates of achievement. Afraid that a "deficiency" in one area or another will ruin a child's future, misguided adults try to "fix" every area in which the child fails to display a high level of ability. Adult emphasis on correcting deficiencies and pushing for extreme achievement ultimately breeds confusion, resentment, and self-doubt in children.

Genuine happiness and a sense of accomplishment in adult life do not result from being forced into one or another childhood mold mandated by teachers or parents. A fulfilling life depends upon the spontaneous pursuit and fulfillment of our unique natural abilities. Parents and teachers can be most helpful by providing a variety of opportunities for children to pursue their spontaneous interests and abilities in a noncoercive, happy learning environment.

Unfortunately, our current demands and expectations for our children are dampening and even killing their spirits. And as the next chapter documents, the children are turning on each other as well.

9

Putting an End to Scapegoating in School

—◆—

Within a week of the Columbine High School murders, I was talking in my office with a young man, Thomas, who to all outward appearances had a good home and family, and was doing outstandingly well in a highly respected public high school. He was a thoughtful, sensitive youngster with a very serious and sometimes sad countenance. His parents had brought him for help because he was depressed and stressed and often felt "like giving up."

"How did you react to the school murders?"

"I'm with Eric Harris all the way," Thomas said curtly, referring to the leader of the Columbine High School tragedy.

"Really?"

"Yeah, I totally identify with him."

Thomas was not exceptional in his reaction. After the Littleton massacre, a large number of students took the opportunity to talk among themselves and to the media about their own experiences as school outsiders and outcasts. The World Wide Web was humming with young people engaging in what one observer called "a fragmented national dialogue over social ostracism and the unforgiving hierarchies of adolescent life."[1]

165

After the shootings, some Columbine High School students searched their own souls about how they treated their fellow students. Patrice Doyle wrote in a school essay, "The way I live my life has come into my head many times. Am I doing the right thing always? Am I making people feel bad by the way I am treating them?"[2]

Even a Music Teacher

Martin was a slender, shy, and artistic youngster. His take-charge father had become so concerned about his son's vulnerability and sensitivity that he had brought him to me for therapy. I tried to help Martin's father understand that vulnerability and sensitivity were positive qualities, especially for an artist, and really for anyone, even if they could bring suffering in difficult situations.

Martin loved to play the trumpet and his dad dropped him off forty minutes early at school each morning to attend band practice. But midway through the first semester of his freshman year, Martin's parents got a note from his school letting them know that their son was being dropped from band owing to lack of attendance. Not only had he been skipping the extracurricular activity, he had been lying to his parents about it. The subject was addressed in a family therapy session with his father:

"What's going on," his father asked Martin.

"I just don't like band anymore."

"Really?" his father said. "I thought you loved it."

"I like the trumpet. I just want to take private lessons for now."

"Son, I'm not sure I can afford private lessons. And besides, why should you get private lessons when you haven't even attended the ones at your school? And your lying to me is even more upsetting."

Silence followed.

"I don't think Martin would lie unless he was very frightened about telling the truth," I suggested.

Martin tried not to show any feelings.

"You're scared?" his dad asked. "Of what, for God's sake?"

"I think it would be a good idea to tell your father," I encouraged him. "Dad, do you promise not to get mad if he tells you the truth?"

His father nodded. "You're right, I shouldn't jump on him if I want him to talk to me."

"You always get mad if you think I'm a quitter. I thought you'd make me go, no matter what."

"Well, I'd like to know why you're not going. Don't I have a right to know that, Martin?"

Martin looked very embarrassed.

"Ask him what's going on in the band," I suggested.

The boy shook his head.

"Did he demote you from being the first trumpet?"

He shook his head again.

"Damn, is somebody picking on you again?"

Now Martin became impassive.

"That big kid?"

"Nobody in particular."

"I don't get it," his father said. "It must be somebody."

"It's, like, everybody. Everybody is teasing me."

"Everybody?" his father said in disbelief.

I tried to help. "I think he probably means that it's so many that it is might as well be everybody."

"Thanks," Martin acknowledged.

"What's the music teacher doing about it?" Martin's father asked.

"Nothing."

"I'll talk to him."

"Dad, that'll just make it worse for me with the other kids. Anyway, he knows about it. I think he likes it. He kind of eggs them on sometimes."

"That's ridiculous . . ." his father started to say, and then caught himself. He was learning to respect his son's social awareness.

We talked together about it and Martin agreed to let his dad talk to the music teacher.

When they came in for the next session, Martin's father began by announcing that Martin was taking private lessons and that they were also looking into a special band program at a local music conservatory. Martin was so good, he might even get a scholarship, his father told me.

"It didn't go well with the music teacher," I guessed.

"Martin was right. The teacher knew all about it. He said Martin had to develop a 'thicker skin.' Sounded just like me before I came here," he said apologetically to his son. "He didn't admit to teasing Martin himself, but I'm sure Martin's right about that, too."

It made me so sad, this wonderful young boy, an outstanding musician, unable to find a safe place to learn music in his own school.

"Martin says it's okay for me to tell the principal, for the sake of the other kids, if nothing else. That man shouldn't be entrusted with the lives of children—and a *music* teacher. I mean, it's not like he's a football coach . . ." Then he smiled. "I guess coaches shouldn't be like that, either."

A Climate of Fear and Violence in Our Schools

Since 1991, the Centers for Disease Control (CDC) in Atlanta have been collecting data each year on the lives of our children by means of a national Youth Risk Behavior Survey. In August 1999 the CDC published data for 1997 for school violence in grades nine through twelve in the United States.[3]

Over the entire year of 1997, according to the CDC, 36.6 percent of students were in a physical fight and 32 percent had property stolen. The rates for boys were higher than those for girls in all categories of physical endangerment. One in ten boys was injured or threatened with a weapon in school and more than one in ten carried a weapon to school during a one-month sample period of time. These disturbing figures indicate that many of our children live in a world rife with fear and violence, especially when they are at school.

There was a slight decline in some indicators of fear and violence in 1997, but the improvement is not uniform, and its causes are uncertain. Some of the positive change may be due to heightened school security. However, the overall climate of fear and violence has not substantially changed.

School Bullies

Most observers agree that the routine humiliation inflicted by students on each other has been growing more destructive in recent decades. In March 1999 a bill was passed in Georgia making school bullying a crime and requiring school officials to alert parents if it occurs. The law resulted from lobbying by Bill Head whose son, Brian, shot himself to death in front of his classmates after enduring years as the butt of their jokes.[4]

School bullies have become such a serious problem that programs around the country teach children how to recognize and avoid bullying. But the worst effects come from more subtle psychological humiliation. Most of the experts agree that bullying is rampant and negatively affects all or nearly all children in school. The reporter Beth Azar, writing for the official newspaper of the American Psychological Association, pointed out, "Boys are often victims of ruthless jeering and insults. Many find that words don't stop the taunting but punches do, because anger is the only emotion that earns them respect."

The weakening of adult attention, authority, and control is the most obvious cause of increased school bullying and humiliation. We have unleashed our children on each other. The peer group takes over the functions of adults. As a result, many young people are more influenced by each other than by their parents, teachers, coaches, school administrators, or ministers.

Teenagers nowadays are more afraid of each other than they are of the adults in their lives. The growth of violent youth gangs represents the extreme of the overall trend that infiltrates every young person's social and educational life.

The intensity of verbal assaults is fanned by the explicit sexual imagery and previously unimaginable violence that permeate modern culture through television, video games, movies, the Internet, and talk radio. Boys and girls are also much more commonly threatened with potentially lethal violence nowadays compared to a few decades ago. In affluent Montgomery County, Maryland, schools, 200 knives were taken from students in 1998 and two students were arrested for making a bomb and bringing it to school. In mid–1999, six high school students were arrested for vandalizing the gym.[5]

Stories about Eric Harris and his co-perpetrator, Dylan Klebold, focused attention on the devastating impact of humiliation and ostracism on young people in school these days. Friends and acquaintances said that both had been the butt of ridicule from more mainstream students, especially the "jocks." The two boys were called the "trench coat Mafia" and were labeled "faggots" by other students. Many observers, including their fellow students, attributed their violent outburst, at least in part, to the humiliation and rejection they endured from other students.[6]

Peer harassment seems to be endemic at Columbine High School as it is throughout most of America's schools. In the aftermath of the shootings, one father explained how he had tried for a year and a half to get the school to stop two athletes from taunting, abusing, and assaulting his son because he was Jewish. The boy's father said he went to the top of the administration, but got no satisfaction until he threatened to sue. Michael Shoels, an African American whose son Isaiah died in the shootings, said that he, too, had tried to no avail to get the school to stop students from making racist slurs against his son.[7]

T. J. Solomon, the Georgia shooter, apparently also had been the subject of ridicule shortly before he attacked his schoolmates. Classmates described how he was allegedly humiliated by an older school athlete. According to one report: "He really picked on T. J. because T. J. was so quiet . . . You know, like being quiet made him weird in the eyes of that little clique of theirs." Solomon took the teasing hard, and even though he had friends, he seemed to have become convinced that he was destined to be the campus pariah.[8]

Most school shooters are known to have undergone bullying and ridicule at the hands of their schoolmates before they became violent.[9] In their profiling of sixteen school shooters, the psychologists McGee and DeBernardo concluded that all of them were social outcasts and that almost all were known to have been teased or to have felt victimized.[10] Examining the profiles of the shooters over the previous two years for *U.S. News & World Report*, Brendan Koerner in May 1999 concluded, "All were kids trying to fit in—kids ridiculed by their peers. Angry kids." This was before further confirmation in the form of T. J. Solomon. Koerner cited as an example Luke Woodham, the 1997 shooter from Pearl, Mississippi, who wrote a letter saying, "I killed because people like me are mistreated every day. I did this to show society, 'Push us and we will push back.' "

At least four school shooters were called "gay" or "faggot" by their peers. Michael Carneal had been called gay in the school newspaper before he stole a .22 caliber pistol from a neighbor with which he killed three students and wounded five others in West Paducah, Kentucky. Most young boys—heterosexual or not—could not endure the humiliation of being called gay in the school newspaper.

How Humiliation Causes Violent Reactions

Shame is the experience of feeling different in a painful, alienating, or humiliating fashion. It leaves the individual feeling rejected, powerless, inferior, or otherwise outside the accepted, meaningful social structure and social relationships. Children will talk about themselves being treated like a "nobody" or a "nothing" or about "not belonging" or "having no friends." Behind these descriptions, the youngsters may be enduring severe taunting.

In the extreme, the individual is shunned, ostracized, or completely rejected by the larger group or its leaders. To avoid facing shameful rejections, children commonly withdraw into themselves. Some youngsters and adults end up distrustful of all others and isolate themselves in a paranoid fashion.

Unlike many other emotional reactions, such as anxiety and guilt, shame and humiliation are self-perceived as to some extent alien—as imposed from the outside. Indeed, humiliation is usually inflicted in very direct fashion by the stronger on the weaker. In their attempts to overcome the sense of being rendered powerless and worthless by others, humiliated individuals often strike back verbally or physically. In the extreme, they may decide to destroy the real or imagined source of the humiliation, not only ridding themselves of the threat, but in the process demonstrating their own potency or superiority.

Shame is woven into the fabric of society and has been called "the master emotion." For the enforcement of social conformity, shaming is probably the single most powerful force in all cultures. Some societies such as Japan are more extreme than ours in relying on shame for inducing conformity, yet all societies use it to direct and shape the behavior and attitudes of children.[11]

Peer teasing is probably the single most potent enforcer of conformity to group norms in most cultures. Being laughed at is one of the most painful experiences in anyone's life. Few children can bear being teased about the way they look, talk, dress, or behave. They cannot endure having their race, religion, or family background ridiculed. Merely having an unusual first name, especially if it sounds foreign, can cause endless embarrassment, leading a child to beg parents to be allowed to use a more acceptable nickname.

The overall result of peer teasing is a uniformity in many habits and attitudes among children in any community. This process is demonstrated in the case of first-generation immigrant families, where the children will typically do everything they can to look and talk "like the other kids" in the new country. In a matter of months, a preadolescent immigrant child can drop every hint of a foreign accent.

172 RECLAIMING OUR CHILDREN

Actions that cause extremes shame can backfire; instead of inducing conformity, they can stir up uncontrollable rage. Sometimes the victim turns to violence. In his 1989 book, *The Creation of Dangerous Violent Criminals*, Lonnie Athens describes the childhood and youth of incarcerated men who had perpetrated extremely violent and hateful crimes against strangers with seemingly little provocation. For example, one man escalated a traffic mishap into murderous rage by beating the other person to a pulp with a tire iron. In every case, Athens found that the perpetrator had been subjected to constant humiliation as a child from older boys and adults, and frequently had been forced as a child to stand by helplessly while loved ones were similarly humiliated. They had also been "trained" by older mentors to believe that it was unmanly not to react violently to disrespect. Their rage, driven by largely unconscious feelings of impotence and humiliation, would burst out against innocent victims who happened, for one reason or another, to stir up their lurking feelings of shame. Even in retrospect, the perpetrators almost always felt that their victims "deserved it" because they had shown disrespect for them—that is, shamed them.

As he expressed on his Website,[12] Eric Harris was trying to gain revenge against people whom he perceived as having humiliated him. In their 1999 analysis of "the classroom avenger," James P. McGee, Ph.D., and Caren DeBernardo, Psy.D., observe that school shooters have been treated as "geeks" and "nerds" by other students. The U.S. Department of Education's 1998 manual, *Building Safe Schools*, remarked, "Students who have been treated unfairly may become scapegoats and/or targets of violence. In some cases, victims may react in aggressive ways. Effective schools communicate to students and the greater community that all children are valued and respected."

Eric Harris and Dylan Klebold, like many of the school shooters, wanted to compensate for feelings of powerless and humiliation by becoming all-powerful and godlike. Feeling like nobodies, they were determined to become somebodies. They were also exposed, like most youngsters, to a wide variety of video games, movies, and TV that made heroes of people who dealt violently with anyone who showed disrespect for them.

Feelings of ridicule and humiliation lie at the root of most personal violence, from the action of an isolated would-be assassin of a president, such as John Hinkley, to those of inner-city children who kill each other over being "dissed" (treated with disrespect). Even when physical beatings are endured, the shameful aspect of the experience will almost always far outlast the healing of the physical wounds. My clinical experience confirms that women who are abused by their husbands often have more painful memories of the demeaning words than of the physical blows. Often the humiliation will feel so overwhelming that the individual will hide it beneath chronic numbness or anger.

The Extent of the Problem

Parents and teachers often have little awareness of the degree to which children and youth are exposed to humiliation from peers and sometimes from teachers, administrators, and coaches as well. Even when parents realize that it's a problem, they are likely to be kept in the dark by their children about just how bad it is.

Shaming takes many forms, from teasing to physical intimidation and even to physical and sexual abuse. A University of Michigan survey found that peer sexual harassment afflicted 83 percent of girls and 60 percent of boys.[13] These high rates for sexual harassment do not include the many other kinds of emotional and physical bullying.

In today's school culture, a torrent of humiliation is heaped on almost any child who is different in any way—shorter, taller, skinnier, fatter, weaker, less attractive, slower, emotionally distressed, or from a different socioeconomic or ethnic background. People with visible physical disabilities are likely to feel that they are standing out like a sore thumb—one that's constantly being hit with the hammer of shame. In most circumstances, anyone from an identifiable minority group is at risk for being persistently shamed by his or her peers.

The Supreme Court Acts on Peer Humiliation

The worsening of the problem of school harassment, and society's attempts to deal with it, are dramatized in the U.S. Supreme Court's ground-breaking opinion holding schools responsible for intervening to protect students from obvious, gross sexual harassment. Issued in June 1999, the opinion may have been influenced by the school shootings in which peer harassment seemed to play a role.

The harassment that brought the case before the court was extreme. The fifth-grade boy at the center of the suit had repeatedly taunted, propositioned, rubbed himself against, and grabbed at the breasts and genitals of LaShonda Davis, his classmate who brought the suit. He allegedly "repeatedly attempted to touch LaShonda's breasts and vaginal area," told her in "vulgar terms" that he wanted to "get in bed with her," and "placed a doorstop in his pants and behaved in a sexually harassing manner."[14]

According to the Supreme Court ruling, a school can be held liable only if it displays "deliberate indifference to known facts of harassment." The ruling applies "only for harassment that is so severe, pervasive and objectively offensive that it effectively bars the victim's access to an educational opportunity or benefit." The harassment of LaShonda allegedly went on for five months while the school took no action to stop the boy despite repeated complaints by the child to her teachers and by her mother to administrators. The behavior ended only when the boy pleaded guilty to sexual battery.[15]

In writing its opinion, the Court purposely set a high enough threshold to exclude routine teasing and bullying. It remains much easier for an employee to sue an employer for sexual harassment than for a student to sue a school. The Court apparently expects students to quietly endure the kind of abuse in school that, if it occurred in the workplace, would land an employer in court. Nonetheless, the decision was an important beginning in alerting the schools and the public to the problem. It put schools on notice that there's a limit to what they can overlook.

The court was sharply divided by a 5–4 vote. The more conservative justices reacted with "furious dissent."[16] Justice Anthony M. Kennedy, who grew up in the 1950s in the California suburbs, declared in his dissenting opinion: "The real world of school discipline is a rough-and-tumble place where students practice newly learned vulgarities, erupt with anger, tease and embarrass each other, share offensive notes, flirt, push and shove in the halls, grab and offend."[17]

Kennedy's opinion is remarkable, first in its ready acceptance of a highly offensive and threatening level of behavior among students, and second for its failure to grasp how much worse it often gets nowadays, including the case that came before the Court. Kennedy's dissent was based in part on his reluctance to bring the legal system into the functioning of schools, but I suspect it also reflects a callousness toward the suffering of our children.

After the Supreme Court decision on the sexual harassment of schoolchildren, school administrators and teachers were divided on the question of requiring schools to protect their students from abuse.[18] One teacher applauded the ruling: "The classroom teacher does need to guard against things like that. We do not simply educate the child. We are teaching the children in our classrooms how to be good citizens, and we're teaching them ways to live."

The Cult of the Athlete

The school shootings in April and May 1999 tended to focus attention on cliques of alienated boys, but it also drew attention to the cliques of jocks and other more mainstream groups who often cause or reinforce the alienation and humiliation felt by many students. The reporters Lorraine Adams and Dale Russakoff of the *Washington Post* followed up the murders at Columbine High School with an insightful examination of what they called the "cult of the athlete."[19] They documented overt sexual, racial, and religious harassment conducted by a number of the Columbine athletes, often in front of approving or condoning teachers and coaches. For example, a football player was allowed "to tease a girl about her breasts in class without fear of retribution by his teacher, also the boy's coach." According to the reporters, many of the athletes were in trouble with the law and "The homecoming king was a football player on probation for burglary."

Adams and Russakoff observed, "Columbine may be no different from thousands of high schools in glorifying athletes." They added, "But some parents and students believe a school-wide indulgence of certain jocks—their criminal convictions, physical abuse, sexual and racial bullying—intensified the killers' feelings of powerlessness and galvanized their fantasies of revenge."

The two reporters documented that the Columbine shooters knew about and felt deep resentment toward routine abuses perpetrated by the school athletes. A fellow student described Dylan Klebold's outrage when a school athlete stuffed his own girlfriend into a locker in front of a teacher who did nothing. Harris and Klebold themselves suffered humiliations at the hands of athletes, including having objects thrown at them from automobiles. In retaliation, the boys began their shooting spree by yelling, "All jocks stand up."

Regardless of the specific role that jock culture played in the various school shootings—and it does seem to have helped to provoke a number of the shooters—in general the jock culture creates a perpetrator-victim relationship that afflicts a large percentage of middle and high school students.

Though the victims are more obviously harmed, perpetrators are also injured by their own behavior. Ultimately, the school athlete turned school abuser learns methods that not only harm other people but also will backfire on him in adult life, when abuse and violence ruin his family life, alienate other adults, result in job loss, and lead to criminal convictions.

In thinking about the "school jocks," we should also remember that perpetrators almost always began as victims. In fact, overcoming humiliation is a major motivation for body building, for learning to fight, and for developing athletic prowess.

The high school senior who owns a six-foot-tall frame packed with muscle may no longer endure much peer abuse, but he might have been subjected to abuse in the past from bigger children or adults. As a younger and hence smaller boy participating in competitive athletics, he would have been constantly exposed to older, bigger boys. As a child in typical athletic training and competitions, he would have been subjected to ridicule and humiliation from stronger or more violent boys. Even as a successful high school athlete, he may be subjected to coaches who use ridicule to motivate students in competitive sports. Growing up in and immersed in a youth culture characterized by competitiveness and peer humiliation, it's no wonder that some high school athletics take advantage of their newfound power and status to abuse less intimidating peers.

Competition and Empathy

As our schools have become increasingly competitive, too little attention has been given to the negative effects of pitting students against each other in their sports, academics, and social life.[20]

The harmful moral and psychological effects of violent sports are the most obvious. High school sports increasingly are modeled on their professional counterparts. Winning becomes primary. Young students are taught to hate and to resent the opposition. Slogans such as "Punish them . . . Kill the bastards . . . Take people out" become reality in the violence of football, basketball, wrestling, and hockey. As Myriam Miedzian points out in *Boys Will Be Boys*, "To play the game as violently as this, boys must learn to repress empathy. They work hard at it."[21]

The competition that characterizes today's schools is indeed very suppressive of the all-important human capacity for empathy. Competition goes beyond sports, infecting every aspect of the academic and social experience. A coach who became a school dean observed: "To compete against another person, my students felt they needed to separate from that person. To beat you in a competition meant that I could not know you or care about you."[22]

Contradictory Roles

Starting in the 1960s, there has been increasing emphasis on men becoming more sensitive, especially in their relationships with women. But this continues to fly in the face of the persistent trend throughout boyhood to equate sensitivity with being a "sissie" or "wimp." Beth Azar put the boy's dilemma succinctly: "Fathers tend to demand that their sons act tough, mothers tend to expect boys to be strong and protective and their friends enforce the rule that a boy doesn't cry. And after being taught not to be 'sissies,' boys are then chastised for being insensitive."[23]

In my clinical practice, I reach out to boys to let them know how much I admire and share their sensitivity, and how I understand that their seeming toughness is driven in part by shame over their sensitivity. Some of my most touching encounters in therapy come at moments when I see the relief on a boy's face upon being reassured that sensitivity and caring are positive traits. Unfortunately, my efforts in this direction are going against much of the momentum of socialization in this country.

Delusional Dominating Personality Disorder

Overall, the competitive atmosphere of today's schools, the diminishing influence of adults in the daily lives of children, the forces of peer pressure, and jock culture combine to perpetuate the value of male domination through humiliation. Boys learn to use ridicule to control girls. Larger, stronger boys learn to brutalize smaller, less socially adept boys. A boy or girl who is seen as "sensitive" becomes fair game.

Those who prosper in these schools often demonstrate what the psychologist Paula Caplan, Ph.D., has called the "delusional dominating personality disorder."[24] Her concept provides an accurate caricature not only of the abusive male but of personality traits inculcated through socialization in males in general.

In addition to a male-centered orientation, Caplan's list of characteristics includes "the inability to establish and maintain meaningful interpersonal relationships," "the inability to respond appropriately and empathically to the feelings and needs of close associates and intimates," and "the tendency to use power, silence, withdrawal, and/or avoidance rather than negotiation in the face of interpersonal conflict and difficulty."

The biological psychiatric approach to diagnosing and drugging children—rather than building relationships with them—epitomizes delusional dominating personality disorder. Caplan, in fact, developed the concept as an effort to counteract the psychiatric diagnostic system that blames the victim, such as the abused child or woman, while it exonerates the perpetrator, such as the abusive parent or husband.

The impact of male-dominated culture in high school is especially devastating on the development of girls and young women. As they enter puberty, many girls feel compelled to forsake their natural assertiveness and become compliant in their dealings with other people, especially men and boys. In the words of Carol Gilligan, they also develop a "crisis of connection" over their basic values of caring and meaningful relationship.[25]

Those girls who become "resisters," according to Gilligan, will be "especially prone to notice and question the compliance of women to male authority." If these young women openly communicate the findings of their critical intelligence, they will pay a heavy price in regard to their popularity with boys and girls alike.

Taking It Out on Girls and Women.   Though boys often treat each other very badly, they reserve some of their most damaging violence for girls and then, as they grow older, for women. Few, if any, assaults are more vicious and destructive than sexual abuse and rape.

The male abuse of women can also take a chronic and debilitating form. Males will spontaneously fight each other, but except in closed institutional settings such as prisons and many schools, it is rare for one man to be able to chronically abuse another the way a husband, for example, can chronically abuse a wife.

The commonly used term "domestic violence" makes it sound as if both men and women are equally involved, but in fact, dangerous physical violence in the family is usually perpetrated by grown men against women and children. When women do become physically violent, it's usually in self-defense or retaliation. Unfortunately, the same cannot be said about emotional violence, an arena in which women seem to be as active as men.

Many girls are subjected to more intense and unrelenting humiliation than boys like Eric Harris and Dylan Klebold. As the University of Michigan study indicated, more than 80 percent of them report being sexually harassed. But girls seldom express their humiliation through physical violence and have not been directly involved in the more publicized school shootings. The result? We have not focused our attention on the plight of girls and young women in our schools.

Boys are likely to endure some teasing from girls, but much of what girls say about boys is done behind the boys' backs, where they never get to hear it. Also, boys typically feel so little respect for girls that they can easily dismiss their teasing. Teasing is far more humiliating when it comes from a person who is seen as possessing higher status and greater power. Besides, however mean or spiteful a girl may act toward a boy, her remarks are rarely backed up by the potential for physical and sexual violence.

More important, boys as a class of people do not experience systematic rejection and exclusion from activities that they would like to join with girls. By contrast, from the time they are toddlers, girls understand that their inferior status excludes them from interesting male-dominated activities, such as playground games and sports, that they would like to join.

Girls very quickly learn that boys look down on them. The very word "girl" is considered a label of disgrace by many if not most boys. Girls see boys humiliate other boys by referring to them in terms usually reserved for girls or by talking to them in a tone of voice usually directed at girls.

As girls grow into puberty, they face a problem unknown to boys—extreme attention to the sexual appearance of their bodies, often accompanied by lewd or otherwise humiliating remarks. Commonly they are sexually manhandled by boys they hardly know. On dates they must often fight for their self-respect and the control of their own bodies. Girls also quickly learn that many or most boys prefer them to act somewhat stupid and shy, and conversely, that boys are threatened by girls who act intelligent and confident.

No Safe Haven for Girls.   Unfortunately, girls cannot necessarily expect a safe haven among their female peers, either. Girls often turn their anger on each other by manipulation and verbal torment, often behind each other's backs, rather than by direct confrontations. Whereas boys will more often say humiliating things to each other's faces, girls will spread hateful rumors. Among school-aged girls and young women, one friendship after another tends to fall apart as they hurt each other with gossip and competition for boys' attention. Teenage girls are often driven to self-hate, self-mutilation, and self-punishment in the form of starving themselves, in large part as a result of peer humiliation.

In a 1999 *New York Times* article entitled "Rethinking America's Schools of Hard Knocks," the author Ethan Bronner cites the "ugly rites of passage" through which our children go. He describes the circumstances under which a fourteen-year-old Bronx, New York, girl had hanged herself: "Friends said she had suffered continual verbal abuse by classmates. Psychologists note that such suicides have been on the rise among the young in recent years."

Because they have not turned to mass violence, the suffering of girls was largely overlooked during the period of self-examination that followed the school shootings of mid–1999. Not only is the everyday humiliation of girls of calamitous proportions in most of our schools and communities, it is likely that they too will become increasingly violent as their needs for self-esteem and security continue to go unmet.

In the suburbs of Washington, D.C., a roadway dispute in June 1999 lead to the brutal beating death of a twenty-five-year-old woman. The alleged perpetrators were two girls: an eighteen-year-old who had graduated high school a month earlier and a sixteen-year-old who had been expelled from an alternative school for fighting. FBI statistics indicate that the number of women arrested for violent crimes doubled from 1988 to 1997. The local state's attorney for Fairfax County, Virginia, declared that he had seen a "monumental" increase of prosecutions of girls and women: "I can remember a day when you could have 100 indictments go through the grand jury and not a single defendant was a woman. But over the last 15 to 20 years, that's changed unbelievably." He added, "The $64,000 question is, 'What is going on out there that's causing that?' "[26]

Violence by girls against their schools may be the next tragic frontier.

A Victim of Jealousy

Because of boys' greater penchant for violence, more media attention is being given to them as victims of humiliation than to girls. In reality, girls suffer far more shaming from a much earlier age. Ostracized and rejected by boys in their peer groups even before reaching school age, girls soon begin to inflict dire humiliations on each other as well. Peer humiliation has reduced many young women to suicidal depression.

Marsha, a dignified, intelligent fourteen-year-old was called a "ho," meaning a whore, every day she went to school. Five or six other girls in her class joined together to systematically humiliate and reject her. Why? Certainly not because of Marsha's behavior, which was much more restrained than that of the girls who were doing the name-calling. Partly it was jealousy. Marsha had developed more fully and possessed an especially warm personality. They may have wanted to drive out the competition.

One of Marsha's "enemies" passed around a note stating that Marsha had been seen performing a "Monica" sexual act on one of the boys in the class. In the parking lot after school, two boys from her class cornered her against a car. One was carrying a heavy stick. They told her she had to have sex with them "or else." When she screamed, they backed off, while calling her "ho." In the school bus that same day, no one wanted to sit near her. When she tried to stand as bravely as possible by herself, one of the boys called attention to her developing body and embarrassed her. When she got home that night, Marsha's only friend had left a phone message explaining that she was afraid to be seen with Marsha anymore.

That night Marsha carved her own initials in her arm with a knife. When her mother noticed the corner of the wound showing at the edge of Marsha's sleeve, she demanded to know what was going on. Marsha snapped back "Nothing, it means nothing, all the kids do it." Besides, she was just trying to make a tattoo, she lied. Meanwhile, in an effort to rid herself of the feminine shape that was drawing so much attention, Marsha began a starvation diet.

Desperate to know what was going on, Marsha's parents called their daughter's friend, and the story came out about the abuse at school. But when they asked for a meeting with the principal of the school, the parents were told, "Girls have to learn to settle these things among themselves." Marsha would have to see the counselor to have a "conflict resolution" meeting with the other girls. The school officers were certain that Marsha was at least as much to blame as the other girls. Marsha, her parents were informed, was "over-sensitive"; the school supposedly had no problems with peer-group humiliation.

Eventually, Marsha's parents resorted to home schooling to save their child from the school life that effectively tortured her. These parents were well off financially. Why didn't they instead try a private school with a reputation for being oriented to the needs of children? Unbelievably, these events took place in a well-known private school that claimed to specialize in creating a caring, cooperative environment. Humiliation and scapegoating occur at all levels in almost every kind of school. It must be approached as a national problem of vast proportions requiring interventions by parents, teachers, administrators, and concerned citizens.

Rethinking School

Contemporary research and clinical experience indicate that the kind of verbal abuse prevalent in nearly all of our schools can cause serious, enduring psychological injury. This kind of abuse has escalated among children and youth in the absence of effective adult supervision.

Many concerned observers have noted that adult supervision and involvement in the lives of children has been declining in the past several decades. "There has never in the history of the civilized world been a cohort of kids that is so little affected by adult guidance and so attuned to a peer world," declared William Damon of the Stanford University Center on Adolescence. "We have removed grown-up wisdom and allowed them to drift into a self-constructed, highly relativistic world of friendship and peers."[27]

In other words, we have stopped taking responsibility for our children and they have filled the vacuum. Lacking meaningful relationships with us, they have developed child-run societies of their own not unlike that depicted by William Golding in his novel *The Lord of the Flies*. In that story, marooned children develop a community dominated by conflict, humiliation, and violence. Ironically, they are rescued by a warship whose officers are dismayed at the children's precocious penchant for violence.

Respect: The Most Important "Show and Tell"

Little children often enjoy "show and tell," a class project that involves bringing something to school that they find interesting and then explaining its importance to their classmates and teacher. Respectful relating is the most important "show and tell" in school, but it's a project that begins with the teachers and administrators rather than the students. Teachers and administrators must regularly tell students about the importance of respect and consistently show them through their own actions how to be respectful under any and all circumstances.

The most painful school experiences almost always involve students' humiliating each other or teachers' and administrators' humiliating students. Often these experiences drive students to express themselves through violence as a means of asserting their own pride and "getting even." By contrast, when people inhibit their tendencies to ridicule or reject each other, conflict resolution can begin.

The Special Humiliation of Minorities

Among the poor in America's inner cities, of course, the infliction of humiliation can reach even more devastating proportions. Girls are even more routinely exposed to severe abuse, as well as to threats of physical violence from each other and from boys and men. Boys all too frequently injure and murder each other over issues of respect and gang membership. Students from racial minorities who attend largely white suburban schools face additional uniquely humiliating circumstances. From kindergarten through higher education, minorities are reminded on a daily basis that they don't quite reach human status in the eyes of many whites.

Racial minorities frequently must endure, in addition to overt harassment and taunting, the humiliation of invisibility. Earlier I quoted Dr. Ron Hopson, professor of both psychology and divinity at Howard University, concerning the feelings of humiliation of black children when they see how much more concern is shown about the death of white children than of black children. The year before coming to Howard University, Dr. Hopson was voted Teacher of the Year at the University of Tennessee. As one of the few black men at Tennessee, he should have been readily recognizable as he walked about the campus. Instead, his own students often acted as if they didn't recognize him outside the classroom.

The experience of not being recognized or acknowledged was so common in his life at largely white universities that Dr. Hopson hardly noticed it until he moved to Howard University's largely black campus. To his shock, and to his enlightenment, black students who hardly knew him nonetheless quickly recognized and greeted him on the campus.

Native Americans, Hispanics, Asians, Jews, and other ethnic minorities are often subject to similar humiliation and rejection as African Americans. Many people have come to sneer at the presumed excesses of "political correctness," but it is important to remember the reasons for establishing the guidelines of "political correctness," namely, the persistent infliction of humiliation on minorities and vulnerable individuals. There are good reasons for people to act respectfully with each other, and to speak respectfully of and to each other. When one group dominates another within a culture, it becomes incumbent upon those in the mainstream to make special efforts to be respectful of those who have been marginalized.

A Blight on All Our Children

Racism is central to our nation's problems, including those that afflict our children and youth. In Chapter 2 I looked at the inevitable spread of violence from the inner city to the suburbs. There are, however, more subtle ways than the spread of violence that racism ends up inflicting harm on all of our children. In a society that promotes democratic and egalitarian values, children will be puzzled and even confused by racist attitudes and by the obvious reality that some groups are not sharing all the benefits in equal proportion. The reality of life in America ends up making a mockery of what we are trying to teach our children about equality and fairness. It discourages their trust in adults and undermines the exercise of their critical intelligence.

The existence of marginalized groups provides an all-too-ready outlet for scapegoating and even violence. When white American youths see white adults bolstering their own flagging self-esteem by feeling and acting superior to minority groups, the youngsters are encouraged to do the same. It becomes easier to blame someone else for their failures and disappointments instead of taking responsibility for improving their own lives.

Racism also creates a scorn for other people that is readily translated into violent acts. As long as hatefulness toward one group is socially sanctioned, it becomes easier to be hateful to others as well. It's almost impossible for a society to say, "These children are good, these are bad; we'll take care of the good ones but not the bad ones." Our culture is too integrated for us to carry out such a charade. Instead, when we condemn one group of children, we end up condemning all of them. We set a tone and express an attitude that must inevitably affect all our children.

Racism reinforces the cult of the individual to the exclusion of community and relationship. It says, in effect, "Some people aren't worth relating to." It creates a myth that some of us "make it on our own" while others "fail on their own"—when in reality society builds in enormous advantages to people born white and affluent, while it builds in equally enormous disadvantages to those born darker-skinned and poor.

On a societal level, we cannot reject the needs of our minorities such as African Americans, Hispanics, and Native Americans without at the same time ignoring the needs of all our children. In the public debate of issues such as eradicating poverty, improving the availability of health care, providing more low-cost housing, or paying more for our schools, racist attitudes often impede federal and state legislation that would benefit all children. The reforms are resisted on the grounds that "they don't deserve it" or "they haven't earned it." Even though greater numbers of white children are languishing in poverty and going without adequate health care, the "they" usually refers to black, Hispanic, or other minority children.

Racism is one of the greatest impediments in this country to making the necessary reforms required to improve the well-being of all of our children. That makes racism a blight on all of our children. In a gross irony, we deprive "our own children" because we resent giving more to "their children." The key to changing all this? All children must become "our children," all children must be treated as treasures to be protected and cherished.

Standing Up as Men for Boys

The environment of peer humiliation, though created by individual boys and girls, is ultimately fueled by the values of domination and control that are perpetuated by men in their relationships to each other and to women and children. Though women commonly adopt these oppressive tendencies, the trend has been set by centuries of male domination and control. If men as a whole rejected these values, our culture would change dramatically for the better.

As men, we need to make clear to boys that we promote values such as love, concern, caring, sensitivity, tenderness, and nonviolent conflict resolution. We can do this, first and foremost, by setting a personal example in how we treat our families, as well as all others in our lives. A boy who has been treated with loving kindness by his father is not likely to turn into an egregious bully. He's also likely to grow up happier. In addition, we can take every opportunity to say aloud to our boys that we love their tenderness and value it in ourselves as well.

For many years, women have been calling on men to put more value on relationship and caring. Since the 1960s, men have begun to respond in large numbers. A growing number of books by men have criticized the values of domination and control that pervade society. The authors have called for the empowerment of values related to mutuality, caring, and sensitivity.[28] Growing male concern for creating a more empathic society is a very positive sign—but as men, we have a long, long way to go before our children can grow up in a world that's more oriented to caring and mutuality than to domination and competition.

Ending School Scapegoating and Slavery

Teaching respectful ways of relating and communicating is a most basic task for any teacher, parent, or caregiver. It must begin with adults setting a good example. Those in power must be the first to show respect toward those who have less power, otherwise insistence on respect becomes an excuse for authoritarian manipulation and control. It will be perceived as hypocritical—and as just another form of humiliation.

We need zero tolerance for humiliation in our schools. Children acting by themselves cannot accomplish this goal. Adults must set the standards of behavior by example and, when necessary, must enforce them with punishments.

Our children too often become school slaves to competitive academic pressure and school scapegoats for the pain and suffering of other children. It's time to transform our schools into places where school slavery and scapegoating are no longer commonplace experiences, and where principles of love and care create a learning sanctuary.

10

Creating Good Schools

—◦—

Imagine a high school brimming over with youthful vitality—lively, imaginative, enthusiastic energy that's not destructive or out of control—a school where teenagers are taught to enjoy learning, to take responsibility for themselves and their work, to greet their teachers with respect and even affection, and to resolve conflicts in a rational and caring way. On a recent visit to such a high school, the students told me about their experiences there:

> On a scale of one to ten, my public high school was a one. This one's a ten; it's awesome.
>
> When I first got here, I couldn't believe it was real. My previous school made me hate learning. Here learning is fun.
>
> We don't have to feel stiff and uncomfortable all day like in other schools. We feel normal here.
>
> Nobody gets ridiculed and humiliated. Sure, there's some teasing and a lot of kidding around, but we don't have the vicious cliques and put-downs like other schools.
>
> If you do something out of line here, they don't punish you right away. They talk to you, listen to you, and try to help you see what you did wrong.
>
> You don't sit at desks staring at a chalkboard all day. You get to talk with each other and with the teacher in class.

189

The teachers don't see us as one big mass of people. They treat
us as individuals.

The teachers don't put you into boxes. They adapt to your personality. They let you be who you are. So kids who come here
with a bad attitude get over it. They find out the school really
cares and wants to help.

The teachers want you to express yourself. They won't come
down on you for disagreeing or being critical.

It's not like the public school or even my other private school; we
almost never get bored and angry.

I was depressed about going to school before I got here.

The school is Thornton Friends School in the Maryland and Virginia suburbs of Washington, D.C., where it comprises a middle
school and two high school campuses. But before I explain how
Thornton Friends creates such a wonderful learning environment, it's
important to understand that many good schools do exist. Although
they are by no means identical, and students, parents, and teachers
may prefer one or another particular model, still it is possible to describe a set of principles that are common to many of the best schools.

A Special Private School

One of my clients, thirteen-year-old Jay,[1] came to me for help after he
and his parents found that stimulant drugs made him "zombied out."
Jay's parents were not fully convinced that a "nondrug approach"
would work, and they worried that Jay suffered from a "learning disorder built into his brain." I told them, "Hating school doesn't mean
there's something wrong in his brain. In fact, he's got a wonderful
brain."

Much of my effort with the family involved bolstering their faith
that without drugs Jay would eventually engage his marvelous mind in
some aspect of learning and school—that he would not be left behind
without a satisfying future. My sessions alone with Jay were at times
more like seminars than like therapy—we'd talk about everything
from the typical "getting along with parents" issues to why adults so
misunderstand what the shock-rocker Marilyn Manson is about. He
called Manson a "free speech abuser"—someone who purposely uses
free speech to defy conventionality to shake up people into really

thinking. I can't say we agreed on everything, but Jay was full of that most healthy and admirable quality discussed in Chapter 5, critical intelligence.

Unfortunately, Jay had hated elementary school and he continued to dislike middle school. Although enrolled in a relatively progressive magnet school that encouraged autonomy and independence, he suffered a persistent combination of lack of confidence, rebelliousness toward authority, and boredom that kept him from engaging with his teachers in a positive way. Although extremely bright, creative, and verbal, Jay took an "I don't care" attitude toward school.

Eventually, in frustration, the school assigned Jay to a special education class once each day. His special education teacher, Jay explained, was "the only teacher who gave a damn about me. None of the other [mainstream] teachers cared." But going to the special ed class only exacerbated his feelings of humiliation while adding to his boredom and frustration with what he called "Mickey Mouse" school.

In our therapy sessions and then at home on their own, Jay and his parents worked on the basic principles of treating each other with respect and sharing as much love as they could. From doing homework to getting to bed on time, typical family conflicts were resolved through caring negotiation, compromise, and mutual concern. Within a few months, they had transformed their family life from a constant state of tumult and turmoil to a sanctuary of cooperation and goodwill. They began to arrive at their therapy sessions more eager to tell me about the fun they were having together than to discuss their relatively rare and manageable conflicts.

After several months of counseling with Jay and his parents, weeks often went by without a serious conflict at home. He developed something unusual for a young teen—the ability to talk sensitively and thoughtfully with his parents about his "problems."

Still, Jay's attitudes toward school did not improve. To his parents' fear and dismay, he nearly flunked the eighth grade. For Jay to do that badly required *effort*, albeit effort in the wrong direction. At the least, it required active resistance to the demands of his school. Once more his parents brought up the possibility of stimulant drugs to "improve his attention span."

But the more I knew, enjoyed, and learned from Jay, the more certain I became that far from being defective, he was as sharp and imaginative as any young person I knew. And the more I came to appreciate Jay, the less I could bear the idea of anyone subjecting his brain to toxic psychoactive agents to force him to conform to school.

My work with Jay and his family indicated that his resistance to school came from two different sources. Childhood conflicts in relating to his father around any kind of project or sustained activity had turned him off to anything that looked like work or that was imposed by authorities. In addition, his own creative imagination felt squelched instead of cultivated by the schools he attended.

When it was time for Jay to enroll in high school, Jay's parents made a last-ditch effort to salvage his interest in his education. They took him for an interview to an unusual private school that emphasized the enjoyment of learning and specialized in bright underachievers. After a day spent visiting classes and talking to students and staff, Jay voiced unaccustomed hope: "They seem to pay attention to the students to make sure they're interested in learning and not just getting higher grades." He was also impressed with the free give-and-take between students and teachers. Teachers weren't "buddies," but the use of first names for everyone made clear they weren't remote and authoritarian. There was a gentle confidence about them.

Other private schools had rejected Jay because he wouldn't readily join into the environment of academic competition and because he wasn't likely to aggrandize the school's reputation with his scholastic achievements. But this new school welcomed him as a challenging work in progress—a young man with the potential to respond to a genuinely engaging, individualized educational opportunity.

Two years later, when Jay was no longer in therapy, he phoned me to ask the telephone number of my fax machine. He wanted to send me a photocopy of his report card. Jay finished his second year with good grades and wonderfully enthusiastic accolades from his teachers. One of Jay's teachers wrote that he himself was learning from Jay and hoped that Jay would critique some of his own writing over the summer.

A Quaker Learning Sanctuary

This school is Thornton Friends School, whose students I quoted at the begining of this chapter. A Quaker high school in the Washington, D.C., area, its declared values are "Trust, Honesty, Community, Scholarship, Individuality, Compassion, Equality, Nonviolence, the Dignity of Work, Careful Listening, and a Sense of Wonder." At this school, these are more than just words. (Though the religion is commonly known as Quakerism, its actual name is the Society of Friends.) Thornton Friends School, in line with the Quaker tradition, seeks to help each student "recapture the sense of the indwelling spirit." Unlike some Quaker high schools that seem to have succumbed to the current competitive emphasis on academic achievement, Thornton Friends remains genuinely child-oriented.

Thornton Friends should not be confused with schools that specialize in helping emotionally or academically distressed youngsters. Certainly Thornton Friends can reach out effectively to many of these young people, but the universal principles of education on which it is based can benefit most if not all students.

Beyond the informal and caring relationships among teachers and students, Jay loved the small classes, averaging nine students each, and the enthusiasm with which the teachers engaged the students. With an enrollment of fifty, the school itself was so small that Jay could learn the name of every student, and get to know a sizable proportion of them well.

Unlike many other private religious schools, where the student body is drawn primarily from the sponsoring religion, only one or two of the students and only a few of the teachers at Thornton Friends were Quakers. The 100,000 practicing Quakers in the United States simply aren't enough to fill the several private Quaker colleges and more than thirty Quaker high schools in America.

Jay's critical intelligence used to make him uncomfortable in school, but not at Thornton Friends School. Quakerism puts critical intelligence at the center of its spiritual values. The religion seeks beneath the surface for enduring truths or reality. As a group that historically has spoken truth to authority, regardless of the danger, on matters such as pacifism and religious conscience, Quakers know that critical intelligence is more than a mental exercise. Robert Lawrence Smith,[2] the retired headmaster of another Quaker school, expressed it this way:

> We know that following our conscience can expose us to ridicule and take away the props that make us feel secure—group identity, conformity, anonymity. I would argue that letting your life speak through your conscience is liberating in the same way that truth-telling is. It frees you from the judgment of others because you become answerable only to God that is in you.

The God Within

Good parenting, good therapeutic practices, and good education—
all of them, I believe, must be based on a profound respect for the individual and in particular each person's potential goodness. Quakers
say that there is "that of God in everyone," that there is continuing
revelation of truth on earth, and that the free and open airing of ideas
is what education on all levels ought to be about. Quakers not only
listen to the God within themselves, they also listen to the God
within others as they speak and share. Learning becomes a sacred
shared experience as the students study a broad range of thinkers,
secular and religious alike. The atmosphere at Thornton Friends is
decidedly more relaxed and playful than at most schools, but it is also
spiritual in its reverence for learning as well as for human beings in
general.

"Meeting for Worship" takes place at the Thornton Friends schools
two mornings a week for about twenty minutes. It is a time for silent
contemplation. Parents are often flabbergasted that forty or fifty students can sit together in a room for twenty minutes without anybody
talking. In fact, the silent meeting becomes very important to many of
the students. According to the headmaster, Michael DeHart, "It's the
one time in their lives when they're not being expected to do anything
but sit with their own thoughts. They grow to like that. Students who
graduate and come back to visit often talk about the meeting for worship as one of the things they missed the most or sought out and
found afterward."

Though not preaching Quakerism, the school openly declares its
principles and ideals. Learning thrives only when inspired by values.
Therefore the willingness to stand for something is key to good
schools. The staff speaks to students formally and also at impromptu
moments about treating each other with respect. Throughout the
school year, Quakers from the community visit the school to talk with
students about Quaker philosophy and how it guides the school and
the relationships within it.

The Daily Practice of Peacemaking

Of course, a certain amount of teasing and conflict occurs at Thornton Friends, but it's much less frequent and intense than at other

places. When asked, Jay couldn't recall a single incident that went unresolved or seemed to leave serious emotional scars. The staff is so involved with the students, he reported, that serious difficulties can usually be headed off. Many of the students receive informal training in how to resolve conflicts, including how to mediate conflicts among their fellow students.

Every school will have its tensions, and it's important not to deny their existence while they fester beneath the surface. Headmaster DeHart believes that "tension is a prompt for moral growth." Tensions should be aboveboard so they can be shared and talked about. He was shocked, he said, when the principal of Columbine High School in Colorado said he was unaware of the "trench coat gang" and related student conflicts. "Students are known here," he explained.

Competing with One's Self

Jay, like most young people, disliked competition and tended to withdraw from it. In my experience, most students who seem to thrive on competition are nonetheless suppressing another side of themselves that yearns for more harmony and cooperation in their lives. Though we often speak of "healthy competition," we rarely examine the implied concept of "health."

Succeeding in competitive situations of course strengthens the ability to compete, and reinforces the idea that competition is good. In other words, those who compete successfully will feel empowered in the arena of competition.

Competition in high school also encourages an outlook on life that favors competition in adulthood. Beyond that, those who succeed competitively often end up with a feeling of entitlement based on their personal experience of superiority. They believe that their greater ability entitles them to many advantages in society and even in personal relationships. In direct contradiction to the competitive principles that guided their earlier success, they may now feel entitled to prevent others from competing with them. In the political arena, successful groups often attempt to limit the capacity of newcomers or the less fortunate to work their way up by competing with those who have already achieved.

Successful competitors too often end up showing disrespect for people whom they see as lacking competitive spirit and ability. This is the essence of the jock culture. Unfortunately, it is carried over into adulthood and the workplace.

To a great extent, competitive values are held dear in our society, but are they really "healthy" when they tend to suppress caring, sensitivity, mutuality, and responsibility for the well-being of others? And what about the vast majority of youngsters who don't succeed competitively in school?

Either because they don't value competition, because they fear it, or because they don't have the personal or physical attributes necessary to triumph, the great majority of students will not fully immerse themselves in the school's competitive culture. Even among those who try hard, very few students will reach the top in the social, academic, and athletic hierarchies of the typical school. There is only so much room at the top—so many spots on major sports teams, so many class presidents or homecoming queens, and so many places in the honor society.

So while competition in school ends up endowing a few fortunate youngsters with a sense of personal empowerment, at the same time it will discourage most children from feeling good about themselves.

The subject of competition is obviously very controversial. Our economic system is built, in part at least, on competition. I won't attempt to come to conclusions about the economic structure of society, but experience with individuals has shown me that the competitive spirit tends to overwhelm many of the most important human qualities related to caring and to relationship. We could do with a lot less emphasis on competition in our schools.

Competition is deemphasized at Thornton Friends. Students are encouraged "to compete against their best selves and not with one another." Grades are given, but so are extensive comments, and no record of class standing is kept. Even the sports league deemphasizes competition and uses innovative rules to limit physical confrontation. For Jay, the lack of pressure allowed him to look into himself for his own personal motivation.

Teaching Through Relationship

Nothing is more important in schools than individual relationships between teachers and students. In its *Guide to Safe Schools*, the U.S. Department of Education states, "Research shows that a positive relationship with an adult who is available when needed is one of the most critical factors in preventing student violence. Students often look to adults in the school community for guidance, support, and direction."[3]

I still fondly remember Mrs. Heart, my kindergarten teacher. Despite my apprehension at the new experience, she made me feel safe and secure at school. She also made it fun. Like many people I've spoken with, kindergarten was one of my best school experiences, because it was the most child-oriented.

I also feel grateful for Mrs. Eula Kielty, my high school Latin teacher. A number of us liked her so much that we talked the school into offering a fourth-year Latin class just to spend time with her. She was also the sponsor of the high school newspaper and her encouragement helped me to think I might someday become a writer. She was a very gentle soul who never said a cruel word and who led through kindness.

During college, medical school, and my psychiatric residencies, the best and the worst times in school were largely molded by my experiences with teachers. I believe this is true for most people.

Relationships among students and teachers are openly acknowledged as the key to learning at Thornton Friends. Learning is expected to take place together in the classroom or in the field, rather than alone doing homework. Homework assignments are light at Thornton, but here students learn more about how to think and to learn than at schools that load them down with work. Students who find the work relatively easy at Thornton, or who display special talents or interests, may find that teachers encourage or ask more of them.

Jay told me, "Because classes are so small, the teachers can actually teach the lesson plan rather than give it as homework. Homework just makes you feel it's so boring. It discourages any interest you have in learning."

Though the college workload may require some adjustment for Thornton graduates, according to Headmaster DeHart it hasn't proved to be an insurmountable problem. Many of the students choose to attend institutions of higher learning, including some Quaker colleges, that follow a more individualized and less competitive academic philosophy.

Learning to Love Life

Learning at Thornton Friends is much more than cramming facts— more, even, than exercising critical thinking. It is about developing a more positive attitude toward life. According to Headmaster DeHart, many students arrive at the school believing that "life sucks." Most end up believing that the world is a good place to be or, at the least, "a better place than they thought when they first arrived." As a way of encouraging a more optimistic view of life, every morning begins with each student in a small homeroom group describing something good that happened the day before.

Community service is a part of Quaker philosophy and Quaker schools, and students are given special times away from school to do something that contributes to the community. The Quaker philosophy encourages both individual fulfillment and contributions to society in the form of service.

Even though most of the students who arrive at Thornton Friends are academically troubled, all or nearly all graduate and go to college. The school aims to "help students become reinvested in being students." "They arrive at Thornton thinking, 'If I don't want anything nobody can have any sway over me,' " Mr. DeHart explains. "We want to help them find a way to be pleased with life and themselves."

Sparing the Rod

Discipline, like everything else, is viewed as a community concern at Thornton Friends School. Students, like all people, are seen as essentially good, and the school anticipates that they will live up to that expectation. Mr. DeHart quotes a school motto of unknown origin: "Responsible people don't need rules."

Punishments are usually reserved for problems that harm the community as well as an individual, such as tardiness, aggression, or using drugs. A common punishment involves loss of lunch privileges outside the school for a day. Serious infractions are dealt with by prolonged discussions between the involved parties, school staff, and families. Meaningful relationship and, Mr. DeHart jokes, "interminable conversation" are the secrets to discipline at Thornton Friends.

Breaches of the peace do result in more severe punishments. A physical fight could lead to a week or two's suspension and an "interminable series of conversations" with everyone involved. "Safety is huge here; school has to be a safe place to be," said Mr. DeHart. There is no tolerance for jostling, pushing, and shoving in the hallways, or for peer humiliation. "Kids don't act aggressively in a vacuum," Mr. DeHart explained. "We're not a therapeutic school, but an aggressive verbal outburst could lead to a minitherapeutic session about what led to the outburst and what new strategies to develop."

Headmaster DeHart could only recall one outright expulsion in his tenure at Thornton Friends. It involved multiple occurrences of possessing, selling, and abusing drugs in school.

When children have significant relationships with adults, they don't want to disappoint those adults. They also don't want to have to "talk" about what they did wrong when they have disappointed adults they care about. But if the conversations are carried on with respect for the children, having to endure talking with adults can be a kind of gentle punishment. It can also be more positive than that. Talking together can help children and adults work out their conflicts and, at times, correct misapprehensions on all sides.

A Haven for the Teachers, Too

For all the same reasons that the students prosper, Thornton Friends is a wonderful place for the administrators and teachers to work. Fifty percent of the governing board must be teachers. Thornton Friends' rules dictate that staff decisions be made in the Quaker way, by determining the "sense of the meeting," in which each individual voice is influential and no one individual voice will carry the day. It is a kind of spiritual consensus reached not by vote but by the sense that all are comfortable with the decision.

If a difficult or seemingly unsolvable conflict confronts the members of the staff, they are sustained by a faith that discussion, silence, and patience will achieve a solution that "speaks in very good ways to the problem." In other words, after some thought and sharing, the issue will be revisited and eventually resolved to everyone's satisfaction.

When teachers are so genuinely and fully involved in the school planning and administrative processes, when they are treated with such respect, it has a positive impact on students. Again, in the words of Headmaster DeHart, "If teachers feel they are powerful, they don't have to exert power over their students."

Contending with Psychiatric Drugs

As many as a third or more of new students are on psychiatric drugs when they arrive at Thornton Friends, but some students top taking the medications as they progress in the school. In Jay's case, after he started attending Thornton Friends his parents no longer worried that Jay had something wrong in his brain that might require drugs for correction. The headmaster explained: "The way schools are currently set up does not allow for natural active curiosity to come out and be developed. Most schools and classes are so big that there's no time and space available to respond to a student who has lots of questions and ideas and who wants to share and explore them. It's harder to change the school than to change the child. So one of the easiest ways is to medicate them to fit in with the program that exists."

A Thornton Friends graduation is like none other I've heard about; it symbolizes the school. A small number of students, staff, family, and friends gather together to celebrate by candlelight. Anyone who knows a student is given the opportunity to stand up to offer a personal appreciation. At the June 1999 graduation—in the shadow of the school shootings and the fear and alienation felt by so many students around the country—inclusion and community were the themes at Thornton Friends. One graduate shared with another, "I can't imagine at any other school we would have become friends but because of Thornton you are my best friend. Because we are so different in key ways, you allowed and forced me to grow and to learn about myself."

Of course, no school is "the ideal school" for every family or student. Just as there is enormous diversity among students, there should be diversity among schools, including in their values. Many parents believe that their children will be better off in schools that emphasize competitiveness and academic prowess as measured in conventional ways. Others may be uncomfortable with the emphasis on critical intelligence. Yet others may feel uncomfortable with the Quaker spiritual principles. Many believe in public rather than private education. Our society and our children need a wide variety of schools with many different approaches. But Thornton Friends fulfills many of the principles that I believe are missing in most public and private education in America today. To an astonishing degree, it successfully identifies and meets the real needs of a broad spectrum of young people for meaningful relationships and inspiring education.

Thirteen Basic Principles of a Good School

I believe we must begin to set a much higher standard for the future of education in America. Even though it isn't at present realistic to expect for all schools, public and private, to begin operating on princi- ples similar to those underlying Thornton Friends and other model learning centers, there is much that can be done now. The following thirteen principles, if implemented, would dramatically improve the character of most of our schools by making them into safer and more engaging educational environments for our children:

Declare, embody, and teach a set of positive ideals and principles. The psychologist Abraham Maslow wrote in the 1960s, "The final and unavoidable conclusion is that education—like all our social in- stitutions—must be concerned with its final values, and this in turn is just about the same as speaking of what have been called 'spiritual val- ues' or 'higher values.' "[4] To ask students to learn without a principled context is to ask them not believe in anything. At Thornton Friends, Quakerism created and permeates the setting, but the principles at different schools could be anything from Catholic to humanistic or agnostic.

Create small communities. Almost all school reform depends on making schools smaller in order to facilitate meaningful relationships among the staff and students. This principle is gaining general accep- tance among school reformers, spurred on by the school shootings in larger schools.[5]

Small schools allow for the possibility of building community among the staff and students. In an interview with me, Fred Bemak, Ed.D., professor of counselor education at Ohio State University, de- clared, "We need to build a community feeling in which everyone owns the school, not just the principal and staff. The students need to feel their own sense of ownership and belonging. That's a true com- munity rather than a principal's self-imposed vision."

At Thornton Friends, relationships are rather close and informal between students and staff; in another, different but equally good, school they could be more formal. The important thing, as stated by the headmaster, is that "the students are known to us."

Keep classes small. Scientific evidence for the value of small classes (13 to 17 students) is supplied by a study of more than 6,000 students in 79 Tennessee schools in diverse communities. Learning in smaller classes brought "substantial improvement in early learning in cogni- tive subjects such as reading and math."[6] The small classes continued from kindergarten through third grade. The academic improvement, measured by comparison to students in larger classes, persisted when tested in later grades. The use of teacher's aides did not produce improvement comparable to that of small classes.

When parents are given a choice, many opt for smaller classes even if it means older, cramped buildings with fewer modern facilities. In western Loudoun County, Virginia, a rural community, parents have successfully fought efforts to plow under and consolidate smaller schools. They are delighted with the result, refusing to trade "small class sizes and a modern family-like atmosphere for a big, modern building."[7]

Almost any improvement in the quality of our children's educational experience will depend not only on smaller schools but also on smaller classes. In many instances, the concept of classrooms and classes will no longer apply. Students will work in open areas as part of small groups working independently on projects, or perhaps alone in front of a computer.

Create an environment in which teachers feel empowered and love their work. Enthusiasm for the subject matter, for teaching, and for the students is far more important than teaching credentials or even a vast body of knowledge in the subject. At Thornton Friends, teachers feel empowered through the group resolution of problems, through participation on the governing board, and through positive relationships with staff and students alike.

Make opportunities for every student to have a meaningful relationship with an individual teacher. Teachers should be chosen first and foremost for their ability to relate to students in a caring, inspiring, and ethical manner. Students' evaluations of teachers, before and after teachers are hired, can play a useful role in selecting and monitoring them.

When Columbine High School put up an electronic message board after the shootings in May 1999, a 1997 graduate wrote about the taunting she had received at the school, and about how much time her mother spent "trying to find someone who cared about me" at the school. A survey of 100,000 students from sixth through twelfth grades by Search Institute found that only one in four students reported that they went to a school where adults and other students cared about them.[8]

In families, churches, mental health facilities, and schools, nothing is more important than a child's individual relationship with a loving, mature adult. It is the single most important factor in the positive growth of a child. School staff meetings should periodically review each child to make sure that at least one of the staff has a special interest in the individual.

Support the students' inherent love of learning. Young people possess a natural interest and curiosity about life. You can't stop a healthy child from learning. Class materials, teaching technologies, homework—every aspect of the learning experience—should appeal to the students' innate inquisitiveness and creativity. To those who think, "Life is not like that" I'd answer, "It can be like that." Many of us do in fact lead lives of never-ending exciting learning, and the more people learn to do so, the better.

Following the Columbine High School shootings, Leon Botstein, the president of Bard College, in Annandale-on-Hudson, New York, told the *New York Times*, "High schools are outdated, obsolete and devastatingly wrong-headed solutions to the education of adolescents. We trap them in a world of jock values and anti-intellectualism, like trying to cram a large person into a small childish uniform." In a similar vein, a technology expert, Jon Katz, pointed out that young people are much more stimulated and empowered by the "electronic culture" than by school. He added, "And school then becomes a nightmare, dull and claustrophobic and oppressive."[9] School should be challenging and fun.

Promote the treasuring of individuals. Students need to be taught to care about and even to treasure each other and all other human beings as unique individuals of essential value. This goal is inseparable from creating an overall learning haven. Creating this kind of sanctuary requires a deep and frequently expressed conviction that all human beings are, in Jefferson's words, entitled to "life, liberty, and the pursuit of happiness." Thornton Friends School draws on the Quaker principle that the spark of God can be found in each of us. Or, as the educator Nel Nodding said, "We should educate all our children not only for competence but also for caring. Our aim should be to encourage the growth of competent, caring, loving, and lovable people."[10]

Even though the exact philosophy behind the treasuring of each and every individual may not be identical in different religious or secular belief systems, the principle of the inviolability and value of the individual human soul must in some way be communicated to students. Meanwhile, many of the other principles and practices noted in this section will further that all-important respect for the individual, especially the encouragement of critical intelligence.

Inspire critical intelligence.   Students should be encouraged to express themselves, even to criticize the school, provided they do so respectfully. The key to "teaching" critical intelligence is restraint on the part of the teacher when students speak their minds. Beyond restraint, a generous interest in the young thinker's thoughts will be like water and sunshine to a budding plant. Being an educator for the young is in many ways a matter of personal restraint combined with nurturing.

Bring parents and community into the school.   The participation of parents, and other community members who have something to contribute morally or scholastically, enhances a student's sense of meaningful education and increases educational opportunities. The U.S. Department of Education in its *Guide to Safe Schools* emphasized, "Effective schools reach out to include families and the entire community in the education of children."[11]

At Thornton Friends School, Quakers from outside the school help to teach its basic principles, and the students go into the community to perform services. Probably Thornton Friends could benefit from more family involvement than the monthly parents' meeting. Volunteers, especially from the population of retired people, could add a great deal to any classroom and school.

Focus on each student's actual growth and development rather than on grades and test scores.   Artificial means of evaluating performance fade into the background within a community of meaningful relationships. When students and teachers really know each other, they can together make more useful and realistic appraisals of the individual student's work, including areas that need improvement. Academic tests measure little more than the ability to take the examination, whereas the origination and completion of individual projects, cooperative work with teachers and other students, and contributions to the school community are much more indicative of the potential for genuine accomplishment in the future adult workplace and life.

Like adults on the job, students should be evaluated on the basis of what they are actually doing from day to day rather than on the basis of tests or formal grades. Unlike adults in the typical workplace, they should be given far greater opportunity to proceed at their own pace, and to make frequent false starts, as they explore and develop their unique interests and abilities.

Emphasize self-motivation more than competition. Competition—whether social, academic, or athletic—is largely of use for developing victorious warriors. The world does not need more warriors; it needs more peacemakers. As we saw at Columbine High School in Littleton, typical American schools with their emphasis on competition inevitably create humiliating relationships and alienation. They end up grossly suppressing the more tender, vulnerable side of everyone involved. Our society and our children are in need of a healthy de-escalation in competition, not more "healthy competition."

Use punishment sparingly. The use of punishments such as detention and suspension reflects a failure to make use of adult relationships with students as the preferred means of maintaining high standards of conduct. The use of punishment should therefore be acknowledged as an indication of failure on the part of those in charge of the school.

At Thornton Friends, Headmaster DeHart joked with me, students fear "having to talk about it over and over again." Much better to fear too much talking than public chastisement, isolation in the principal's office, demerits, detention, suspension, or expulsion. Whenever possible, serious infractions should be dealt with through serious expressions of concern by adults who are willing to engage the youngster with the aim of resolving conflicts and teaching improved conduct.

Create sanctuary. Four years before the school shootings at Columbine and Heritage high schools, the psychiatrist Sandra Bloom advocated that our schools must become sanctuaries to foster emotional safety and psychosocial development.

A school should insist that all communication express the kind of care that all vulnerable beings need. There should be no tolerance for threats or acts of aggression, or for peer humiliation and ridicule. The staff and other students should be mutually devoted to creating this safe environment, this sanctuary. Any breaches in safety should be immediately responded to. Each threat to sanctuary should become an opportunity to teach students about human pain and suffering, about how suffering perpetuates violence, and about how violence can be replaced with more caring and successful strategies.

A Special Public School

Communities can develop their own alternative public schools, not only to meet special requirements but eventually to become models for the local educational system. In the Maryland suburbs of Washington, D.C., there is another school, this one a public school, that exemplifies many of the basic principles of a good educational facility. But it doesn't look much like Thornton Friends. Remember, diversity is a key to providing our children with inspiring education.

Clarice was fifteen when her parents noticed a marked change in her appearance and behavior. She began dressing in black, even painted her bedroom black, and began hanging around with students who looked to her parents like members of a drug culture. Although they had no direct evidence, Clarice's parents confronted her about drugs and alcohol. She responded with indignation that the very suggestion was an insult to her. A week later, Clarice's mother tried to awaken her for school and found her in bed nearly comatose from an overdose of street drugs and alcohol.

In the emergency room, the doctors pumped her stomach and called for a psychiatric consultation. The psychiatrist interviewed Clarice for a few minutes—she was resentful and uncooperative—and talked with her parents as well. He recommended immediate admission to the psychiatric unit in the hospital.

A Narrow Escape

Clarice's parents had always tried to recognize her autonomy; now they held a private discussion with their daughter in the ER treatment room. Clarice became hysterical and pleaded with them not to "ruin my life" by "treating me like a nut case." She had friends who'd gone to mental hospitals and now all they did was take psychiatric drugs along with their street drugs and alcohol. She begged her parents to take her home right away.

When Clarice's parents informed the psychiatrist that they were not going along with his suggestion for hospitalization, he threatened to call the county child protective services to bring charges of child neglect against them. Clarice's parents were stunned. They had never heard of such a thing—that they could be charged with negligence for refusing psychiatric treatment for their own child.

The three of them—father, mother, and daughter—became united in a mutual fear, that psychiatry could take over their lives. They did something otherwise unimaginable to them. They made believe they were taking their daughter to the bathroom and instead sneaked her out the window. They went home and called a lawyer. At the attorney's suggestion, they called the chief of the emergency room to say that they planned to get their daughter help of their own choosing. He seemed reassured and no action was taken against them.

The following day, somewhat united by the harrowing experience of the night before, Clarice and her parents agreed that help was needed. Clarice explained she couldn't remain sober if she went back to the high school. Drugs and alcohol were everywhere, and she would be surrounded by her drug- and alcohol-abusing companions. But where else could she go? She was determined not to "become a mental patient."

Rising from the Ashes in Twelve Steps

Clarice's parents called around to their friends, and located and made an appointment with an addiction counselor. In making the calls, they learned about Phoenix, the only public high school in the nation that offers a Twelve Step (Alcoholics Anonymous, or AA) approach to helping children who want to recover from drugs and alcohol. The name Phoenix is taken from the mythical bird that periodically rises from the ashes of its own funeral pyre to regain its youth in an immortal cycle.

Most communities of any size have regular Twelve Step meetings. Larger cities offer meetings several times a day. Twelve Step programs are based on a set of ethical principles and a set of traditions presented in *Alcoholics Anonymous*, the "the Big Book," first published in 1939, that underpins Alcoholics Anonymous.[12]

Written in the past tense in a way that lends them a unique aura, the steps include ethical and spiritual guidelines such as "We came to believe that a Power greater than ourselves could restore us to sanity."

Most AA groups encourage a broad interpretation of the nature of that "Power," including higher ideals, the AA group itself, or a loving God.[13] As a result, many successful participants in AA maintain a non-religious but usually spiritual attitude toward their experience.

Additional guiding AA principles encourage deep soul-searching. Two of the steps are: "Made a searching and fearless moral inventory of ourselves" and "Admitted to God, to ourselves, and to another human being the exact nature of our wrongs." AA principles promote right action and service. The twelfth step states: "Having made a spiritual awakening as the result of these steps, we tried to carry this message to alcoholics, and to practice these principles in all our affairs."

AA meetings encourage "fellowship," or community. At each meeting, the individual is free to express personal thoughts and feelings without anyone evaluating, contradicting, or correcting what's been said. Traditionally, the group says, "Thank you for sharing" after each person speaks. At special celebrations, when an individual has been sober for a specific period of time, testimonials may be given on behalf of how hard the person has worked, how much he or she has accomplished, and how much the person has contributed to others in recovery.

Individuals "in recovery" are encouraged to seek out and to draw strength and guidance from a mentor, called a "sponsor," who has a longer period of sobriety than they do.

There are two Phoenix campuses based on the Twelve Steps in Montgomery, Maryland. Phoenix I was founded by Brian Berthiaume in 1979, and Phoenix II was opened under his leadership several years later. Until 1990 he was the program coordinator for both, but he now heads Phoenix I in Silver Spring, Maryland. Phoenix I has thirty-five students and a staff that includes Mr. Berthiaume, an assistant, and three teachers. Despite the small ten-to-one student-teacher ratio, the school costs the county only a little more per student than the regular schools.

Mr. Berthiaume functions as the on-site principal, chief administrator, and the clinician on duty. Students must attend a therapy group each day, of approximately seven students. The school was originally designed to handle eighteen students at a time, and the growing number forced it to seek help from an outside agency for additional drug counseling. Students are also expected to attend Twelve Step meetings outside the school on a regular basis and to have a sponsor. They also attend Twelve Step meetings in school, and these, according to Mr.

Berthiaume, are often more productive than the counseling groups because they focus on the individual rather than on the peer group. The students are also required to take a weekly urinalysis to test for drug abuse.

Parents must attend a parent group meeting once a week. It's a source of networking and mutual support that plays a central role in the child's recovery, as well as the family's stability. Report cards take the form of discussions of each student's progress made in a sensitive manner in front of all the students and families at a meeting held each grading period.

To say that the students and staff have an open relationship would not quite capture the degree to which they communicate freely to each other and about each other. I've heard students do "clinical analyses" of Mr. Berthiaume, who in turn displays extraordinary caring and patience under fire.

A School of Last Resort

In comparison to Thornton Friends School, which tends to draw children who have academic difficulties and more moderate psychological problems, Phoenix specializes in helping some of the most difficult youngsters of all: those suffering from drug and alcohol abuse and addiction. If they don't make it at Phoenix, they are likely to land in the juvenile justice system.

As a result, Phoenix has a far more conflicted and intense environment than a typical school. There's zero tolerance for physical aggression, but it's hard to control the constant nattering and ridiculing that take place among youngsters struggling with drug abuse and related emotional problems. These problems, however, are confronted as much as possible in the daily group therapy sessions, in occasional school community meetings, and in individual counseling.

The disciplinary system is based on a series of levels of privileges. Good behavior gets the most privileges, including the right to sit in soft chairs and couches, and to bring food or drink into class. When Clarice cursed at one of the teachers, she got in-school suspension and was forced to sit by herself, "watching everybody else have fun." She was also asked to participate in a discussion with her teacher to resolve their conflict.

At first Clarice "bitched and moaned" endlessly about the school. It was "crazy making" to be with so many angry, upset youngsters who were constantly "pushing each other's emotional buttons" in class and in group therapy. She also resented the frequent required urine tests.

But it was soon apparent to Clarice that the school was trying to meet the students' real needs without overstressing them with academic work. Clarice enjoyed the relatively light homework assignments of reading books and writing a personal journal. Unless a student fell behind during classroom work, math problems and other rote assignments were not made a part of homework. With help from her teachers, Clarice got all her more rote exercises finished in school and could look forward at night to settling down with a book and her journal.

Phoenix Rising

Over the next few months, Clarice began to understand and to value what she was learning at Phoenix about principled living and about her own personal psychology. She became devoted to her AA meetings, going every day, and has now been sober for five years. She hasn't attended AA for a year or more.

Sobriety is the aim of Phoenix. When the student, the student's family, and the staff agree that sobriety can be maintained, the student must return to the mainstream county schools. After two years at Phoenix, Clarice began her junior year at her regular high school. Within days she came home in tears to tell her mother and father, "I can't do it. It's against everything I've learned and everything we've learned as a family. The teachers and students don't respect each other, and all the students are compulsive about something—sex, sports, drugs, hating school, or even getting grades. No one's open with anyone else. And it's not safe. I'm always getting leered at. A boy leaned on me in line," she said, shuddering and pointing to where he'd pushed himself against her body.

Clarice's parents had always favored public education. Now, however, they asked Clarice if she would like to be home-schooled, and Clarice responded with relief. Two years later she graduated with her high school degree from a university extension program. All of the work had been conducted by fax machine and telephone with the help of a local tutor. Her tutor, a graduate student, became a close friend. Clarice achieved mostly A's working on a level nearer to college than high school. Because of AA and her wide circle of friends, she had no trouble maintaining an active sober social life.

Unlike Clarice, nearly all of the Phoenix students have been through the mental health system before their arrival at the school. Therefore, most are taking psychiatric drugs at the time they enter Phoenix. But many—entirely on their own—eventually decided to stop taking them. They come to see psychiatric drugs as a crutch no different from illegal substances.

Like 75 percent of the students who enroll in Phoenix, Clarice successfully completed the program. From the Phoenix viewpoint, the criteria for success are that the student has been drug-free for long enough to seem stable, is achieving good grades, and is either graduating or going on to another school.

Lessons from the Yeshiva

Barry Mehler was a thirteen-year-old boy "spiritually dying in the suburbs" when he moved to the New York City with the aim of becoming a rabbi. He spent five years living and studying in Yeshiva Chofetz Chaim in Queens. There, the goal of the education is the ethical development of the individual. In a unique approach to teaching children in small classes of eight or twelve students, no one could move ahead to the next subject—or even to the next page of the book—until every student understood the material. So learning became a group effort often focused on the student who was doing the most poorly. The teacher and all the other students would gather round to help the slowest student. In the beginning, that was Barry, and the support worked educational miracles for him.

Many other factors enhanced the educational experience at the yeshiva, including several thousand years of Jewish tradition and the study of the Torah (the Hebrew Scriptures). But the communication of the values depended on relationships, including the teachers' love of the students and the students' mutual efforts. Although not participating in the school itself, the scholars at the yeshiva became exemplars of the importance of learning.

Barry Mehler is now professor of history in the Department of Humanities at Ferris State University in Missouri. When he arrived in 1988, a large percentage of the students enrolling in the university were ill equipped to deal with academics, and 50 percent of them were failing to complete the first year. Dr. Mehler returned to his roots at the yeshiva to invent the Structured Learning Assistance (SLA) Program.

As a part of their introductory history course, students with grades less than a C must attend four hours of seminar per week, where they learn, in the context of their actual history course, how to read, take notes, and study. Similar to the yeshiva classes, SLA teaching utilizes students helping each other. In groups of three to five, the students learn to encourage and to teach each other. For many, it's their first experience with group studying.

When the program was initiated, a control group of similar students not in the SLA Program was compared with those in the program. The SLA student group averaged a full grade higher. For many, it was the first time in their lives that they received good grades. The Structured Learning Assistance Program is permanent now and Dr. Mehler is extending it into the high schools.

A Shared Emphasis on Relationship

The schools I have described vary greatly. Thornton Friends is a private school that can serve a broad range of children. Phoenix is a special school for high-schoolers who want to recover from drug and alcohol abuse. The yeshiva is intended for Jewish education. But as diverse as these schools are, they embody a consistent set of principles.

These schools share essential qualities of a good school that I summarized earlier in the chapter, especially those pertaining to relationship. Though the Structured Learning Assistance Program may seem bare of spiritual principles, in fact it grows from Barry Mehler's belief in relationship as a guiding principle in education. In each of the schools, a very high premium is put on relationship and community, as well as on respecting individuality. Great effort is put into creating a safe space. There is also a therapeutic aspect to each of these settings. Thornton Friends deals with occasional important conflicts in a therapeutic manner, whereas Phoenix aims at being a fully evolved therapeutic milieu.

Of course, many parents and students may have serious objections to any one school's religious, ethical, or academic grounds. Ideally, we need a very broad spectrum of schools to meet the varying needs of students and families in our complex, evolving society.

A Special Man Among Children in the Inner City

School life within the confines of the inner-city ghetto is impacted by special problems and hazards. Our citizens who live there are afflicted by larger political problems—including the breakdown of institutions in our urban centers, racism, and poverty—that cannot be solved by educational reforms alone. With this caveat in mind, I want to address some of the ways that school life under these heavily compromised circumstances can be made more relevant to the needs of the children.

A Need for Men

The lives of urban poor children—white, black, and Hispanic alike—are among the most dreadful in America. A 1999 study by the Children's Rights Council ranked the fifty states and the District of Columbia as places to raise children.[14] The council drew its conclusions on the basis of the measured rates of abuse and neglect, inadequate prenatal care and infant immunizations, high school dropouts, poverty, infant and child mortality, juvenile crime, divorce, and teen birth. Washington, D.C., an intensely segregated, predominantly African American city, rated last.

Is there an underlying theme to this kind of global disorder in a community? Ron David, M.D., a pediatrician and former chief medical officer of D.C. General Hospital, the hospital for the indigent in the nation's capital, has pondered the answer to that question. The key, he has explained in workshops we have done together, is not poverty itself, not even inadequate health and educational services, but the breakdown of relationships in the community. Groups who immigrate into America, even if they live in poverty, do not begin to show signs of this social and economic deterioration and accompanying rampant ill health unless their culture and then their family life begin to come apart.

In an article on the health care of African Americans, Dr. David quoted South Africa's Bishop Desmond Tutu: "I would not know how to be a human being at all, except I learned this from other human beings. We are made for a delicate network of relationships, of interdependence. We are meant to complement each other. All kinds of things go horribly wrong when we break that fundamental rule of our being." Dr. David adds, "In essence, the sense of coherence which defines health can only be developed and nurtured in the context of mutually supportive, loving human relationships."[15]

In school, in their families, in their communities, what do poor, urban black children need most of all? It can be stated in a sentence: Ultimately they need to have white people stop imposing their racist viewpoints on their lives. Racism is the biggest overall hindrance to the development of the African American community and its children. They have been excluded from the benefits of participation in America and humiliated in the process of trying to participate.

In their daily lives, the impact of racism is felt by children through its negative impact on their families. Black men have been most injured by racism in America, and what black children are missing most of all are devoted adult men. They need meaningful relationships with male parents, father figures, and mentors. Of course, like all children, they need mothers as well as fathers, but in the black community, active fathers are comparatively few and far between. Children also need more African American men as school administrators, teachers, coaches, ministers, counselors, big brothers, and neighbors.

Why are there so few competent, available black men in the inner city? The greatest damage done by the destruction of the urban black community has been to young black men of age to be husbands and parents. As Andrew Hacker observed, "The pool of 'marriageable' black men gets smaller every year."[16]

As hard as it is to believe, on any given day in an urban center like Washington, D.C., or Baltimore, approximately one half of African American young men will be under the control of the criminal justice system—under indictment, on probation or parole, or in jail.[17] The vast majority of these men will have been convicted of nonviolent drug crimes. There is enormous evidence that white young men are rarely arrested under the same circumstances. And if arrested, they do not face such serious charges or sentences. Large numbers of black men are also being killed off, often in gang wars involving drugs.

In the absence of husbands and fathers, other men will have to fill in to help care for and guide children. That's where men like Lieutenant Colonel Charles Collier come in.

A Hand from the Advantaged

Charles Collier is a forty-nine-year-old retired air force officer. He's African American, educated, handsome, single, has no children, and receives a retirement income. As a man with so many advantages and opportunities, he has nonetheless turned away from more lucrative and prestigious pursuits to devote himself to those children who most need him: at-risk black children of the Washington, D.C., area.

When Lieutenant Colonel Collier retired from the service in 1994 after twenty-four years, he had already earned a master's degree in counseling. Now he's finishing his Ph.D. at George Washington University. Two years ago he received the Doctoral Student Outstanding Research Award and last year the Outstanding Doctoral Level Student Award. I met him the year he was the elected president of the D.C. Counseling Association.

Until recently, he was on the staff of a clinic in the D.C. area, where he worked with youngsters like V.T. The boy was fifteen when a judge sent him to the clinic for training in anger management and conflict resolution. Since the age of eight he'd been in three different foster homes. Because of sexual abuse by his father and physical abuse by his mother, he'd been taken from his birth family.

Many children in urban schools are given "social promotions" despite not mastering the academic content of the grade level. Caught up in this process, V.T. was about to enter high school without having learned to read. He also had few or no social skills. Without parents to take him anywhere, he knew little of life outside his neighborhood.

Lieutenant Colonel Collier brought V.T. into a therapy group of six other boys that met twice a week at the clinic. He also became a personal mentor to the boy, taking him to the movies, to a recreational park where he could race miniature cars, and to the Pentagon athletic club to work out with him. V.T.'s foster parents were so poor, he'd never been to a restaurant—not even to a McDonald's. It was mostly on these outings that V.T. began to talk about the abuse already documented by child protective services. Lieutenant Colonel Collier also met with V.T.'s foster parents to help them understand and relate to the boy. He visited V.T.'s school as well.

As Lieutenant Colonel Collier likes to put it, "The boy knew right from wrong." V.T. became a role model for other members of the group, often taking the lead to make suggestions to the others about handling their rage. He taught the other boys that it was a sign of strength to walk away from fights.

V.T. has been improving ever since he came to the clinic. Instead of C's and D's, he's getting A's and B's at school. He never gets suspended anymore. He is no longer in treatment but he stays in touch with Lieutenant Colonel Collier.

Getting Fed at the Air Force Base. Some readers may have realized that this kind of intensive professional intervention will never be able

to meet the needs of large numbers of poor children. Lieutenant
Colonel Collier is aware of this, too.

After meeting him, I introduced him to Dr. Ron David, who at the
time was the chief medical officer of the D.C. General Hospital.
Quickly the two men developed a new pilot program for one the public elementary schools through Dr. David's role in overseeing the
health clinics and school nurses of the city.

The elementary school has several hundred students, nearly all of
them African American, and is located in downtown D.C. near areas
scourged by the riots of 1968. Like many schools in areas of poverty
through the nation, the building is a dilapidated structure with bath-
rooms that are closed for repairs, holes in the gym floor, and a library
that's hardly worthy of the name.[18] The school does, however, have a
good supply of donated computers, some of them obtained by Lieutenant Colonel Collier as items discarded by the Pentagon.

Most children who attend the school live across the street in public
housing amid unspeakable poverty and misery. One mother had to ask
the counselor for a white shirt for her child to wear at his upcoming
graduation from elementary school. Happily, the counselor had a box
of donated civilian clothing. This grinding poverty results from a
combination of limited welfare payments and welfare reform. Much
of it is also due to the personal incapacitation of many single mothers
by chronic trauma and stress, including racism, physical and emotional abuse at the hands of others, the ravages of drug and alcohol addiction, and lack of any support network.

The pilot program is aimed at boys and girls in grades four, five,
and six, with the emphasis on boys, many of whom lack effective
same-sex role models at home and are in special danger of getting involved in violent activities. The interventions are based on individual
and group counseling, parent and teacher training, tutoring and mentoring, and various incentive programs, such as the squad-leader concept. The selection of squad leaders aims at transforming especially
troubled and troublesome youngsters into effective leaders in the
overall school intervention program that ultimately involves larger
numbers of children. All the squad-leader students have their own
military-style uniforms that they are entitled to wear to school three
times a week. These were donated by the air force.

The squad leaders learn conflict resolution and anger management.
They use their skills in school and share their knowledge with other

students. But they are learning much, much more than just anger management and conflict resolution.

Lieutenant Colonel Collier began to recruit volunteer mentors from the local community, in this case Boling Air Force Base, near Washington, D.C.[19] The ten air force noncommissioned officers (including two females) spend time as mentors at the school and in extracurricular activities with the children. Sometimes they take the boys to a military baseball game at Boling Air Force Base. Some of these kids have never held a baseball glove. They also love being taken to military events where they can sit in airplanes, learn about airplane maintenance, meet pilots, and eat.

The program successfully completed its first year and is being expanded to other schools. At the end of its first year, the program held its first annual mentoring picnic with twenty-two children and six adults.

The boys are learning the amenities that we take for granted in children of their age, such as how to say hello, to shake hands, and to eat out. The games and activities with the mentors are encouraging them to learn to read. Until then, they had seen no reason to read.

The boys are incredibly naïve about life outside their ghetto neighborhoods. After visiting an air force base one of them asked, "Do they feed you every day in the air force?" It turns out that many of these children get no other food than their free breakfasts and lunches at school. They take home food to eat overnight and on the weekends.

Lieutenant Colonel Collier's program is thriving and should prove to be a valuable pilot project for other schools. Soon he will finish his dissertation and become Dr. Collier. The model program he's developing could and should be a part of every school. Even in my rich suburb of Bethesda, Maryland, many if not most of the boys could use more contact with men like Lieutenant Colonel Collier whom they can admire and trust.

Conformity and Control in Education

Many critics of the public school system, including Jonathan Kozol, have noted the manner in which public schools produce conforming students who will become docile citizens rather than independent thinkers capable of expressing critical intelligence.[20] Schools have been accused of purposely suppressing the cultures of minority groups, particularly of African Americans and Native Americans.

The journalist Diane Granat confirmed that minority parents often believe that Ritalin and other drugs are being forced on their children to make them conform.[21] She quoted Dixie Jordan, a Native American parent, who warned about the impact of a government conference that advocated psychoactive medications for children: "We call it the racism pill. This is a pervasive feeling in many minority communities because schools have not created an environment that is hospitable to our children."[22]

Roland Chrisjohn, Ph.D., and Sherri Young, M.A., describe in graphic detail the use of residential schools in Canada to suppress First Nation peoples by stripping their children of their culture and then by attributing the disastrous psychosocial results to "mental illness." They documented how these government programs were genocidal: "The creation of Indian Residential Schools followed a time-tested method of obliterating indigenous cultures." The suffering produced by the obliteration of culture in the schools, and through other government programs, resulted in vast suffering among the people. The government covered up the results of its actions by "pathologizing these individuals, studying their condition, and offering 'therapy' to them and their communities."[23]

Speaking at the 1999 annual conference of the International Center for the Study of Psychiatry and Psychology and in personal interviews, Dr. Chrisjohn has made clear that this educationally inspired genocide, as well as the "pathologizing" of the results, continues to take place in the United States and Canada.

Within the inner cities of America, many black leaders over the years have voiced to me the opinion that the urban school system is the ultimate societal tool for enforcing racist views. By providing inadequate education to inner-city children, it keeps them "in their place" at the bottom of American society. The lack of useful education has blighted the hopes of black Americans, especially as the value of unskilled labor has declined.

The more gross and obvious assault on the culture and even the lives of First Nation peoples and African Americans should remind us of the power of public or state education to control all of a country's citizens. Indeed, much of what we call "mainstream America" can be understood as the homogenized thinking produced by public education.

With the new White House–sponsored plan to further empower schools and teachers to identify children for psychiatric evaluation and treatment, Big Brother's shadow looms larger and larger over America's schoolchildren.[24] What has happened to African Americans and Native Americans is an extreme example of trends in our society generally. It should encourage us in our determination to transform our schools for the benefit of everyone. We need to loosen the conforming grip of biological psychiatry on all of our schools and instead turn them into learning sanctuaries that inspire the critical intelligence of all of our children.

Scaling Down the Size of Schools

When it comes to our schools, small is beautiful—and big tends to be ugly. Eric Harris and Dylan Klebold went to Columbine High School with 1,900 other students, Kip Kinkel to Thurston High School with 1,400 others, T. J. Solomon to Heritage High School with 1,300 others, and Luke Woodham to Pearl High School with 1,000 others.

Though many students may rally around a competitive football or basketball game, most of our schools have become too large to inspire a sense of social and academic community or a feeling of personal significance and safety. We will have to return to smaller schools, not just to help prevent violence but to implement programs that discourage peer abuse and encourage positive relationships among students and with the faculty.

After the shootings at Columbine High School and Heritage High School, Vice President Al Gore started supporting the smaller-school movement. He urged school districts to stop "herding all students . . . into overcrowded, factory-style high schools [where] it becomes impossible to spot the early warning signs of violence, depression, or academic failure."[25] Our schools have become factories for the production of academic performers who conform to parental and educational standards without regard for their true needs or desires. Second-class citizenship is the fate of those who fail to make the expected grade.

In several cities in the last decade, including New York, Chicago, and Los Angeles, high schools have been opened with student populations of 500 or fewer. In some more rural counties, the trend to create large county schools has been resisted all along.

In larger schools, students must compete for far fewer places in sought-after teams or organizations. More students are competing for the same number of slots on football teams, newspaper editorial offices, or the class officer slate. A larger proportion of students are shut out of these activities.

In smaller schools, students tend to get better grades, become less involved in gangs and fights, have lower dropout rates, and enjoy more participation in extracurricular activities. They also tend to share more openly with their teachers. "It doesn't matter what category you measure," reports Kathleen Cotton of Northwest Regional Educational Laboratory in Portland, Oregon. "Things are better in small environments. Shy kids, poor kids, average athletes—they all are made to feel like they fit in."[26]

Meanwhile, we are stuck with thousands of enormous, industrial-size schools. In some cases, these behemoth schools are being split up into "schools within a school." This movement attempts to solve two of the problems of large scale: first, what to do with existing huge facilities that cannot easily be sold or dismantled, and second, what to do about functions that benefit from economies of scale, such as science and computer resources, libraries, and gymnasiums.

In one approach to building "schools within schools," high schools with two thousand students are divided into four or five smaller schools sharing the same building. Each of the separate units can have its own special focus, such as art, science, or humanities. Each has its own principal and teachers, while sharing some of the more expensive resources, such as the library or the gymnasium.

What to Do About the Dinosaurs?

Schools—including their large physical structures—are as firmly enmeshed in their own bureaucratic structures as any institution in America. Corporations, by contrast, must transform themselves to meet newly emerging needs, or they go out of business. Even the federal government has had to change, if ever so slightly, in response to public outcries against arbitrary power, useless agencies, and economic waste. American schools, however, have been cemented into their molds by state and federal bureaucracies, by county school boards, by teachers' unions, by teachers' colleges, and by a lack of motivation to respond to the needs of their customers.

Large interest groups vie for control over schools. Organized psychiatry and the drug companies want to force themselves and their products on children. The psychology establishment wants to maintain a foothold in the arena of evaluation and diagnosis, and the medical establishment has joined psychiatry in promoting the use of drugs to control behavior. The teachers' unions want to maintain security and seniority. Contractors want to build big buildings. Conservatives pull one way, liberals another, and libertarians yet another.

Our schools seem as huge and as intimidating as the dinosaurs that roamed and dominated the earth for millions of years. Will it take a cataclysm—the equivalent of a giant comet striking the earth and darkening the sun with dust and debris—to make our present cumbersome schools extinct so we can replace them with more child-oriented versions? It will certainly take a widespread awakening among Americans.

Ultimately, major changes will almost certainly depend on giving parents a wider range of choices of where to send their children, so that various school alternatives will have to compete among themselves. Most school systems provide few if any options to parents, and so do not have to tailor themselves to parental wishes or needs. Mandatory education for children—in the absence of a selection of alternatives—has generally resulted in a stultifying formula.

A great deal of debate has swirled around the use of voucher systems in part as a method for increasing the range of choices of schools. In effect, the government provides each family with a set amount of scholarship money per school-age child to defray some of the cost of sending their children to a school of their choice. Public and private schools must then compete for students, and it is hoped that this competition will increase and improve the alternatives.

There are many complicated political and economic issues surrounding vouchers, such as the potential consequences of undermining public education and the constricting effect of continued state control over standards for accrediting all schools. I want to emphasize that increased parental choice by itself will not lead to the kind of dramatic educational improvements that are required for the sake of our children. We must have a paradigm shift—a new vision—about how to educate children. We must make education more child-oriented, more academically and ethically inspiring, and more encouraging of critical intelligence. Otherwise we will end up using our vouchers to re-create the same old thing.

John Taylor Gatto was an award-winning teacher in New York City before he resigned to become a critic of the basic concept of public schools based on national standards and agendas. In his book, *Dumb-*

ing Us Down: The Hidden Curriculum of Compulsory Schools,[27] he argues that our current public school system cannot be salvaged because it has become an intractable monopoly force that oppresses our children's freedom, individuality, and identity. He believes that public education is not education at all. Instead, it crushes the spirit of inquiry and alienates education from the family and from spiritual values. He wants us to look toward local solutions created and chosen by individual families rather than imposed upon them by the government. Though local choice would certainly lead to great descrepancies in quality, he believes it would ultimately encourage the spirit of independent thought and return spiritual values to education.

Gatto's observations help to underscore the impossibility of teaching critical thinking and independence within large, compulsory, bureaucratic systems. Above all else, we need to rethink education in terms of how to really empower our children to grow up to be ethical, independent, and yet socially minded adults.

As the adults most directly affected by our schools, parents must organize among themselves to lobby for the improvement of our school systems. They must insist that schools meet the genuine needs of children for sanctuary, for guidance with higher ideals, for meaningful relationships among themselves and with teachers, and for engaging educational experiences. Parents in general need to get more involved in their children's schools and in local school politics.

Not only are our children failing to reach their potential, what's worse, their love of learning and their spirit are being crushed in their schools. Therefore, there's no option other than to seek solutions, whatever the economic cost and whatever the personal effort on the part of each of us.

The goal must reach beyond eliminating the more outrageous conditions in our schools. We must provide schools that inspire and guide our children to become independent, thoughtful, caring human beings who possess the ability to continue to learn and to prosper in the modern world. From institutions that oppress the individual and discourage empathy and learning to institutions that empower the individual and encourage caring and education—this is the dramatic turnaround needed in our nation's schools.

11

Creating Sanctuary in Our Families

There's some good news in how angry and even violent our children have become: They are reminding us that they need us. From the poverty in which so many children live to the lack of parental engagement in the home and the high suicide rates among teens, there is no lack of evidence that children have been sliding down our priority list for too long.

The overall message of a 1999 "think tank" on violence conducted with sixty youngsters on the Internet was summarized by an adult participant in the program: "The overwhelming reason they cited for youth violence was that students feel isolated from their parents. The youth explained that feeling disconnected, unsupported and unloved led to poor communication skills and aggression."[1]

The psychologists James P. McGee and Caren DeBernardo have provided useful information and analyses concerning the school shooters. They tried to profile the adolescents' families from the available data. Drawing on information about twelve shooters, they concluded that their families did have serious problems:[2]

Family background and relationships, which may appear superficially normal, are often quite dysfunctional. Divorce, separation and/or frequent episodes of intense friction between parents, and parents and child, are the norm and parents are at risk for becoming the Classroom Avenger's first victims. . . . Explicit or covert anger and hostility are the prevailing emotions in the family, accompanied by parent-child power struggles and battles over control.

Although McGee and DeBernardo's description of a conflicted family may fit the backgrounds of some violent schoolchildren, the researchers did not have sufficient information to make such a broad generalization about all the families. Details of the home life of many school shooters remain unavailable to researchers. Despite the formative importance of family, other factors such as peer abuse, the use of prescription and illicit psychoactive drugs, and a violence-prone society also contribute to the development of violence in children. Furthermore, the researchers' description of family conflict is so nonspecific and commonplace that it would apply to millions of families who do not produce violent children.

With the above caveats in mind, clinical experience confirms the view that a supportive family life is one of the best protections against a child's becoming dangerously out of control or seriously emotionally disturbed.

In August 1998, the U.S. Department of Education published *A Guide to Safe Schools*, which was based on input from eighteen organizations concerned with children, families, and schools. Among their findings was the conclusion that "students whose families are involved in their growth in and outside of school are more likely to experience school success and less likely to become involved in antisocial activities."[3]

Refocusing Ourselves

Even though more caring relationships and less conflict between parents and children will reduce violence and improve academic performance, the almost exclusive focus on the two criteria of reducing violence and improving academic performance is in itself an indicator that society has misdirected its attention. As mentioned in the beginning of this book, we need to be much more interested in the quality of life—the happiness—of our children. Our children know when we are concerned about their "behavior" or their "performance," rather than about them; they need us to be genuinely concerned about *them*.

A Stay-at-Home Father Reclaims His Family

Mr. Louis Collins was working as a public health administrator when his wife, Sharon, started her pediatric practice in Cedar Rapids, Iowa.[4] After the birth of their first child, the Collinses considered their future and it didn't seem to offer much family life with both of them working. In 1981 Mr. Collins took what for a man is a giant step: He chose to stay at home with his children.

A strong individual who was a medical corpsman in 1967 in Vietnam, Mr. Collins is no wimp. But in the years after he made his choice, he was often looked at as an oddity. As the difficulties of raising children in our society have become more acute and as the role of fathers has gained more recognition, Louis Collins has started getting much more positive responses.

According to the U.S. census, about 200,000 men have left full-time jobs to raise children. There's even a newsletter, *At-Home Dad*, that helps fathers to make the adjustment from outside work to the household. With the increasing earning power of women, and the greater recognition of the need for a paternal presence in the American family, the trend will hopefully increase.

The Collinses also home-school their children. A number of factors, from peer hazards to materialistic values to inadequacies in the public schools, have pushed increasing numbers of families to home-school their children. In fact, the number of home-schooled children is approaching 1 million.[5] In the Collins household, Louis has the primary responsibility for teaching the children, but Sharon also helps out.

Home schooling can be more than merely an escape from the emotional and educational battering of the public schools; home schooling can be a tremendous opportunity to bring up children with strong ethical principles and family ties, and a stronger sense of self-esteem. Louis Michael, nineteen, the Collinses' oldest child, has successfully finished his first year of college.

The Collinses are a model for parents who want to claim—or reclaim—their children. The talent, intelligence, and self-confidence of the children confirm that having an at-home father, as well as home schooling, can be a tremendous advantage.

Needing Help to Be a Father

Fathers who don't seem able or willing to raise their children are be-coming an increasingly common phenomenon, but often the problem is blamed on mothers, because they are the ones who bear the brunt of the child's lack of discipline. In modern American society, it is very difficult for a mother to discipline a young boy if the father is not in-volved or, worse, if the father is undermining the child's discipline.

The week after the massacre of students at Columbine High School in Littleton, Colorado, I received a frantic phone call from Mrs. Mar-vin. Watching the news coverage of the young murderers, Eric Harris and Dylan Klebold, confirmed her worst fears about her son, Richie.

"I thought he was going to hit me today. I had to call the police to calm him down."

"How old is he?"

"Fourteen and big!"

"Where was his dad at the time?"

"At work, but it wouldn't have made any difference if he was home. He just withdraws inside himself and doesn't do anything."

I suggested they come and see me, and asked, "Will Dad come in, too, if you ask him?"

"Yes."

I made arrangements for an appointment and then suggested, "You might leave Richie home for the first session. We're the adults . . ." I started to give a pitch for our responsibility for helping Richie.

"Leave him home? He'd attack his little brother. Besides, didn't you hear me that Richie is the problem? He's like that Eric Harris. All he wants to do is to play with his computer."

"Well, it's up to you. You can certainly bring him with you."

Since it seemed like an emergency, I agreed to see the family that very day. Richie, his mother, and his father were soon sitting in my waiting room.

"I think you ought to talk to him alone," Richie's mother urged.

"Is that okay with you?" I asked Richie.

"Why not?" He came into the office and I closed the doors to the waiting room.

I let him look around the room, chatted a little to make him more comfortable, asked him his age and grade, and so on. He asked me if

I was a psychiatrist or psychologist, and knew that a psychiatrist has a medical degree and can prescribe medications.

I asked, "Did your parents explain to you why you're here?"

"I know why I'm here."

"Why?"

"My mom freaks out when I don't do something she wants. Then I 'lose it' sometimes."

"I heard the police were called yesterday."

"I wouldn't play my clarinet."

"What?" I said in disbelief.

"I'm not kidding you. She has this idea I'm supposed to practice twice a week and if I don't she corners me, gets in my face, and then it starts."

"Are you saying that when your parents talk to me, your mother is going to say, 'He wouldn't practice his clarinet'?"

"Yep."

It seemed most honest not to hide my disbelief.

"She thinks I'm going to be a murderer," he continued. "Did she tell you that?"

"As a policy, I don't tell family members what they say to me privately. That way everything you say will be private, too."

"I got it," he agreed.

"How do you know she thinks you'll be a murderer?" I continued.

"She told me, 'You're like Eric Harris.' "

"Oh," I said. "Have you ever hurt anyone?"

"Once my mom fell down when I pushed her away."

"Is that going to be her explanation?"

"Maybe."

"Where does your dad fit into all this?"

Richie went on to describe a family in which the parents were in constant conflict over multiple issues. He was able to explain that his father never disciplined him and his mother, when attempting to discipline him, often lost her temper. "He ought to discipline *her*," Richie explained with disdain.

After we chatted a few more minutes, Richie agreed to have his parents come in to share their interpretation of what was going on in the family. He said he looked forward to hearing what they had to say.

Richie's mother and father sat on the couch; Richie, on a chair.

"Okay, Dr. Breggin, did Richie tell you about the time he pushed me down?" his mother said, launching her major concerns.

Richie responded for me: "I told him you got in my face and I shoved you away."

"Is that what happened?" I asked.

"I had to get in his face," she said. "He won't practice his clarinet."

"I hate the fucking clarinet," he said.

"You promised if I got you lessons you would practice every day."

"When did he promise that?" I asked.

"Last year," Richie said. "And she's going to hold me to it until I die—or reach eighteen."

"You made an agreement. You have to learn to keep agreements," mother declared.

"I don't want to play the goddamn clarinet," he screamed.

"Then you can't be on the basketball team either." She perched on the edge of her chair as if only my presence was keeping her physically out of his face.

I looked over at Richie's father, who was being as inactive as a tree stump in a thunderstorm.

I looked at Richie, who mouthed for my eyes only, "I told you so."

"Well, all of this is pretty amazing," I observed. "Dad, what are you thinking over there?"

"Nothing," his wife said, turning on him. "As usual, he's thinking and doing nothing."

The three of them now sat quietly simmering. Within a scant few minutes, I had witnessed one of their typical conflicts. Only my presence had kept it from escalating.

I suggested to them that we talk about the shoving incident, since it understandably frightened Richie's mother and since it was extremely important for a strong young boy to learn to control himself.

After a few minutes of discussion, I said that I had some thoughts about how to prevent any future shoving incidents. All three looked interested, if a little apprehensive about what I might say.

"First, Mom, you should never get into an adolescent boy's face. Never. You should leave the room first."

"Second, Richie, you should never shove your mother, even if she gets in your face. Never. You should leave the room first."

"Third, Dad, when a father doesn't exert any authority in a family with an adolescent boy, all hell is going to break loose. Dad, you should never sit by when your wife and son are going at each other. *You* should never leave the room when there's a conflict going on. Right here, these last few minutes, you left the room without even having to get up."

"Wow, that all makes sense," Richie said.

His parents looked more cowed than ecstatic.

"I'm just supposed to let him give up his clarinet? And then what if he stops doing his homework?" Richie's mother challenged me. She was obviously very frightened that her son teetered on the verge of being completely irresponsible.

"Mom, for Christ's sake, I got all A's and B's last semester. I do that *for myself*. What makes practicing the clarinet such a big deal?"

"You got all A's and B's last semester and, Mom, you're harassing him about the clarinet?" I was genuinely dismayed.

Richie's mother looked embarrassed; his father said nothing.

"How many of the fights are about the clarinet?" I asked.

"A lot of them, most of them," Richie said. "The rest are about my being on-line, you know, the computer."

"It's not good for him," she protested. "He could be watching anything!"

"Yeah, right, Mom, I'll end up like Eric Harris."

Richie's father still said nothing.

"And what about his picking on his little brother?" his mother demanded.

"The brat is a pain in the ass," Richie said.

"How old is your little brother?" I asked.

"Four."

"You're picking on a four-year-old?" I asked. "That's like a professional wrestler picking on you," I observed matter-of-factly.

Richie seemed startled by the image. "Yeah . . ." he said thoughtfully.

We took a few more minutes to talk about what went on between Richie and his little brother. It turned out that, owing to his mother's temper and his father's lack of involvement, Richie had to manage the relationship with his little brother mostly on his own. It was no wonder he got impatient.

"I'll make you a deal, Richie," I said. "I'm going to urge your mom to let you quit the clarinet because it's just not worth ruining your relationship over. I'm also going to ask you to stop teasing or in any way embarrassing or shaming your kid brother. In fact, I insist that you stop. It's wrong to pick on a child, even if he's being a pain in the neck. Somehow this family has gotten out of control, and you're taking it out on a little kid. What your mom is doing to you isn't fair and what you're doing to your brother isn't fair. Your mother gets in your face and you take it out on your brother. You've got to break that chain and stop picking on your brother, no matter how much stress there is in the family. You know it's wrong, and you'll feel a lot better about yourself being a good big brother who protects his little brother instead of harassing him."

For me, that was a long speech. I waited somewhat apprehensively for a response.

"It's a done deal," Richie abruptly announced.

"Don't make fun of the doctor," his mother interjected.

Richie said nothing.

"You weren't making fun, were you?" I asked.

"No. You got good ideas. I always knew I shouldn't pick on my kid brother. I just never understood where it was coming from."

"It's also coming from your father, who should have stopped it a long time ago," I said.

"Yeah, I got that, too," Richie said. "I'm getting a lot out of this."

I looked from his mother to his father but got no such support.

"Okay, Richie, this is great," I said. "I want you to give me a call next week and leave me a message saying you've been a good big brother and you've backed off from any conflicts with your mother."

"That's it?" Richie asked.

"That'll be a lot. If you stop picking on your little brother—and promise never to lay a hand on your mother even to defend yourself—everything will go better for you."

"I can do that. Do I have to come back again?"

"Only if your parents think so. I think you'll do fine if they straighten out their act. Especially, your father needs to get involved."

"First you'll have to wake him up," his wife said.

"I'm awake, goddamn it!" Richie's father said his first meaningful words, very loudly.

"Wow," Richie said. "Wow. Good luck, Doc, but I think I'll wait outside." As he left, Richie pointed toward me and told his parents, "Listen to this guy."

I explained to Richie's mother, "We have to figure out a way to get you out of your son's face and out of the details of his life. And I know only one way to do that." I turned to Richie's father. "You must learn to get involved in this family. You've left a big hole that your wife is trying to fill, and it's ruining the family."

"You know all that from half an hour?" he growled.

"He's right," his wife confirmed. "Even Richie sees it." And then to me, "I couldn't believe how Richie was listening to you."

"He's desperate to have a father. He wants a mature man to tell him what's right and to insist on his doing it. So I played father, in part to help him, in part to show the both of you what's needed."

"That's all that's needed, I play the father and everything will come out all right?" he said, ridiculing the idea.

"It's not something to play at. You *are* the father," his wife corrected him.

He shut up, stony silent again.

"Doesn't it make you feel awful to sit by on the sidelines while your wife and son go at each other?"

His wife looked grateful for the question. A minute passed while we waited for his answer.

It began with a kind of slow panting. The man was building up to something. His breathing got deeper and yet faster, so that the breath was audibly sucking through his chest. His face was filling with color. I glanced over at his wife, whose eyes were glued to her husband's face. It was as if we were watching a volcano building toward eruption.

At the peak of strong breathing, with his faced filled with color, he howled, "I want to be a father!" It was loud enough to be heard outside the house.

Then we all rested for a few moments.

"Good," I said.

"Thank God," his wife said.

"Where do we begin?" he asked.

I asked him to tell me and his wife what kind of struggle was going on inside him about being an active father. He talked about how he always retreated from intense feeling or conflict. He said he wanted to change.

We talked for a while longer about the kinds of things to insist on from Richie. From what I'd already seen, I suggested the following:

First, mutual respect should become the top priority. Both parents must insist that everyone in the family act with respect toward each other.

Second, Richie's mother should be temporarily relieved of all issues of discipline and control pertaining to Richie, to enable his father to establish himself as a disciplinarian with his son. Later, when things cooled down between Richie and his mother, the two of them would be more able to relate in a reasonable and respectful fashion.

Third, Richie's father should have serious discussions with his son to reinforce Richie's treating his little brother better and his never laying a hand on his mother, even in self-defense.

Fourth, since Richie was doing well in school, and more or less carried out the limited household chores assigned to him, nothing else should be expected of him. He should be able to spend as much time on his computer as he wanted and as little time on his clarinet as he wanted.

I saw the couple for the second time the following week and they reported that Richie was already doing much better. Many months later, when seeing me for couples therapy, they agreed that Richie was continuing to behave well while enjoying the family much more. They attributed the changes in Richie to his father's at last becoming an effective influence in his son's life. This freed up Richie's mother to focus more on loving her son rather than on controlling him.

Meanwhile, Richie's parents realized that their own problems ran much deeper than conflicts over childrearing, and they continued to work on improving their own relationship. Over a period of months, they learned to identify and to stop the ways in which they hurt each other and to replace them with loving communications and deeds.

It cannot be said too often: A child's behavior will improve within a short period of time if the parents take responsibility for learning better ways of parenting. If the youngster is a preteenager, very rapid improvements are almost guaranteed. Though Richie was already fourteen years old, he was so eager for effective male influence in his life that he calmed down as quickly as a younger child would in response to his father's new involvement in his life.

Often the child has a better understanding of what's happening than the parents, who are locked into patterns of behavior that go back to their own childhood. Once again, children and adolescents often express more critical intelligence than the adults in their lives. Their opinions and insights should be taken seriously.

Creating Sanctuary in the Family

Many of our children do not feel safe at home. They sense conflict in the family with the potential for separation and divorce. Too often, they witness or experience emotional and physical abuse, or are subjected to sexual abuse. They lack a consistent flow of unconditional love and discipline is inconsistent, lax, or arbitrary and oppressive. The children are simply not a high enough priority and must survive on whatever we happen to have left over for them. Often children are treated with disrespect. Too often, parents in frustration withdraw love from their children.

The principles required for creating sanctuary and a good family life are not much different from the principles required for good school programs. I encourage parents and others who relate to young people to review the thirteen principles set forth in Chapter 10. Everyone's emotional and physical safety must come first. Toward this end, two principles should be paramount:

First, parents should focus on creating respectful relationships with their children. Being respectful in everything, from tone of voice to the choice of words, is key. When parents have mutually respectful relationships with their children, disciplinary problems can usually be resolved by negotiation and agreement. The first step in creating mutually respectful relationships rests with the parent, who must treat his or her children with the same respect that would be shown toward a powerful, wealthy adult relative upon whom the parent was dependent.

Second, parents need to remain aware of their child's need for unconditional love from them. In a child's development of self-worth, nothing is more important than feeling loved by parents through the ups and downs of family life. Even when enforcing discipline, a parent should remain in touch with being loving.

Problems of the Modern "Family"

Providing an ideal sanctuary for children requires an extended family and the proverbial village—neither of which is available to the typical modern family. Nonetheless, we should strive for the ideal.

Especially since the 1950s, the very concept of family has become complex and difficult to define. Many children will experience separation and divorce, sometimes more than once, and will have a variety of adults living with them with whom they have no blood kinship. All this puts considerable pressure on single parents to provide meaningful, beneficial daily relationships with the children in their care.

After a separation or divorce, nothing is more important than the continued active involvement of the nonresidential parent, which is usually the father. If at all possible, parents should help their children maintain positive relationships with both sides of the divorced family, and with each other.

Children cannot bear watching their parents turning angrily on each other. It creates overwhelming anguish. The joint determination by separated parents to maintain a cordial relationship with each other is probably the single most difficult, and the single most important, strategy for easing the pain of separation and divorce for children. Separated couples, suffering from their own thwarted emotional needs and hurt feelings, are often tested to the limits of their emotional capacity when it comes to acting maturely toward each other. How well they pass that test will influence their children for the rest of their lives.

There are some practical measures that can help to ease the painfulness of divorce for children. An effort should be made for separated and divorced parents to live near each other, preferably in the same school district to facilitate transportation by school bus regardless of which parent the child is visiting or living with. A live-in helper can also relieve some of the pressure on a single parent, but the cost is beyond the means of most parents, and live-in help can also cause stresses and conflicts.

Single parents can strive to bring other adults into their children's lives. It can be helpful to build a relationship with another single-parent family to exchange information and approaches, to share holidays and other family activities, and at times to fill in for each other. Consistent, loving child-care providers make a huge difference. A Big Brother or Big Sister volunteer can help. Activities that involve other adults, such as church or Boy Scouts, may provide mentors and parent like figures.

Perfection is unobtainable in family life. Every relationship has its difficulties, and today's families have more than their share of multiple, complex relationships. But awareness of an ideal can help us monitor ourselves and keep us moving in the right direction. Sanctuary is one of the most useful ideals. It reminds us that children need, above all else, a safe, child-oriented space filled with love and consistent, rational discipline. Even if we must acknowledge that we can only approximate it to the best of our ability, the family as sanctuary is the ideal that we must strive to implement.

Parents Always Matter

Therapy or counseling can be especially effective when both parents, and even the extended family, become involved. With all the adults working together, it quickly becomes apparent that "the child's problem" is really "the family's problem"—and it is certainly the family's responsibility to ameliorate and overcome the child's problems.

Even if the family is not the source of the child's difficulties, the family remains the ultimate source of the healing. Thus, when children have been traumatized by persons or events outside the family, including schools that don't meet their needs and adults who have bullied or abused them, the family will have to mobilize to help the child recover. This point cannot be overstated: Whatever the cause of a child's problem, the solution lies in the hands of the adults who take care of the child.

Only One Parent

When a child is troubled or acting out of control, it becomes especially difficult to improve the situation if both parents are not willing to work together for their child's sake. Sometimes in a case where a father has removed himself from a child's life, I see the youngster in individual counseling while also working with the mother. But if at all possible, it would be more effective for another adult male to enter the child's life on a more regular basis as mentor or parent figure.

Jimmy's mother looked worn out when I first met her. She was unkempt, her hair hadn't been combed, and her eyes lacked any luster. Ten-year-old Jimmy, on the other hand, was full of energy. He bounced as though sitting on an air compressor that periodically bumped him into the air. Then he got to his feet, checking this and that item around my office. There are few things in my office that I worry about a child breaking, but he found them, my pair of ceramic great blue herons tucked away on a bookcase behind the couch. In a blink of the eye, Jimmy was behind the couch holding aloft my blue herons.

I found myself saying impatiently, "Jimmy, please, be careful with that."

Jimmy's mother nodded at me as if to confirm: "See, nobody can handle that child." Instead, she said, "That child was *born* with a bit of the devil in him."

Jimmy shot his mother a smirk that said, "Born devilish? Okay, watch me!" He faked dropping my treasured herons on the floor, giggled, put them back, and came flying back over the couch.

I pride myself in being able to calm down all the children who come to my office within the first session simply by relating to them, but it looked like I had met my match in Jimmy. But his mother's remark about the devil—and Jimmy's defiant reaction to it—told me that they revved each other up. So I asked Jimmy's mother if I could visit alone in the office with her son for a few minutes. Her response was telling:

"If you dare! The last doctor said it was neurological and there was nothing we could do about it except medication . . . Glad to get out of the way," she said as she hustled from the room.

Jimmy stood in the room pirouetting in his efforts to spot the next place to make trouble. Instead he began to look with fascination at the plants, colorful molded birds, and chimes hanging from the ceiling.

"This place is cool," Jimmy observed as he backed slowly onto the couch.

"Jimmy?" I asked, "where's your dad?"

Stone still, hands planted on his waist like an actor, he declared, "I hate him and he hates me."

"How dreadful for you."

"He doesn't bother me," the little boy snarled.

For ten minutes—now glued to his seat—Jimmy told me about visiting his father the past weekend: the fights they had, the awful things his father said to him, how his father preferred his new wife's children. A large piece of the child's tragedy unfolded in front of my eyes.

"I don't want to talk about him anymore," Jimmy concluded and started to grab things up from the teak table beside the couch. He began banging two tiny bronze ducks together.

Then he looked up.

"Why are you looking at me that way?" he asked in puzzlement.

I had to think a minute before I realized I was on the verge of tears. "I feel incredibly sad," I told him.

"You're feeling sorry for me?" he demanded defiantly.

"Oh, no. I admire your energy. Your honesty. Your courage. I feel sad that such a wonderful child has so much hurt inside that he can't sit still with it. But you calmed down when you were telling me about your dad—about how badly your dad treats you."

Remember, this is a ten-year-old, but I could see he understood me. He began to sit much more comfortably.

He started to fuss at things on the table again.

"Let me keep you company," I explained softly. An adult might wonder what I meant by "keep you company," but he seemed to know. He sat back and looked at me again while his hands toyed aimlessly with a crystal from my table.

"It's good to sit quietly with you," I said. "I'd like you to have at least a few minutes of peace each time you're here with me."

We talked some more about his father, and then about his mother, who often screamed at him in frustration and impatience, and about school, which he claimed to hate almost as much as he hated his father.

"Let's get your mother back in here," I suggested after more than half an hour.

Immediately I saw the child's anxiety and energy rising up.

"It's much harder for you to be relaxed with your mom around, isn't it?"

He shrugged.

"Would you like to meet my dog Blue before we bring in your mom?"

His sour face split into a broad grin.

My Sheltie, Blue, would be leaning against the other side of the pair of heavy double doors that separate my office from the remainder of the house. When I opened the doors, Blue came marching in expectantly, ears back, tail up. When he saw it was a child, he immediately lost that alert mode. No trouble here. He bowed in front of Jimmy, the way Shetland sheepdogs do with some people.

"He likes you, trusts you—so he's bowing."

Jimmy got down on the rug and began to pet him. As old as Blue's bones had become, he found Jimmy's touch gentle enough to be relaxing. Meanwhile, I went to the waiting room to escort Jimmy's mother back into the office.

"He calmed down with me," I told his mother, "and now look at him with Blue."

"Oh, he loves dogs," Jimmy's mother said. "He's very good with animals."

"Then he wasn't born with the devil in him," I commented. "At least not when it comes to dogs."

"I didn't mean that . . . I meant, well, you know. It must be genetic, something in his nervous system, something neurologic, like the other doctor said."

"How could he have a 'neurological' problem if it goes away when he pets a dog?" I asked rhetorically.

Out of the corner of my eye, I could see Jimmy starting to get ready to be "hyperactive."

"It's okay," I reassured Jimmy, and he went back to petting Blue.

"It's not about his nervous system or he wouldn't calm down with me. Or with Blue. Or with you and me right now," I explained. "It's about the conditions he's been living in, the stresses at home, and with his father, and in school."

"I told the doctor about how mean Daddy gets," Jimmy informed his mother.

"He's not exaggerating," his mother confirmed.

"Mom says she'd like to kill him," Jimmy said casually, still petting Blue.

"I was only—" his mother stammered with embarrassment.

"You say it a lot," Jimmy jumped in.

"I guess I shouldn't."

"I understand your frustration when his father hurts Jimmy so much—but no, it's not good for him to hear that from you."

"But if it's not about his nervous system, what's it about?"

"It's about relationship. He found something in his relationship with me—and with Blue—that lets him calm down. I want to help you find the same way of being with him."

"He was calm with you? He threatened to kill the last doctor I left him alone with."

"Kill?" I emphasized the word.

"You think he got that from me?"

I shrugged. It's always hard to know exactly where kids get things from. However, it was important that Jimmy's mother was thinking about the impact of her own behavior on her son. That was important progress.

"He calmed down with Blue, too," I went on. "Blue and I must have something in common that helps Jimmy to calm down."

Jimmy laughed at the idea of me and Blue having something in common.

"You and Blue—you're both old and gray," Jimmy chimed in.

"Jimmy! Mind your mouth!" his mother snapped.

"We *are* both old and gray," I affirmed, "and we both like you, Jimmy."

There was a brief silence. Jimmy's mother looked puzzled about why I wasn't offended.

"I try," his mother said defensively. "He won't calm down like this for me, except sometimes."

We talked about the times that Jimmy did calm down with her. It turned out that the times always involved getting his mother's undivided attention. Ever since the divorce, his mother observed, Jimmy needed a lot of attention. I reassured her that Jimmy's response was "normal"—that being "needy" and "demanding" was the natural and even healthy response of children who were traumatized by separation and loss, and that it was much better than if Jimmy were acting withdrawn and unwilling to ask for attention.

I talked with Jimmy's mother about how to create more peaceful spaces for herself and her son for the purpose of their giving undivided, loving attention to each other. For the mother, it was in part a matter of priorities—taking the time to be together with her son with nothing else on the agenda to interfere or to stir up conflicts and tension. I also tried to show his mother how Jimmy's "bad behavior" almost always amounted to a cry for genuinely needed attention. Instead of reacting angrily to the behavior, Jimmy's mother needed to give much more of herself to her son. Jimmy, meanwhile, listened with obvious pleasure while his mother received help in improving their relationship.

I reassured Jimmy's mother, "It doesn't mean you're not trying. It doesn't mean your a bad parent. You're dealing with negative factors that you cannot control, like the way your ex-husband treats you and Jimmy, and also the impatience of the teachers and the school."

I explained to Jimmy's mother that it's very hard in general for parents—mothers or fathers—to raise children on their own. Many mothers are forced into this position by separation from fathers who do not remain intimately involved with their children; but it would be even more difficult for most men to function effectively as single parents.

Very few men voluntarily choose to raise children on their own. Even most *married* men seem tried to the end of their patience when circumstances require them to spend a day or two taking care of their children on their own. It can be a healthy turning point in the marital relationship when a father, after only a day or two alone with the children, realizes how much work it requires for his wife to do child care as her regular daily occupation.

"You don't think there's anything really wrong with him?" Jimmy's mother asked again.

"Jimmy, do you think there's something wrong with you?" I turned to the child for an opinion.

"I wouldn't be getting dragged around to so many doctors if I had nothing wrong with me."

"I don't think there's anything wrong with you, Jimmy. You're responding to a lot of stress. I want to help you see that there are ways you can calm yourself down. And I want to ask your dad to come in to see me, because I think your behavior has a lot to do with what's going on with your parents. I don't think there's anything the matter with you. I think you're wonderful."

I asked Jimmy's mother to send a message to his father that I wanted him to make an appointment to see me. He lived in New York City but sometimes made business trips to Washington, D.C.

Many fathers would have gone out of their way to travel to their child's psychiatrist. This father did not. But since visiting his father was often emotionally traumatic for Jimmy, it would be difficult to help Jimmy without his father's involvement in therapy.

Even without his father's involvement, Jimmy calmed down over a period of a few months, and there was a lot more peace at home. Sometimes I would visit for a few minutes alone with him, but generally I emphasized meeting with Jimmy and his mother together in order to help them learn to relate without agitating each other. I also visited him at school, where he remained uncomfortable and hence "hyperactive," but I had limited success in getting his teachers to reevaluate their approach to Jimmy.

At school Jimmy needed, above all else, a benevolent, meaningful relationship with one of the teachers. All the completed assignments, all of the appropriate behavior, all the smiley faces on his papers would not come close in importance to one teacher taking a personal interest in him; but I couldn't make it happen.

The woman assigned to counsel Jimmy was decidedly authoritarian and aloof, and Jimmy hated and feared her. I tried but couldn't manage to build rapport with the counselor, so how could I expect Jimmy to do so? I was able to make a good connection with one of the administrators but learned that there were no other counselors in the school.

Jimmy's father never responded to my requests that he meet with me. Jimmy's teachers remained aloof and often negative toward him. Ultimately, his mother seemed to give up, too, and despite the gains we had made in improving their relationship and calming Jimmy down at home, she dropped out of therapy before we had completed our work. From her last communication, it seemed she was feeling overwhelmed by the stressors in her life. Her departure left me pondering over what I might have done to provide more effective help to the family. Perhaps I could have worked better with the teachers. Perhaps I could have been more aggressive about getting in touch with Jimmy's father. Meanwhile, how can we expect children like Jimmy to succeed when the adults around them seem to consistently let them down?

Opening Our Homes to Our Children and Their Friends

Nowadays, young people often have no supervised place to go because their parents are always out on Friday and Saturday nights. But some parents do otherwise. We know parents who decided to stay home on weekends for the duration of their children's adolescence to provide an open house for them and their friends. Even if their own children were out somewhere, other youngsters would often drop by. From getting to know their children's friends, the parents developed a sense of what was happening in their world. Over several years, the parents often found themselves becoming confidants and mentors to some of their children's friends. Best of all, their own children always knew where to find them on a Friday or Saturday night. It was a source of security for the youngsters, even if they were doing something away from home.

The parents who ran the open house allowed the teenagers to visit together, listen to music and dance, play computer or video games, watch TV, and relax together. But mostly the teenagers wanted a place to sit down and chat among themselves with music in the background and something to munch in hand. They needed a safe space of their own. That's all it took to provide them a refuge and an opportunity to visit with each other.

The adults did not have to hang around with the youngsters in the middle of the living room, basement rec room, or deck; they merely had to be in the house to make occasional rounds, to greet new people, to remind everyone about the rules of the house, and to be available in case of a rare emergency. They didn't even need to provide snacks; the youngsters brought their own.

Staying home and welcoming your children and their friends to hang out, as they wish and when they wish, provides something that in most communities is not otherwise available. Even if it were available somewhere else—say, a teen center—there are great advantages in having safe hangout space in your home and the homes of people you know. If numbers of families began to do this, it could transform life in the community for teenagers.

In various ways, parents must change their work and recreational activities so that they can really focus on their children. The justification that "I'm working so hard for your future"—for example, to pay for college—is self-defeating. It too easily becomes an excuse for avoiding genuine engagement within the family.

A generation or two ago, parents happily anticipated being free of parental responsibility when their children reached young adulthood. Now many parents look forward to sending their children off to day care before they reach age four. It's as if we cannot wait to get rid of our children. This tendency—this desire—must be reversed. Instead of molding their lives to fit the shape of our needs, we need to shape our lives to meet their needs.

Learning to Resolve Conflicts with Our Children

The great majority of problems faced by parents fall into the category of *conflicts* with their children. With younger children the issues surround topics such as being obedient, not hitting, paying attention when adults speak, being respectful, doing the chores or homework, putting away clothes or toys, cleaning up the bedroom, coming to dinner when asked, and getting up or going to bed on time. Additional issues surface with older children, including curfews, use of the automobile, and drug and alcohol abuse.

Even failures to do well at school are best understood as conflicts between a child's behavior and the expectations of parents and teachers. Children who have failed to learn to resolve conflicts at home are likely to bring their difficulties to school. Teachers and parents with expectations that exceed the child's ability or motivation also end up in conflict with the child.

Though these sources of contention and strife are likely to be labeled disciplinary or school problems—with the focus on the children's failings—they are in reality conflicts between adults and the children. The conflicts can escalate to violent proportions with both adults and children resorting to extreme measures such as hitting and rejecting each other. Failing to understand the potential for conflict resolution can lead both adults and children to take self-defeating, destructive stands.

Since these are conflicts, the best solutions lie in conflict resolution based on love and a mutual concern. The individuals must learn to trust that when people care about each other they can figure out solutions that meet everyone's significant needs.

If hostility has made everyone withdraw from each other, finding ways to revive love must be the first priority. It requires at least a tentative acceptance of the possibility of resolving the conflicts. A professional counselor with an understanding of conflict resolution can be helpful in creating that hopeful environment.

Unfortunately, parents often fail to see their difficulties with children as conflicts. Often, they view the child as irrational, stubborn, disobedient, and oppositional, while they assume they do not and cannot play any personal role in resolving the conflict situation. Even when the adults have a benevolent feeling toward the child, they are likely to dismiss the child's resistance to their authority as childish and in need of correction. They will fail to focus on reaching better understandings and mutual agreements and in taking the role of mature leader rather than enforcer.

Children can quickly grasp the concept of conflict resolution. It is taught to youngsters in many elementary and junior high schools. For parents accustomed to believing that it's their duty to make unilateral decisions and to enforce them, it can be difficult to learn to share decision making while maintaining parental moral authority.

It cannot be overemphasized: The great majority of problems between parents and children are best viewed as conflicts that require resolution. The approach is conflict resolution based on sound ethics, reason, and love, instead of punishment or behavioral control. This may seem obvious when stated in such a straightforward way, and yet parents whose children seem to have "problems" will be told by teachers and mental health professionals that the "problem" lies in the child, when it really lies in the child's relationships with adults.

Here are some suggestions and guidelines on what to do and what not to do to avoid severe conflicts with your child:[6]

Don't do time-outs.   A well-known, often used behavioral technique is the so-called time-out in which the child is forced to stay alone for a few minutes or more. Though the intent is to de-escalate the situation, the child is likely to perceive it as a punishment, even as a shameful rejection and ostracism. If children do on occasion respond to time-outs by calming down, parents and other caregivers become encouraged about the efficacy of the approach and end up resorting to it with increasing frequency. A parent will hear a commotion in another room, run in, see that one of the children is especially angry or upset, and order that child into a time-out: isolation in another part of the room or even in another room entirely. The child ends up responding angrily to being ostracized, resulting in further escalation.

At times any severe punishment will stop a child's ongoing behavior. Time-outs will occasionally accomplish that. But time-outs are wrong in principle. Children don't need time-outs, they need "time-ins." When a child is upset, unable to control emotions, fighting over toys or perceived humiliations—the child needs the intervention of a caring adult who can calm the situation and show the child better approaches to resolving conflict.

Will a child learn to get upset or even nasty just to get a "time-in" attention? No. When a parent responds to a child's distraught behavior with a combination of firmness, tenderness, and concern, the child learns to respond positively in return. Then, when the child becomes upset, bored, or lonely in the future, he or she will have learned to reach out more directly for the parent's genuinely caring attention.

Why? Because the child knows, from the experience of "time-ins," that the parent is available to give genuinely caring attention. No child will consistently prefer provoking conflict to seeking and obtaining quality attention.

Don't regularly resort to punishments. Punishments demonstrate our willingness to inflict emotional or physical pain on our children. That's not spiritually elevating to them or to us. Punishments tend to stop ongoing behavior without showing the child how to act more positively. A child who is already beaten down will respond to punishment by becoming submissive. While this may end the stress of the moment, it is very bad for the child's mental well-being. If the child has spunk, he or she is likely to resist punishment. This creates a very destructive cycle of punishment and rebellion. There may be occasions, such as a child's violent outburst that causes injury, when a punishment may be useful to emphasize the gravity of the event. But this should be a rare, last-ditch resort. The need for punishment reflects that the situation is already out of control.

Punishments always indicate that we have run out of patience, imagination, better strategies of communication, or love. When parents feel at the end of their rope, that's the one circumstance in which I can imagine a use for time-outs—but for the adult, rather than child. When you feel like you've got to punish your child, take a deep breath, count to ten, maybe even leave the room—and then return to your child when you have regained your sense of proportion and your capacity to engage your child in a loving way.

In relationships, we tend to get back what we give. If you try to force your child to behave in a certain way, your child has two basic choices—to submit or to force back. If you try to engage your child in ways that encourage your child to relate rationally and lovingly, your child is likely, over time, to learn to respond in a similar fashion.

If for any reason you are frequently unable to give a needed "time-in" to your children, then your relationship with them is too rushed, harried, or conflicted. You need to slow everything down, make more time for your efforts to dress or feed your child, and focus on relationship instead of getting things done.

Don't enforce heavy homework schedules. The process of turning children into school slaves—children who suffer under the yoke of oppressive daily routines and excessive homework—is turning parents into school slaves as well. When parents feel that they are in severe conflict with their children over homework, it's often best to get out of the homework business. Refuse to enforce compulsive submissiveness to the demands of the schools. In many cases, parental attempts to enforce homework regimens are ruining parent-child relationships.

Refusing to enforce homework can of course create conflicts with teachers and administrators. However, a parent can, in a thoughtful fashion, communicate to the school that the relationship at home has been suffering from too much conflict over homework. Teachers can be enlisted in encouraging the child to complete homework without relying on parental involvement. Also, another adult or a tutor can sometimes be involved to help with homework without putting that stress on the parent-child relationship. Children sometimes enjoy learning from a skilled, enthusiastic tutor, whereas they would rebel against their parents offering similar help. Even if a child's grades temporarily worsen, getting homework completed is not nearly as important as improving the relationship between parent and child. This is true for children regardless of their age. Older youngsters if anything have even more need, not less, to find their own motivation for studying while preserving a harmonious relationship with their parents.

It is a mistake to emphasize academic expectations, especially in the first few years of school. Parents need to demand a reduction in pressure on their children. They need to refuse to make second-graders do hours of homework. As a parent, I wouldn't become a slave driver, even if it meant my children didn't "excel" at school.

Share educational adventures. Ted's father and mother came to see me because their son was "hyperactive" and "aggressive" in school and with other children. In addition, schoolwork never sustained his attention.

The family had seen two psychologists, both of whom encouraged Ted's father to get involved in physically active things with his son, such as wrestling, playing ball, and biking. These activities were supposed to help Ted "blow off steam." But when I met Ted and his parents, it became quite apparent that contrary to being a natural-born athlete, Ted, like his father, was a quiet, artistic person. In fact, Ted's aggressiveness was most likely an attempt to cover up and compensate for his sensitive nature.

It turned out that Ted and his father shared a common artistic interest in drawing and sketching, and I urged them to figure out ways to enjoy this together. Within a short time, instead of running around outdoors, they were sitting together sketching nature scenes. Soon they were taking an art course together, and Ted began to display an unexpected capacity to focus his attention on creative projects.

Many parents are especially concerned because their children do poorly at completing school projects, such as writing book reports, building model forts, or carrying out a science project. Often the children try to get their parents to do the work. In the extreme, the children become so frustrated, resentful, and lacking in confidence that they don't want anyone trying to help them.

Rather than fighting over school projects, it's far better for us as parents to think of the kinds of projects that we ourselves enjoy—hiking, fishing, gardening, listening to music, going to the theater or movies, visiting a museum, playing tennis or golf, taking a vacation to an animal sanctuary—and then share our interests with our children.

At the same time, it's important to help your children figure out what interests them, so that you can join in doing things of their choice as well. With younger children, this requires patient trial and error. Ideally, it can become a mutual affair, each of you sharing the other's interests. More often than not, you'll have to compromise and spend most of your time on activities and projects that your children especially enjoy.

Overall, parents can best teach their children and encourage their academic interests by doing interesting things together a lot of the time.

Teach and exemplify respectful relating. As emphasized in the chapters on school, displays of disrespect probably cause more anger and hatred between people than any other offense. We have seen how outbursts of extreme school violence have been motivated, in part at least, by feelings of being rejected, ridiculed, and humiliated by peers. In general, if you can create or recapture a respectful relationship with a former antagonist, let alone a friend or family member, you will be well along the way to resolving your conflicts.

Teach your children about the importance of respect. Then provide a model for your children by being respectful to them under any and all circumstances. Keep in mind that you should at all times be sensitive to your children's vulnerability to anything that smacks of shame or ridicule. Never take the easy route of enforcing your wishes by embarrassing your child. The cost is too high in terms of your child's spiritual well-being.

Remember that respect must be mutual and that those in power must be the most careful, at all times, to show respect for those with less power. To insist on respect from children without providing it oneself is hypocritical and oppressive. To insist on mutual respect is empowering to everyone involved.

Focusing on What Matters

When parents are involved in destructive conflicts with their children, I urge them to stop enforcing nearly all of the rules and regulations they have been imposing on them. Forget about getting homework done. Forget about chores. Forget about bedtime. At least for a few days or weeks, stop trying to enforce any rules other than those pertaining directly to safety, such as prohibitions against violence or drunk driving. Instead, focus entirely on respectful relating and communicating. Emphasize the *style* and the *intent* of communications: All communications in their form and in their spirit should be respectful and even thoughtful and caring. Without resorting to threats or punishments, *explain* how you want to build a respectful, caring environment.

I find that this approach works regardless of the age of the child. For example, the parent of a three-year-old may already be locked into endless battles over eating, bathing, going to the toilet, and going to bed. I recommend trying to handle all of these kinds of conflicts through loving relationship. Make eating, bathing, going to bed, and even going to the bathroom into something fun to do together. If that doesn't work, don't force the child into anything. Meanwhile, do insist on two or three basic rules, such as talking respectfully, no hitting, and wearing your seat belt. It is astonishing how much a frightfully violent relationship with a child can be quickly calmed by adherence to a few simple principles. Simplify the rules, keep the child company during difficult times, and enforce only a very few things.

With teenagers it is no different; it's simply a different set of rules that need to be simplified and hopefully agreed upon. Often, parents quickly realize that they only really need to emphasize respectful relating, physical safety, and nonviolence, and everything else will eventually work out. Teenagers in turn are usually very able to see the rationality behind agreeing to be mutually respectful and nonviolent with their parents while their parents give up trying to coerce them about homework, bedtime, or other issues that the teenager must ultimately learn to handle independently.

At first my recommendations may seem utopian to parents embroiled in conflict with their children. Forget about discipline in general and focus on respectful, nonviolent communication? But after a few minutes, it usually sinks in. "That would be a miracle!" parents are likely to respond on realizing that I want to help them have gentle, kind, thoughtful, rational communications with their children.

But what about flunking out of school? What about her awful friends? What about cleaning up his room? What about all the time they waste in front of the TV or on the Internet? Usually the parents realize that they have been unable to control these kinds of activities anyway, and that it's futile to keep trying. Then I try to help them understand that if they can reestablish a respectful and even caring relationship with their children, they will have accomplished the most important task of parents. Once that relationship has been reestablished, most young people will then be willing, at times at least, to discuss most of the other sources of conflict in a rational manner. I like to put it this way: "If you've got a good relationship with your children in the next few years, you'll have given them everything you can, and you'll actually be enjoying each other."

If you decide to adopt these principles, make clear that you've changed your priorities, and your main concern is now that everyone in the family—parents and children alike—relate to each other with kindness and with respect for each other's vulnerabilities. That means *no one tries to get what they want by being threatening, nasty, disrespectful, or even whiny*. Only thoughtful, respectful communications will be given a positive response. Negative behaviors will not be given any response, or will be acknowledged as unsatisfactory. All participants must learn that nothing will be obtained by mean, cruel, or disrespectful communications.

In other words, create peace. Make sanctuary. That should be the entire focus when members of a family are at each other's throats. Once peace and harmony are established, even at the cost of people not doing "what they're supposed to do," individuals can begin negotiating about how to handle the daily conflicts of living together. Once respect is established, you can begin to find more loving solutions for problems like doing the homework or the chores. At any rate, neither homework nor chores is as important as a genuinely caring, respectful relationship with your child.

To reiterate: Achieving this kind of sanctuary in the home must begin with all of the adults in the household. If the children are used to being treated disrespectfully, it's futile to demand respectful relating from them. The good news is this: It is entirely possible to build homes around the ideal of mutually respectful relating and communicating.

Questions to Ask Yourself

When have you ever welcomed being punished against your will for a mistake you made or for something you did wrong?

Most likely, you wanted forgiveness and you hoped the other person would trust you to do better the next time. If you harmed the person—for example, by breaking something that mattered—you might have wanted voluntarily to make restitution. But you would have resented anyone screaming at you, "You've got to pay for it!" Children want and need the same trust and respect.

When was the last time you wanted your boss or spouse to force you to take a "time-out"?

You may on occasion take "a break" for yourself to get away from an escalating conflict situation, but you would never want a bigger, stronger person to force you to stand in the corner or to go to your room. Children feel the same way. They may on occasion want to take a time-out, but not under compulsion.

Have you ever enjoyed being forced, night after night, to bring home two, three, or four hours of boring extra work upon which you would be evaluated by your boss in the morning?

Many of us do on occasion bring home extra work but how many of us would willingly put up with the amount of homework given to children on a nightly basis? Remember, our children are already worn out and tired by busy days at school by the time they get around to their homework. Tragically, today's children often work longer, harder hours at elementary and high school than their parents do at their jobs. Mother and father are flaked out in front of the television, while their kids are struggling with math or English.

I confess to working very long hours almost every day of my life on my clinical practice, writing, medical-legal consultations, psychiatric reform work, and so on. But I love what I do. My work is my play; it gives me energy. But that's not how most children feel about their homework—and I didn't feel that way about mine, either, when I was a child. Fortunately, I lived in an era before public education turned children into school slaves. I could gradually learn to love to work, but at my own pace and on my own terms.

Would you persistently act in a nasty fashion toward someone who always tried to treat you in a fair, kind, and understanding manner?

Parents grow afraid that treating their children with the utmost thoughtfulness will ultimately spoil them or bring out the worst imaginable behavior. But that's not how human nature tends to work. Children, like adults, usually to try to please people who treat them well. There are always ups and downs in this regard with children so that sometimes they will seem to treat us badly no matter how nicely we treat them. Sometimes they will be so upset with others in their lives, such as peers or another adult, that for the time being they cannot accept our kindness. But in the long run our children will respond positively to our treating them with respect and unconditional love.

As a parent, you will rarely go wrong if you ask yourself, "How would I want to be treated by my parent if I were the child in this situation?" If you believe, "I'd want to be hit or yelled at," then you need to get in touch with how you really felt when those things were done to you as a child.

Listening to Our Children's Voices

Children need adults devoted to listening to their voices and meeting their genuine needs for unconditional love, rational discipline, engaging ways to learn, and lots of play. There is no way around this—children need us, lots of us. We have to pay serious attention to the feelings and communications of the children in our care and in the process keep renewing our relationships with them. Often this will require us to change our attitudes and our lifestyles, but the rewards are enormous: enjoying love-filled relationships with our children and seeing them prosper through our care.

12

Helping Our Most Disturbed and Violent Children—Lessons for Helping All Our Children

———•◦•———

In the past, I have written that nothing reflects the humaneness and ethics of a society as much as how it treats its children. That view can be taken a step further: Nothing reflects a society's moral attitudes toward children as much as how it treats its most difficult children. In America, our routine treatment of psychiatrically labeled children reflects shame upon us. Tragically, it is but one aspect of our general failure to provide our children with meaningful adult relationships.

The model programs in this chapter aim at reclaiming our most disturbed and violent children but they can teach us a great deal about reclaiming all of our children. All children—from those who are thriving to those who are feeling overwhelmed—need the kind of safe, loving environment that these programs strive to create for the children in their care.

Saved from Death by Love

As infants we require emotionally satisfying relationships in order to survive and then to thrive. As this story will demonstrate, even the provision of food will not keep a child alive in the absence of a caring relationship.

What happens to us in infancy often establishes the basis, for better or worse, of our evolving lives. When an older child or young adult arrives for psychiatric help, the stressors and trauma of infancy have usually been obscured by time. Parents have a natural tendency to forget how they themselves may have hurt or failed to protect their children. Or in retrospect the parents may attribute the problems to the baby's being unaccountably "fussy" or "colicky." Sometimes, however, severely disturbed infants will be brought to the attention of child health or welfare agencies, and the impact of early trauma and deprivation will be immediately apparent.

Natasha was five months old and in danger of dying. Her weight was that of a two-month-old and her development was also lagging far behind. She didn't make eye contact or smile, she was unresponsive to being held, and her body was more like a sack than a bundle of energy. Natasha had been brought to the Judge Baker Guidance Center, a part of Children's Hospital Medical Center in Boston, with a diagnosis of failure to thrive. Though there was no evidence for an underlying physical disorder, Natasha was not growing. She was becoming physically and spiritually stunted.

Dr. Richard Goodman was put in charge of Natasha's treatment.[1] Now a psychoanalyst in private practice in Boston who works with children and families, Dr. Goodman at the time was a therapist and then staff director of the unit. It was more than a decade ago, shortly before "managed-care" companies and biological psychiatry took over the field of mental health. When necessary, patients could stay in the unit for up to three months, they could be treated with intensive psychological and social therapy. Psychiatric drugs were rarely given to children or teenagers.

In the intake interview, Natasha's mother confessed to feeling overwhelmed by the challenge of taking care of a baby. Being a single parent working full time was difficult enough. But Natasha's mother herself had never been properly mothered. She was becoming depressed over her failure as a parent and, much like her baby, could not make eye contact with Dr. Goodman.

As Natasha's mother held the bottle, her motions were wooden and spiritless. She didn't lock onto the baby's eyes with wonder and delight the way new mothers usually do.

After four or five weeks of therapy, Natasha's mother could revel in the experience of making direct eye contact, however fleeting, with her daughter and of occasionally eliciting a smile from her. "Then we knew we were connecting with the baby," Dr. Goodman told me. At about the same time, Natasha's mother also began to make eye contact with him.

Over the next two to three months, baby Natasha gradually gained weight and learned to make regular eye contact, smile, wriggle, and hold her body like a more normal infant. At three months, she was discharged and continued to do well over a one-year follow-up period.

What happened? Was this a miracle of modern medicine? No, it was a miracle of love. Dr. Goodman taught Natasha's mother how to relate to her child and inspired her to do so. He showed her how to hold, cuddle, coo over, and smile at her baby. He demonstrated how to make feeding into a loving ritual, with hugging, stroking, talking, smiling, and lots of eye contact. At the same time, he related to the mother as well, giving her caring support in her efforts to parent.

When Natasha's mother was at work during the day, hospital staff acted like an extended family, fussing over the baby and providing for her needs. At night, Natasha's mother slept on the ward in the same room with the child.

Like all good therapists, Dr. Goodman was building an empathic relationship with the mother and child, and helping them to relate better to each other. Dr. Goodman did more than offer a role model for the mother; he offered, he said, a "direct emotional relationship that filled past deprivations" in the lives of mother and child. He was "touching their lives to support aspects of them that had never been touched before."

Healing relationships are inspiring for everyone involved. When Dr. Goodman reached deeply into his own capacity to care and helped to bring about a wonderful result, it touched him as well as those he was helping.

Childhood Leaves an Imprint

If Natasha had survived her childhood without her mother's receiving help, the infant would have brought into adulthood the scars of her early deprivation. But as already noted, it would probably have been difficult to identify them. Psychiatrists who believe in genetics and biology would have discounted the importance or ignored the existence of the early deprivation.

Although the original devastating relationship problems in infancy are usually long forgotten by the time adults seek help, improved relationships remain key to healing the older child or adult. Regardless of the cause, human beings in profound emotional distress are most effectively healed by safe, caring, meaningful relationships. In fact, the more desperate an adult's condition, the more likely the problems extend back into early childhood or infancy, and the more surely the "infant" continues to need to be healed.

Research Confirmation of Our Human Needs — Even in Animals

The story of Natasha's difficulties and subsequent healing has been confirmed by clinical experience and research from multiple sources over several decades. Studies of infants and small children have shown that separation from parents can cause them to wither emotionally and, in the extreme, to die.[2] Observations of chimpanzees and apes in the wild have shown that, much like human children, they withdraw into depression when a parent is ill or absent, and eventually will fail to thrive and die. They, too, can be revived by renewed parenting from another animal or, in some cases, from a human being who rescues them from abandonment and provides caring attention.[3]

Almost any parent's experience will confirm that raising an infant requires enormous personal resources and reserves. Whenever the parent is even a little bit "out of sorts," the infant is likely to respond by fretting or failing to eat or sleep. Nowadays parents often lack an extended family to step in when they start to feel exhausted or stressed by parenting chores. In a vicious cycle, the baby then reacts to the parent's stress, and both parent and child increasingly cause upset in each other.

Again, as most parents can verify, when another person intervenes in the middle of this downward spiral, the infant or baby often responds instantly to being held or played with by the newcomer. That's probably because the new caretaker isn't overstressed and locked into escalating conflict with the child.

Really Getting to Know Children

There are programs for helping older children and teenagers that apply the same relationship principles—including no use of psychoactive drugs—that Dr. Goodman used with Natasha and her mother. Jennie was only nine years old when she was admitted to Seneca Center, near Oakland, California, where Tony Stanton, M.D. is the consulting psychiatrist for the children's residential program. Seneca Center takes relatively young children, those age six to thirteen, who have failed everywhere else. Nearly all are violent when they arrive. If Seneca were not available to help them, many would eventually end up in juvenile detention or a state mental hospital.

As young and innocent as Jennie seemed, when she stepped into a room, her response "was to attack the first person she saw," Dr. Stanton told me. "You would look at her and wonder, 'How could this be?' She was a cute little blond child." The answer lies in part in Jennie's chaotic home; Jennie's mother had been unable to protect her child from her boyfriend's physical and sexual abuse.

Before Jennie arrived at Seneca Center, a mishmash of drugs and three years of previous residential treatment had failed to control her rage attacks or to enable her to function in school. Dr. Stanton immediately began to withdraw Jennie from three different psychiatric drugs, one at a time.[4] The staff went to work developing relationships with her in a small cottage for six children and in Seneca Center's school.

Dr. Stanton has succeeded in removing all two hundred of his children from psychoactive drugs at Seneca House. Like most of the other children, Jennie became drug-free in a little more than one month. This kind of relatively rapid withdrawal from psychoactive drugs requires careful supervision, often in a residential setting. Meanwhile, her previously persistent violence became occasional. Now that she wasn't taking psychoactive drugs, Dr. Stanton explained, "You saw the child's basic being that had been covered over by all the abuse and drugs. She was delightful. The staff liked her very much."

Within a few more months, Jennie was no longer violent at all and was doing spectacularly well in school. Her stay at Seneca Center lasted two years before she was released to a foster home, where she continued to do well and to thrive in school.

Seneca Center was founded on the belief that children could be helped through relationships and firm, clear limits. Dr. Stanton and his colleagues have developed a treatment philosophy based on the conviction that distressed and emotionally upset children are suffering from deprivation and trauma, and they need "safety, predictability, and engagement."

Children need to feel protected from the aggression of others. Children also need to feel that adults will intervene to help them to control their own aggressive impulses. When children do feel safe, they can begin to identify what they really think and feel, and to share these thoughts and feelings with others.

Dr. Stanton, like most experienced clinicians, believes that it is important to intervene quickly in a nonpunitive way at the least threat of violence. Aggression should not be allowed to escalate. Instead of severe punishment, the control of aggression should be maintained and there should be a sufficient number of caring, engaged adults in the child's environment. Dr. Stanton also finds that children who are raised in a safe environment do not become violent.

Instead of diagnosing children, Dr. Stanton emphasized getting to know their individual stories. He has found that diagnoses, rather than helping to describe a child's problems, actually obscure and minimize them. Dreadful realities in the child's life are reduced to a category such as "ADHD," "major depression" or "conduct disorder," all of which distract from the underlying tragic stories.

In place of a diagnostic label, Dr. Stanton created a two- or three-page Table of Life Events for Jennie. As with most of the other children, the summary of Jennie's life was filled with heart-rending details of loss and abuse. Having the child's story so readily available helps the staff keep in mind why the child needs empathic caring.

Drawing lessons for all children, Dr. Stanton observed, "The more we address children's actual lives, and make sure that they have safety and predictability, as well as true engagement with adults, the more they thrive. We need both to empower our children and to be curious about their actual lives. This is what is being lost these days throughout our culture."

Dr. Stanton rejects the idea that some children need to be medicated to control their behavior at school or at home. When he finds that a child is on medication, it makes him ask, "Is the child really safe? Is he really in a predictable environment? And is he really with caretakers who are deeply involved with his life?" In a 1999 report about Seneca Center, Dr. Stanton wrote, "We do not believe it is of any use to blame anyone for a child's difficulties. We do feel, however, that families and society need to look carefully at the context of children's lives and to take responsibility for assuring their safety and nurturance."[5]

There is no difference in essence between the needs of severely disturbed children and those of all children. All children need the safety, predictability, and engagement that the staff strive to bring into the lives of the patients at Seneca Center. A good therapeutic setting temporarily substitutes for an effective family and intensifies the process of healing for children who are in dire need.

The Critical Moment of Healing

Although Seneca Center is located in California, Dr. Stanton lives and also works part time in Bremerton, Washington, at the outpatient clinic of Kitsap Mental Health Center. In 1995 Vance Sherman, M.D. joined Dr. Stanton in the clinic and became attending psychiatrist for the mental health center's ten-bed adolescent unit.

The Kitsap Mental Health Center inpatient ward treats about 130 youngsters a year, typically for a maximum allowable stay of thirty days. The children are older than those at Seneca Center, ranging in age from twelve to seventeen years old. They include the most disturbed and violent youngsters in the community.

Twelve-year-old Ricky had grown up amid emotional and physical abuse. After he became violent at home and rebellious at school, his mother sent him to visit his grandparents in Washington State and then refused to take him back. The grandparents brought Ricky to a psychiatrist, who eventually put him on four psychiatric drugs at once, two of them FDA-approved for adults only. When he continued to get worse, the boy was admitted to the inpatient unit at Kitsap Mental Health Center.

The first task in treating hospitalized children, Dr. Sherman explained to me, is to create a safe environment. The second is to find at least one staff member who is capable of engaging the child or teenager. The third is to involve the youngster in structured activities that build healthy relationships with staff members and with other youngsters.

Like Ricky, most of the youngsters are on psychiatric drugs when they arrive at the hospital. If they stay for the full thirty days, Dr. Sherman is always able to withdraw them from drugs. Those who are discharged too soon are withdrawn in the outpatient clinic. With daily monitoring, Ricky was able to stop taking all four drugs in the surprisingly short time of two weeks. This could be accomplished safely because of the intensive clinical supervision in the inpatient unit.

Since he had no family to return to, Ricky stayed for an extended three-month treatment period in the in-patient unit. When Ricky was free of drugs, it became apparent that he had few or no social or con- flict resolution skills, and had a limited ability to handle frustration. The behaviors that had been called symptoms of various "psychiatric disorders" were manifestations of his lack of psychosocial develop- ment. Over the three months he spent on the unit, he improved so rapidly that by the end he had become a role model for incoming children.

Ricky was next transferred to a therapeutic foster home and re- mained in the school associated with Kitsap Mental Health Center, where the teacher took a special interest in him. Testing showed that the twelve-year-old was reading on the level of a senior in high school. Ricky's previously unrecognized superior ability had left him bored in school. Six months after his discharge from the hospital, he continued to do well in both his foster home and in school. He was soon "main- streamed" to the local public school.

Before coming to Kitsap Mental Health Center, Ricky had been given multiple psychiatric diagnoses, including ADHD, oppositional defiant disorder, and bipolar disorder (manic-depression) with psy- chotic features. From Dr. Sherman's viewpoint, it makes no sense to give any psychiatric diagnoses—except perhaps posttraumatic stress disorder—to children who have been subjected to or are recovering from stress.

In Dr. Sherman's experience children who are given labels such as bipolar disorder, schizophrenia, and major depression have been "traumatized and overwhelmed" by their life experiences. Most have been victimized by sexual or physical abuse and severe neglect in chaotic homes. Many of the homes that caused these marked distur- bances in children were grossly disordered and violent. Commonly, one or both parents suffered from drug or alcohol abuse.

Dr. Sherman observes, "There's no doubt at all that trauma can make children crazy. A history of trauma is the major characteristic of children who come to us for help. Almost all of them have been physically and sexually abused. It's very different from working with adults because with adults you're too removed in time from the original stress and trauma. Adults frequently have lost the context of what was causing such 'overwhelm' in their lives. As adults, their lifestyle, including harmful relationships, and illegal or prescription drug use, covers up what originally happened to them. With children, you see them in the middle of the crisis and the trauma that's causing it. As a doctor who doesn't drug children, you can see how their feelings are caused by what's going on in their lives. You're not blinded into believing in genetic or biochemical theories. Instead, you really see the results of the trauma.

"Drug therapy in my experience only serves to sedate the child's expression of frustration about his current life situation. It makes for a more manageable inmate. The tragedy is that when children are drugged with substances that suppress their emotions it prevents them from benefiting from the most important aspect of the therapy—engaging the staff and peers. I really see drugs as an impediment to that process of engagement with the staff and their peers, and their own families. Relating with people in more healthy ways is what gets the children's psychosocial development back on track."

When a child first arrives on the ward at Kitsap Mental Health Center, there's almost always a brief lag before, all of a sudden, he or she starts doing better. In a very predictable fashion, Dr. Sherman can pinpoint the moment at which a child is about to make these major improvements. The moment occurs when one of staff members says, in one way or another, "I really like this kid." In Ricky's case, he was initially so difficult to reach that it was not until the second month that several of the staff began to feel that way about him.

The Importance of Families

If at least one staff member at Kitsap Mental Health Center always finds a way to care about and to like the individual children who are admitted to the unit, why haven't other people done the same before the youngsters got into so much difficulty? In some cases, of course, parents or other adults have loved the children but have been unable, for varied reasons, to reach them. Often the child's living conditions in the home or foster-care situation have been too destructive for anyone to offer effective help. Ricky's mother, who had serious personal problems of her own, let Ricky get "out of control." She then abandoned him to her own parents, who were too elderly to handle a rambunctious twelve-year-old child.

Because families are the key to long-term healing, the clinic tries to involve parents in the treatment from the time of admission. Families then become the entire basis of the treatment after the child's discharge from the hospital into the clinic. "We try not to identify the child as the problem but instead we work with the whole family system," says Dr. Sherman. The therapeutic work is similar to what takes place in my private practice, as I have described in this book. The aim is to identify harmful interactions within the family and to replace them with more empathic, rational, and loving ones.

In rare cases, such as Ricky's, the clinic may recommend the removal of the child from the family. However, when families cooperate to learn new ways of engaging their children and creating a more peaceful and organized home life, the child and family prospers together.

Creating a Spiritual Outpatient Sanctuary

The psychologist Kevin McCready, Ph.D., is the founder and director of the San Joaquin Psychotherapy Center in Clovis, California, near Fresno. For over a decade, Dr. McCready has been treating children and adults—including the most disturbed—without resort to psychiatric drugs.

The San Joaquin Psychotherapy Clinic provides services five days a week during the daytime only, but is often able to help adults and children who have not benefitted, or who have gotten worse, from repeated hospitalizations and heavy drug regimens. By means of a combination of individual and group activities, people who need intensive care can receive it throughout the day. Usually they are able to withdraw from psychiatric drugs.

Dr. McCready builds his treatment on a strong philosophy of individual self-respect and responsibility. He avoids making clients feel like "mental patients" who cannot take care of or control themselves, and encourages them instead to take responsibility for their actions. Even emotionally disturbed individuals who have previously seemed "out of control" often reach a new level of functioning in response to these higher expectations from the professionals who staff the clinic's therapeutic environment.

Dr. McCready believes that parents must rebuild their faith in themselves and learn to take care of their own personal needs as the first steps toward helping their children. He compares this to the familiar emergency instructions that airline flight attendants give to passengers before takeoff: First put on your own oxygen mask, and then your child's. A parent gasping for spiritual air is no more able to adequately take care of a child than a parent gasping for oxygen.

To build healing relationships with their child patients, Dr. McCready and his staff use counseling, play therapy, games, art, seminars, and trips outside the clinic. Parents are counseled about how to strengthen their own ability to relate to their children.

Dr. McCready's own spirituality inspires and permeates his work. His clinic is his calling and its practices are spiritual as well as psychological in their aim. Staff and the patients come from a variety of secular and religious backgrounds. All, however, share an appreciation for and commitment to overcoming emotional problems by developing positive aspects of our humanity rather than suppressing passion with drugs.

For Dr. McCready, compassion is an essential ingredient in any healing relationship: "The word 'compassion' means 'to suffer together.' " Suffering, he explained to me, is the common denominator of human existence that brings us together: "Our shared suffering gives us our understanding of each other." Instead of suppressing passion with drugs, Dr. McCready encourages painful feelings to be shared in order to develop self-understanding and to build relationships. As Drs. Stanton and Sherman have observed, and as my own practice confirms, Dr. McCready finds that most children are easily withdrawn from psychiatric drugs.

I have known Dr. McCready as a close friend and colleague for many years, have participated in seminars with him, and have given workshops for the benefit of his clinic. The San Joaquin Psychotherapy Center clinic offers a model program for treating children, adults, and families with caring human services. Wholly committed to psychosocial therapy without resort to drugs, Dr. McCready's clinic often helps people who have despaired of ever finding help. It welcomes patients from around the country and from overseas. (Dr. McCready and his clinic can be reached at the following address: Kevin McCready, Ph.D., Director, San Joaquin Psychotherapy Center, 3114 Willow Street, Clovis, California 93612. Phone: 559-292-7572.)

Open Forum Counseling

Many families and children do not need the intense treatment offered by clinics and hospitals. Yet they may be too distressed to get all they need from parenting books, groups, or classes. For some of these families, individual counseling can be very helpful; but not everyone can afford it and good counselors can be hard to locate.

There are many alternative approaches to helping families and their children. One model is the child guidance clinic prototype developed by the psychologist Alfred Adler in Europe before World War II.[6] These clinics continue to operate throughout the world, including the United States, under the name Open Forum Counseling.[7]

Consistent with the healing approaches described in this book, Adler insisted on parents' and teachers' accompanying children to the clinic, and he oriented his therapy around the family. He believed that children, like adults, could be addressed in a rational manner about their problems and about ways to solve them. He emphasized "social interest"—caring or meaningful relationships. He de-emphasized punishment and authoritarian control in favor of relationship, mutual understanding, and reason.

In order to help more people, Adler asked individual families to volunteer to work with him in front of a group of parents, children, teachers, clinicians, and community members in the spirit of helping each other. These demonstrations were aimed at strengthening, encouraging, and educating everyone who attended.

Linda Jessup, a registered nurse with a master's in public health, is executive director of the Parent Encouragement Program in Kensington, Maryland, an Adlerian family education center.[8] Ms. Jessup explained to me, "Adler believed that learning is the basis of almost everything human beings do. The demonstration counseling takes an educational approach to working with children and their parents to help them learn to get along and cooperate harmoniously in a family." Jessup described the model as helping to "spring people out of the mode of being broken. The family is called the co-educator family. It is not there to get fixed but to educate an audience of observers about problems that all families share. Instead of being a 'problem family,' you are family that has something of value to learn and, most important, something to contribute to other people's learning. The idea is that difficulties are not to be hidden, not to be ashamed of, but to be shared so that everybody benefits."

The Open Forum's public setting helps families and their children feel better about themselves when they discover that their problems aren't unique. Because the family demonstrations are viewed as educational rather than therapeutic, people are more willing to participate in an open, sharing manner.

Great emphasis is placed on adults', including therapists', admitting that they too make mistakes.[9] A child's self-esteem can be helped by hearing therapists admit to having faults.

As I find in my practice, Ms. Jessup reports that children respond to respectful attention by participating more actively than their parents could have previously imagined. Children who are "terrors" in other settings will settle down and participate enthusiastically, and make particularly insightful observations.

Helping the Most Seriously Disturbed Individuals

Advocates of psychosocial approaches (those based on human services rather than physical interventions) are often asked to show that their methods can "work" with the most severely disturbed individuals. In fact, the value and superiority of psychosocial approaches in healing the most disturbed patients, children and adults, has been well documented in the literature.[10] Indeed, the greatest achievement of psychosocial approaches lies in their effectiveness for adults labeled acutely or chronically "schizophrenic," for these patients tend to be much more difficult to help than children. Thus, if even these adults can be helped by meaningful relationships, it becomes easier to understand their effectiveness with children.

In the Snake Pit

Because I place so much emphasis on psychosocial and spiritual approaches, skeptics wonder whether my experience has been confined to "easy" patients in my private practice. To the contrary, for many patients who come to me—adults and children alike—I am a doctor of last resort. They have gotten worse after years of psychiatric drugs, electroshock, and multiple hospitalizations. But perhaps more to the point, I originally learned about the power of healing through relationship when working with the most difficult patients of all, chronically disabled inmates confined to the back wards of a state mental hospital.

My introduction to psychiatry began when I was a young college student volunteer working with the most disturbed, distressed, and potentially violent children and adults in an old-fashioned "snake pit" state mental hospital. The adults were confined to the male and female violent wards, and the children were housed separately in a large dismal building.

These children and adults were at the end of society's road to nowhere. Most were considered beyond help and, from the community's viewpoint, untouchable. Even in the hospital, no one wanted to have anything to do with them. Their lives were lonely in the extreme.

With rare exceptions, these adults would live the remainder of their lives locked up in dark, barren dungeons devoid of the most simple amenities and pleasures. Many of the children would eventually end up as chronic inmates in adult hospitals or prisons.

It was 1954—my undergraduate freshman year at Harvard College—when I first stepped onto the wards of Metropolitan State Hospital in Waltham, Massachusetts. This was the inaugural year of the Harvard-Radcliffe Mental Hospital Volunteer Program and we began by flooding the asylum with hundreds of fresh faces. We wanted to perk up the inmates with relationships as well as social and recreational activities.

Soon after getting a foothold in the hospital, we stole the keys to the back wards to provide ourselves regular access to the wards without being supervised or managed. In our youthful enthusiasm, one day two of us took the whole women's violent ward into town on an unauthorized outing and returned without incident several hours later.

Many of us developed close relationships with patients and learned, through them, that there was little difference between college students and hospital inmates, except perhaps for grave misfortunes in life. As much as any people I have worked with, they usually proved worthy of the trust we gave them. In the face of the harsh realities and often abusive practices of the hospital, college students and patients banded together to keep each other out of trouble with the authorities.

During my four years in the program, with many hundreds of students coming and going, not a single one of us was ever hurt by a patient, even when we stayed individually by ourselves on locked violent wards. None of us, as far as I know, was ever seriously threatened or endangered by a patient. But, in contrast, there were frightening encounters with the hospital staff.

On several occasions, students came upon ward personnel physically assaulting a patient. Each time, the perpetrators backed off at the sight of the volunteer. We began to find that our mere presence helped to make the institution a bit safer for the inmates. In a more frightening encounter, one of our female volunteers, a Radcliffe student, was mistaken for a patient by a male hospital attendant. The attendant tried to bully her into having sex with him by threatening to transfer her to a worse ward. To his chagrin, he then realized she wasn't a patient. To this day, much of the supposed violence of psychiatric patients in hospitals is in reaction to humiliation and abuse at the hands of staff.

As director of the volunteer program in its second and third years, I created a special experimental project called the case aide program. A select group of fourteen students, including me, were assigned our own individual patients to work with throughout the school year. Almost all the inmates carried severe diagnoses like "paranoid schizophrenia" and "psychotic depression." They were, after all, state hospital inmates with little hope of ever getting out. Many were older adults, but some young adults were also involved.

Without any recourse to psychiatric drugs—the so-called antipsychotic drugs had not yet inundated Metropolitan State—we helped eleven of fourteen patients get out of the hospital. Only three of them returned during the one-to-two-year follow-up period. We didn't need a controlled clinical trial to show that this was a significant accomplishment because Metropolitan State, like most hospitals of the era, hardly ever discharged any of the longer-term patients. In any event, the new drugs could not have accomplished what we did. Even after the "antipsychotics" had been given to tens of thousands of patients for years at a time, few of these people were discharged until a change of administrative policy forced them out a decade or more later.[11] The drugs merely made the patients more docile and hence manageable. By any standards, our results were miraculous.

Remarkably, the case aid program was then incorporated into an undergraduate credit course at Harvard College. Students worked with their own individual patients while taking a psychology seminar.

The success of our college volunteer case aide program was based on relating to the patients—providing caring companionship. Not yet jaded by professional training, we described and wrote about ourselves as offering love to our patients. We also tried to identify and to meet their needs for such ordinary things as the right size shoes or

clothes, health care, recreation, and contacts with family—all of
which were typically neglected by the hospital.

The case aide program and the entire Harvard-Radcliffe Mental
Hospital Volunteer Program continued to operate effectively long
after I graduated from college and then medical school. In 1961 the
volunteer project was described by a major presidential commission as
one of the potential solutions to the crisis created by thousands of inmates languishing without effective help in the state mental hospitals.
A year later we published a book about the program.[12]

In the 1970s, biological psychiatry began its takeover of the profession. The marvelous Harvard-Radcliffe Mental Hospital Volunteer
Program, like all other successful psychosocial interventions, was
plowed under by advocates of biological theories, drugs, and electroshock. It no longer exists.

Soteria House: Creating Shared Meaning

Thus far I've shown how disturbed infants, children, and youths as
well as chronic hospital inmates can benefit from relationship interventions rather than drugs. What about young people undergoing
their first diagnosed episode of "schizophrenia"? This is the arena in
which the drugs are supposedly indispensable.

The psychiatrist Dr. Loren Mosher is now a consultant with Soteria
Associates in San Diego, California. In the 1960s, as director of the
center for schizophrenia research at the National Institute of Mental
Health (NIMH), Dr. Mosher created Soteria House, a residential
treatment program that proved it could help the great majority of
people undergoing their first "schizophrenic" episode without resort
to psychiatric drugs.[13]

Soteria House was made part of a scientifically controlled clinical
trial to test its efficacy. Some patients were sent through the regular
psychiatric hospital treatment program and others, randomly se-
lected, were placed in Soteria House. All of the hospitalized patients
received psychiatric drug treatment for an extended period of time. At
Soteria House, an effort was made to keep all patients off psychiatric
drugs, but approximately 10 percent ended up receiving them for an
extended period of time.

The Soteria patients were treated noncoercively in a homelike setting in a house on a residential street. The staff were chosen for their
ability to listen, to care, and to be tolerant of differences, rather than

on the basis of professional training. The positions ended up being filled by nonprofessionals because they tended to fit the required personal characteristics better than professionals.

Dr. Mosher explained to me that "schizophrenia" can be viewed as a breakdown of the person's ability to create a shared meaning with other human beings. Therefore, he said, "the basic intervention at Soteria was the establishment of a relationship in which shared meaning and understanding emerged. When you and the other person share an understanding of what is going on [between you and in life], you have an engagement." Engagement heals psychosis.

In my clinical experience, engaging someone who seems irrational and bizarre requires a welcoming attitude toward any and all communications. Many virtues must be practiced by the therapist: patience, gentleness, tact, understanding, empathy, a willingness to take seriously almost any unexpected viewpoint, a curiosity about where the perspective developed and what it means in the person's life, a comfort with the other person's distrust, and a willingness to share your own related views in a thoughtful, sensitive manner.

To relate to a person who has been emotionally injured and driven into private fantasies also requires the creation of a safe and comfortable environment. To do this, the therapist or companion must be willing and able to be present without controlling the other person's thoughts and behavior.

Measured by criteria such as the patients' ability to return to their families and to work, and to live independently, Soteria's largely drug-free approach worked as well or better than drug treatment in psychiatric hospitals. More important, it inspired patients to believe in themselves and in other people—rather than in doctors and drugs. In addition, the drug-free patients were not exposed to the extreme risk of developing drug-induced permanent neurological disorders.[14]

Soteria House was so successful that, like the Harvard-Radcliffe Mental Health Volunteer program, it became a threat to the psychiatric establishment. Biological psychiatry intervened to crush it. Its research funding was withdrawn, insurance companies refused to pay for its services, and eventually Dr. Mosher was removed from his post at NIMH. Despite many scientific papers proving the efficacy of Soteria House's approach, nothing like Soteria House is operating anywhere in the world today.

Because of the legalities involved in enrolling children in an experimental program, Soteria House treated only a very few youngsters under the age of eighteen. However, many young adults eighteen and older went through the program successfully. According to Dr. Mosher, several other Soteria-like programs for children were effective, but they too failed to receive support from organized psychiatry or the insurance companies. They, too, no longer exist. Dr. Mosher is certain that children benefit at least as much as adults from the Soteria approach.

Replacing Coercion with Respect

All successful healing programs attempt to minimize the use of restrictions and coercion. In part because oppressive techniques are so common in therapeutic settings, the federal government funds Protection and Advocacy agencies in each of the states. I met Linda "Pax" Linson, who has a master's degree in psychology, when she was director of a regional office for the Protection and Advocacy System in Fairbanks, Alaska. One of her tasks was to advocate for children with disabilities, which often brought her into the schools and mental hospitals.

Ms. Linson points out that from foster homes to prisons, we tend to treat our most vulnerable children as if all that matters is their outward behavior rather than how they actually feel and think. "The tendency is to correct the behavior by placing restrictions on the children. But cracking down on these kids makes them worse. It causes them to be violent."

According to Ms. Linson, treatment too often ignores the fact that the child's anger and violence often originally resulted from too much irrational manipulation, as well as outright brutality. "My experience is that when we provide those same youngsters with respect, we find that their problematic behaviors disappear. In 99 percent of the cases, if you can find a way to empower the children—to give them some responsibility and to get rid of the restrictions—they start to live up to a higher standard of conduct."

The Grateful Therapist

During more than thirty years in private practice, I have developed an increasing sense that being a therapist is a sacred trust and an honor. It is also an extraordinary opportunity to care about and to help people while getting to know them on levels that we seldom have the opportunity to share with anyone. I believe that a good therapist is a grateful therapist.[15]

Despite my many years in private practice, I've yet to experience anything close to burnout. Counting back to when I first became a volunteer in a state hospital, I've been in the field for more than forty-five years without any sense that it's been long enough, let alone too long. Instead, I am renewed from day to day by working directly with people who want help.

I experience daily wonderment at being able to meet people for conversations that plumb the depths of the human experience, while managing to help them through my presence as a caring person. It involves patience and tact as well. In one of our conversations, the psychoanalytic therapist Bertram Karon called it "treating people with unambiguous kindness."

Of course there's more to therapy than just "being there." Therapy is enhanced, I am sure, by the wisdom and skill accumulated and honed from years of clinical practice and living. But the key lies in being present as a warm, welcoming, empathic human being who inspires others to have confidence and faith in themselves.

None of us can radiate a healing presence all the time, but when we do, we are at our best as therapists, parents, or teachers. All helping relationships require this healing presence.[16]

Creating Ideal Healing Centers in Varied Settings

As this chapter demonstrates, the healing of even the most severe mental and emotional disorders does not require treatment in a traditional psychiatric hospital or the use of medication. Medical supervision or consultations can be useful and sometimes are necessary during the process of withdrawing children or adults from drugs, but even in supervising drug withdrawal, experience and knowledge are more important than a medical degree.[17]

Havens that offer healing to distressed and disturbed children do not need to be directed or supervised by physicians, although they many wish to have physicians available for consultations. Drs. Sherman, Stanton, and Mosher are psychiatrists, but their approach to therapy did not require medical training. Dr. McCready, a psychologist, runs an intensive, multidimensional day clinic that enables patients to discontinue psychiatric medication. Soteria House was created by Dr. Mosher, but it was run on a daily basis by a social worker, Alma Menn. Drop-in centers have also been created and managed by former patients who call themselves psychiatric survivors.[18] In reality, healing havens could be developed within a variety of contexts such as community clinics, schools, and churches.

There are strong historical precedents for basing therapeutic havens or asylums on nonmedical principles. From the mid–eighteenth to the late nineteenth century, the best asylums were operated more like schools or churches. They based themselves on "moral principles" and so the era and the approach was called "moral psychiatry."[19] These humane institutions drew on a combination of Enlightenment principles of liberty and rationality as reflected in the writings of Thomas Jefferson, combined with Judeo-Christian principles of love, kindness, and charity as found in the Bible. Unlike the case with modern materialistic psychiatry, these higher ideals were openly espoused as the guiding principles of treatment.

Moral psychiatry was not without flaws. It often operated on very authoritarian religious principles and restraint and toxic drugs were not always completely eliminated. But as far as historians can ascertain, these asylums were far more humane and human-service oriented than modern psychiatric hospitals, used far fewer restraints or toxic agents, and proved at least as effective in helping the most disturbed patients as the best contemporary mental hospitals.

Alcoholics Anonymous (AA) provides a more modern model for a combined therapeutic and spiritual approach that allows for a variety of secular and religious convictions among its participants. Many young people flock to AA meetings even though they remain skeptical about the existence of a Higher Power. In Chapter 10, we saw how a public school—Phoenix in Montgomery County, Maryland—was based on a Twelve Step approach to the healing of children who abuse drugs. Phoenix provides better "treatment" for children with drug and alcohol problems than any medical setting could.

I am not arguing for a takeover of the mental health field by organizations with specific religious or spiritual viewpoints. I am Jewish, and I espouse humanistic values such as love and spiritual values such as a belief in ideals beyond the individual. My aim is to liberate all ethical and spiritual orientations—religious and humanistic alike—from the dominating presence of biopsychiatry. What we need is a variety of ethical therapeutic approaches rooted in both secular and religious principles.

Finding the Right Professionals

Local clinics, schools, churches, and other groups may at first find it difficult to locate health professionals who do not advocate drugs and diagnoses. Nonetheless, in my experience there are many of them in most communities. Although they typically try to keep a low profile in order to avoid attack and ostracism by local psychiatrists, there are ways to locate them, such as holding a conference.

Professionals from outside the community can be brought in for a conference on subjects such as "Counseling Families and Children Without Resort to Psychiatric Drugs."[20] The conference can become a springboard for the creation of a referral list of like-minded professionals within the community or for the planning of a clinic in the church or community that refrains from using drugs.

Even More Than Other Children

There are many good reasons *not* to view severely distressed children as inherently different in their needs from other children. When we get to know a very disturbed child, we discover a large window into our own human vulnerabilities and needs. The most disturbed and desperately in need of help are as human as the rest of us—just more obviously so.

If we believe that some children are impossible to reach through caring relationship, we make them something less than human. This in turn justifies inhumane, abusive practices such as beatings, physical restraints, humiliating incarceration in psychiatric hospitals and juvenile centers, psychoactive drugs, and electroshock. Many of the children at facilities like Seneca Center, Kitsap Mental Health Center, and the San Joaquin Psychotherapy Center—as well as in my own clinical practice—have spent many prior years suffering the adverse effects of authoritarian therapists, psychiatric drugs, and even inhumane residential confinement.

Furthermore, the idea that *some* children are unreachable creates a slippery slope. Before we know it, the mental health profession and the drug companies will expand the notion to include *many* children. In fact, this process has already begun. In the 1970s, there was a public uproar, outraged books, and congressional hearings about one hundred thousand children being prescribed Ritalin.[21] Now hardly anyone even remembers that controversy. Instead, *millions* of children are taking stimulant drugs with hardly any outcry at all.[22] Biological psychiatry has also pushed for more electroshock and psychosurgery for children.[23]

Finally, drastic treatments, including the more powerful psychiatric drugs and electroshock, have no proven value in the treatment of children who are severely disturbed. No drugs are FDA-approved for treatment of childhood diagnoses such as depression, mania, manic-depression, autism, schizophrenia, and conduct disorder.[24] Similarly, none are approved for treating suicide or violence.

Especially since the school shootings in the spring of 1999, fear of violent children and youths has been used to justify drugging even greater numbers of children. But, as demonstrated in Chapter 7, anti-depressants and stimulants very frequently *cause* behavioral abnormalities in children, including violence. A fear of violence in young people should discourage the practice of prescribing psychiatry drugs to them.

What do disturbed and violent children need? What all children need—kind and gentle care. They should get the best we have to offer—empathic relationships with trustworthy adults.

All Our Children

From infancy to old age, human relationships are the most powerful healing force for psychological and spiritual suffering of every kind, including extremes of violence and psychosis. This becomes particularly obvious in the treatment of children because they are usually quickly responsive to caring interventions.

Because children have the same basic needs regardless of the setting into which we put them, the characteristics of a model "mental health program" are similar to those of the "model school" described in Chapter 10, as well as the successful family described in Chapter 11.[25] Families, schools, and therapy centers alike should be based on providing sanctuary and caring individual relationships between children and adults.

13

Devoting Ourselves to Children

———◀•◆•▶———

Our personal identity builds upon our experiences with other people, from parents who nurture and guide us to friends who sustain us to teachers who inspire us and leaders who give us direction. For children, these relationships are the primary factors in their growth and development. For adults they determine much of the quality of our lives and what we accomplish.

Because relationships are so basic to who we are, they can also injure and even destroy us. Too often, our children suffer from insufficient or harmful interactions with us. From family and school life to government policies, we need to reassert the importance of children; we need to commit ourselves to meeting their needs, even at the sacrifice of some of our other adult interests.

The Litmus Test for Children's Issues

When making decisions about children, we need to ask ourselves, "How will these choices affect our *relationships* with the children? Will these decisions ultimately further mutual love and respect—or will they inflame conflict and estrangement?" For example, a family may seem to be running efficiently and even peacefully, but if the parents are not engaged with their children, the family will fail to raise healthy, secure, and caring youngsters. Similarly, a school may promote academic performance, but if the teachers fail to create inspiring relationships with students, the school will not empower the youngsters with sound ethics and a love of learning.

Making relationship primary becomes more complicated when dealing with larger institutions such as schools, therapeutic havens, or community centers. The complexity can become overwhelming when dealing with yet larger societal issues, such as the inadequate health care, poverty, and violence in the lives of our children. However, I believe that the primary question still remains, "How will policy decisions on these issues affect relationships between adults and children?"

Even on a national policy level, relationships should be of primary concern. Policies aimed at providing children with better access to schools, health care, or food will prove positive in the long run only if they strengthen, rather than disrupt, the child's relationships in the family and community.

All existing and proposed national policies should be required to pass the litmus test of their impact on our children's relationships with us. If concern for children were put first, national policies in many arenas, from education and health care to gun control, would take a decidedly different direction. Seemingly urgent adult interests would be made secondary to the interests of children.

Political principles often come in conflict with each other. Freedom from government control over the ownership of guns and automobiles, for example, conflicts with the need for children to be protected by compulsory trigger locks and safety seats. The balance between the principle of liberty and the principle of love or caring is difficult to maintain, and there are no simple resolutions of the conflicts.[1] But the cacophony created by demanding lobbying groups has been allowed to drown out the cries of our children. It's time to right the balance in favor of our silenced and unheard children.

What Parenting and Other Relationships Can Do

The family is the natural center of any child's psychological, moral, and spiritual development. When children run into difficulties, as parents we are their first line of defense and their best potential source of nurturing, guidance, and healing. The parenting relationship can be more basic than food in the lives of children: Without a loving caretaker, an infant may actually reject nourishment and fail to thrive.

In short, our children need our *personal devotion*. They need it from the day they are born until they become mature adults. Often they continue to need us long after they have grown up, much as we continue to need them, for love and spiritual sustenance.

Beyond Parenting

Without diminishing the enormous value of even one meaningful relationship in a child's life, we must also face the limitations on how much we can accomplish as individual parents, teachers, or caretakers. Being the best possible caregiver is not enough to guarantee that children will do well. To think that parents or teachers by themselves can make all the difference is a prescription for disillusionment and failure.

Being a good parent will help in almost every way, but it cannot fully protect your sons and daughters from dying in gun-related accidents while visiting in a neighbor's home, being killed in car accidents caused by someone else, or developing diseases such as asthma or cancer that are caused or aggravated by environmental pollution. Your parenting won't always prevent your children from being enticed into drugs by peer pressure. Nor will it completely protect them from the consequences of inadequate health-care insurance, abandonment by their mother or father, peer ridicule and abuse, racism and sexism, poverty, or the economic necessity of your working outside the home to feed and clothe them.

Children are exposed to so many other people and influences that parents or other individual adults cannot by themselves create complete security. And in a world of such complex technology, parents cannot teach their children everything they need to know. Instead, society must mobilize in new and creative ways on behalf of children.

Misinformed, overtaxed, or abusive parents and teachers can cause serious distress in a child. But even then, the ultimate cause often lies in society itself, which demands so much of parents and classroom teachers while failing to develop policies that strengthen families and schools.

The Distracting Impact of Violence

There has been a great deal of emphasis, and rightly so, on the damaging effects of exposing children to violence in the media, video games, and other entertainment sources. But there's another side to this. Why are children so mesmerized by violent action heroes? Is it built into human nature? Or has the widespread neglect of children stimulated frustration and aggression in them, making them more vulnerable to the lure of violence?

So many of our children are unhappy, we need to mobilize on their behalf whether or not they pose a risk of violence or display obvious signs of distress. Above all else, we need to focus on ourselves—including society as a whole—as the source of both the suffering and the healing for our children.

The specter of children committing violence against each other appalls and frightens us. It therefore motivates some of the most hasty and ill-conceived reform efforts. We become willing to accept almost any program that promises to prevent our children from becoming a victim of a school shooting. If our schools turn into locked fortresses with security guards, key cards, and surveillance cameras, at least they're safer, we think. If one third of the students end up taking psychiatric drugs, we can tolerate that. We will even compromise our rights as parents and allow our children to be psychiatrically screened through the schools to winnow out anyone who might hurt them.

Biological psychiatry and its financial backers among the pharmaceutical companies want us to trade our liberty and our children's brains for the illusory hope of preventing violence. But biopsychiatric control of children is not only wrong in principle, it hasn't worked. The epidemic diagnosing and drugging of our children is worsening our children's lives, sometimes actually causing children to become violent, and is leading to further deterioration in our schools and families.

The Many Faces of Child Abuse

The current emphasis on culling out violent children overlooks the basic truth that they themselves are often victims of abuse.[2] The underlying problem isn't our children's violence—it's a combination of society's failure and inadequate or abusive relationships with the adults in their lives.

That children are commonly exposed to physical, emotional, and sexual abuse by adults is widely understood. That they are often exposed to peer abuse is becoming more generally recognized. In addition, children are regularly exposed to more subtle forms of coercion that are seldom appreciated. One overlooked source is biopsychiatry and another is our schools.

Medical Child Abuse

The psychiatric diagnosing and drugging of children should be viewed as a form of technological child abuse—conformity enforced by physical suppression of the brain. I do not blame the millions of parents and teachers who have been hoodwinked by organized psychiatry and medicine. Instead, I hold my colleagues responsible for this national catastrophe, especially those mental health professionals who enjoy leadership roles in professional associations, universities, government agencies, and industry. I call upon them to find the courage to stand up on behalf of children. The combined efforts of a relatively small but ethical fraction of the health profession could stem the tide of medical child abuse.

A Children's Inquisition

We have replaced social reform with a children's inquisition run by the mental health establishment. Instead of being interrogated by inquisitors, they are "evaluated" by mental health professionals. Instead of being put on the rack and imprisoned, they are drugged and hospitalized.

When almost every classroom has several children taking psychiatric drugs, the other students will try to figure out how they are supposed to behave to avoid being labeled "crazy" and "drugged." When most children have many friends and acquaintances who have been diagnosed and drugged, the lesson is not lost on them. Thus the negative effects of biopsychiatry extend beyond the millions of children who are prescribed drugs.

All children who live in this inquisitorial atmosphere will tend to doubt and to suppress their own unique ways of being. They, too, will tend to reinterpret their internal landscape in terms of whether or not they have "ADHD," "clinical depression," or some other mental disorder. Ultimately, they will become afraid of their own emotions, while feeling compelled to conform to a bland version of "normality."

By looking at them through the psychiatric lens, we are teaching our children to view themselves diagnostically, robbing them of the moral, social, and spiritual context of their own lives. How can children hope to mobilize their moral strength to overcome internal conflicts or aggressive impulses if they believe that these problems emanate from a broken brain? How can children tap their own courage and determination to become better persons, if they are taught to see their suffering as a matter of biochemical imbalances? To reverse this dreadful trend, we must take back responsibility for our children, reclaim them from the "experts," and dedicate ourselves to providing children with the adult relationships that they need.

Snuffing Out Critical Intelligence in School

Our schools also coerce children on a daily basis through the suppression of their vitality and critical intelligence. Even if they were paid to endure it, few adults would choose to spend a week, let alone endless years, subjected to the mindless conformity and rote learning demanded by most schools. "Schooling" is what the psychiatrist Dr. William Glasser calls the enforced submissiveness that is "killing students' love of learning" in most of our schools.[3]

We must join together to insist that our schools become learning sanctuaries and centers. This means becoming more active as parents and as citizens in the educating of our children, and insisting that our schools become more child-oriented.

The Need for Concerted Action

In our individual lives as adults, as well as in our social programs and national policies, we too often fail to display a deep and abiding concern for our children. There is no easy way to overcome this societal crisis. Progress will be made one person at a time, one program at a time, one genuine leader at a time, until there's sufficient momentum for the emergence of a national movement on behalf of children.

Of course, there are many private and public agencies that are concerned about the well-being of children. But their effectiveness on behalf of children is dwarfed by the influence of lobbies that promote the agendas of the gun industry, health insurers, organized medicine and psychiatry, the pharmaceutical industry, alcohol and tobacco companies, and a host of other powerful interest groups.

Because these interest groups have such great financial and political influence, none of the high-profile children's advocacy groups have come out against the mass diagnosing and drugging of our children. Among professional groups, the International Center for the Study of Psychiatry and Psychology (see Appendix B) is the exception in rejecting the chemical suppression of our children. As long as this massive experiment in social control is allowed to continue, our children's voices will remain largely silenced and their needs will go unmet.

In the 1930s, the devastating impact of the Depression on the elderly led to the creation of social security as a safety net to prevent extreme poverty and starvation among them. This was followed by Medicare, universal health insurance, for older citizens. With increasing numbers of people living into old age, Congress has become more responsive to senior citizens as a voting bloc. As an overall result, far fewer elderly now live in poverty or go without food or health care. The success of this determined effort to rescue our elderly from desperate conditions can inspire us to anticipate what could be done on behalf of children with a similar vision and concerted effort.

Many policy makers and voters seem to assume that if we take care of everything else—such as foreign affairs and the economy—children will do fine. It's not so. Probably it's more nearly the reverse: If we took better care of raising our children, we'd have a better domestic economy and fewer foreign crises. Why? Because our children would grow up to be more capable, more rational, and more devoted to peaceful conflict resolution.

Rescuing Young Inmates

Children fill our foster homes, special schools, juvenile detention centers, and psychiatric wards. Their care in these institutions too often confirms our willingness to abandon those who are most in need of us—those whom we have already hurt the most.

Prisons for juveniles are not always welcome in small communities. Though they generate jobs, they bring a potentially dangerous population into the area. Most communities are more concerned about security at these facilities than about how they treat their young inmates. But in the summer of 1999 something extraordinary took place in the small town of Dalton, Georgia: The townspeople became concerned about the living conditions of the boys and girls confined in their local detention center.

After hearing reports of "overcrowding, assaults, self-mutilation and suicide attempts," a group of citizens put up more than $100,000 to sue the state to improve the lives of the children, age nine to thirteen, some of them crammed five at a time into rooms that were built for one.[4] In the trial before a federal judge, the nightmarish story was told of a slightly built nine-year-old who tried to kill himself after being sexually assaulted by a seventeen-year-old.

The judge warned the Georgia Department of Juvenile Justice to settle the case by meeting many of the demands of the citizen group. The state agency complied, agreeing, among other things, to reduce the overcrowding, improve safety, and provide better educational and psychological services.

This story demonstrates the grim reality of how badly our society treats its most vulnerable and injured children. But more important, the people of Dalton show us how adults in a community can care about children with whom they have no personal relationships. Altruistic actions of this nature provide a hopeful sign and point us in the direction of community responsibility for all of our children.

Taking Back Responsibility

Neither the police nor psychiatrists have the answer to our children's problems. Relying on them will ultimately increase conflict and alienation. Instead, every institution of society—from families and schools to churches—must work toward the creation of beneficial, meaningful relationships between adults and children.

Reclaiming our children and rescuing them from violence and despair requires a change of heart not in our children but in ourselves. Our children will then manifest the effect of our good efforts in their own improved lives.

Only a moral awakening in society will make it an honor and a blessing to devote oneself to children as parents, teachers, counselors, or mentors. Only a cultural paradigm shift and a galvanizing national effort will make every legislature and government agency, every school, church, and family give first consideration to the needs of children for positive relationships with adults.

This societal transformation must begin with great numbers of individuals deciding to place a much higher priority on the children in their lives. No single individual can conceive of everything that needs to be done to improve the lives of our children; and no one leader can make them come to pass. We need millions of people imagining, talking, and planning together to bring new vitality and direction to every institution in society that touches on the lives of children. In short, the transformation begins with each one of us and ultimately must involve all of us.

Our children need more of us—our unconditional love and unambiguous caring, our serious attention, our moral leadership, our precious time, our economic resources. Whether we are parents, teachers, counselors, ministers, police officers, mentors, politicians, government administrators, or leaders of great corporations and universities, we must make children a higher priority in our personal lives and in our social and economic policies.

The African proverb "It takes a village to raise a child" must now be expanded to "It takes a nation to raise a child." Eventually, we may realize that it takes the whole world. Child abuse and neglect, domestic violence, and other family problems, as well as inadequate or harmful schooling, afflict children everywhere. Racism and sexism, religious and cultural conflict, starvation, war, and pollution are obviously global problems. Even children favored by good fortune will experience the inevitable stresses involved in growing up, and they are likely to realize that so many others in so many other places are suffering without relief.

Nowadays when we speak of "our children" we tend to think of the sons and daughters we have raised as parents. We must no longer be indifferent or intolerant toward any of the children. The concept of "our children" must come to include all of the children in this nation and ultimately, the world.

Appendix A

Biography of
Peter R. Breggin, M.D.

Dr. Breggin is a psychiatrist in full-time private practice since 1968 in Bethesda, Maryland, where he treats children, adults, and families. He is a well-known critic of biological psychiatry, including psychosurgery, electroshock, and medication, and is a strong advocate for psychological and social human services. Dr. Breggin is the founder and director of the International Center for the Study of Psychiatry and Psychology (ICSPP), an organization of several hundred reform-minded professionals that has been called "the conscience of psychiatry." He is also editor-in-chief of the new peer-review professional journal *Ethical Human Sciences and Services* and serves on the editorial boards of several other journals. (See Appendixes B and C for information on the ICSPP and *Ethical Human Sciences and Services*.)

In addition, Dr. Breggin is the author of many professional articles and numerous books, including *Toxic Psychiatry* (1991), *Brain-Disabling Treatments in Psychiatry* (1997), *The Heart of Being Helpful* (1997), *Talking Back to Ritalin* (1998), and, with coauthor Ginger Breggin, *Talking Back to Prozac* (1994) and *The War Against Children of Color* (1998). He is also the author of *Your Drug May Be Your Problem: How and Why to Stop Taking Psychiatric Medications* (Perseus Books, 1999), coauthored by David Cohen, Ph.D.

Dr. Breggin has participated as a medical expert in a variety of criminal and civil legal cases involving the harmful effects of psychiatric drugs, constitutional rights of patients, malpractice, and product liability. He lectures widely throughout North America and Europe. His views are regularly covered in the national print media, including the *New York Times*, the *Washing-*

ton Post, Time, Newsweek, and *USA Today,* and he frequently appears as an expert on television programs such as *Oprah, 60 Minutes, 20/20,* and *Larry King Live.* His work is cited in scientific and academic sources such as *Science, Science News, Nature,* and the *Chronicle of Higher Education.*

Dr. Breggin was trained at Harvard College and Case Western Reserve Medical School. He took his residency in psychiatry at the Massachusetts Mental Health Center and the State University of New York, Upstate Medical Center. He is a former full-time consultant with the National Institute of Mental Health (NIMH) and has held teaching appointments at Harvard Medical School, the Washington School of Psychiatry, the University of Maryland, George Mason University, and Johns Hopkins University.

More about Dr. Breggin and his work, including a complete résumé, can be found at his Website: www.breggin.com.

Appendix B

The International Center for the Study of Psychiatry and Psychology

———◆———

The International Center for the Study of Psychiatry and Psychology (ICSPP) is a nonprofit international center for professionals and others concerned with ethical and scientific issues in human research and services. On the board of directors and advisory council of the Center are more than two hundred professionals in the fields of counseling, psychology, social work, pediatrics, neurology, and psychiatry, as well as former members of the U.S. Congress and other leading citizens.

Founded in 1971 by its director, Peter R. Breggin, M.D., it began its reform efforts with successful opposition to the international resurgence of psychosurgery. In the mid-1990s, ICSPP organized a campaign that prompted the U.S. government to withdraw its Violence Initiative, a government-wide program that called for intrusive biomedical experiments on inner-city children in the hope of demonstrating biological and genetic causes of violence. ICSPP's most recent reform efforts have been directed at the growing international trend toward psychiatric diagnosis and medication of children. Because of its many successful efforts on behalf of truthfulness and justice in the psychosocial and biomedical sciences, ICSPP has been called "the conscience of psychiatry."

ICSPP has several divisions in North America, Europe, and Australia. It offers a general membership, publishes a newsletter, and periodically distributes news releases and press packages about contemporary issues in the human sciences. In September 1998, ICSPP held its first annual international conference, "Counseling and Psychotherapy Without Psychiatric Drugs," in Bethesda, Maryland.

In 1999, ICSPP commenced publication of its peer-reviewed journal, *Ethical Human Sciences and Services: An International Journal of Critical Inquiry.* In keeping with ICSPP's goals, this journal gives priority to scientific papers and reviews that raise the level of ethical awareness concerning research, theory, and practice. It also examines important issues in contemporary human services with critical analyses that span the psychosocial and biomedical sciences. (For further information on the journal, see Appendix C.)

You can obtain information about ICSPP membership and activities by accessing the ICSPP Website (www.breggin.com) or by writing to ICSPP headquarters at 4628 Chestnut Street, Bethesda, MD 20814. General memberships are $25 in the United States and US$35 internationally. Members receive a newsletter, a discount on the journal, and announcements of activities. They also share in the satisfaction of supporting the Center's reform efforts.

Appendix C

Ethical Human Sciences and Services: An International Journal of Critical Inquiry

The mandate of *Ethical Human Sciences and Services: An International Journal of Critical Inquiry* (*EHSS*) is to understand and address the genuine needs of human beings in an ethical and scientific manner.

EHSS publishes scientific research, literature reviews, clinical reports, commentary, and book reviews that draw on broad ethical and scientific perspectives, including critiques of reductionist theories and practices in various schools of thought and ideology. It spans the fields of psychology, counseling, social work, nursing, sociology, education, public advocacy, public health, and the law, as well as medical fields such as psychiatry, pediatrics, and neurology, and biomedical sciences such as genetics and psychopharmacology.

This peer-review journal seeks to raise the level of scientific knowledge and ethical discourse, while empowering professionals who are devoted to principled human sciences and services unsullied by professional and economic interests.

The editor-in-chief is the psychiatrist Peter R. Breggin, M.D. The senior editor is David Cohen, Ph.D., professor of social work at the University of Montreal. *EHSS* is the official journal of the International Center for the Study of Psychiatry and Psychology. On the editorial advisory board are more than fifty international ICSPP members, including Fred Bemak, Ed.D.; Phyllis Chesler, Ph.D.; Graham Dukes, M.D., Ll.D; Alberto Fergusson, M.D.; Giovanni de Girolamo, M.D.; James Gordon, M.D.; Thomas Greening, Ph.D.; Richard Horobin, Ph.D.; Lucy Johnstone, Dip.Clin. Psych.; Bertram Karon, Ph.D.; Kate Millett, Ph.D.; Loren Mosher, M.D.; Craig Newnes, Dip.Clin.Psych.; Candace Pert, Ph.D.; Steven Rose, Ph.D.; Dorothy Rowe, Ph.D.; Thomas Scheff, Ph.D.; Clemmont Vontress, Ph.D.; Lenore Walker, Ed.D.; and Wolf Wolfensberger, Ph.D.

The journal welcomes the submission of unsolicited manuscripts. Please send manuscripts and direct editorial inquiries to the editorial office: Peter R. Breggin, M.D., editor-in-chief, Ethical Human Sciences and Services, 4628 Chestnut St., Bethesda, MD 20814, U.S.A.

Domestic subscription rates are $44 individual and $88 institutional. Outside the United States, rates are US$52 individual and US$100 institutional. To order a subscription, contact Springer Publishing Company, 536 Broadway, New York, NY 10012-9904. Telephone: 212/431-4370; fax: 212/941-7842.

Notes

---·•·---

Literature citations in the Notes refer to entries in the Bibliography, p. 313.

Chapter 1

1. According to Belluck and Wilgoren (1999), Eric Harris appears to have been the leader as reflected in the violence planned in his journal, his Website filled with threats, and his more hostile speech at school. Dylan Klebold was more shy, usually talking only to Eric in class but may have influenced Eric in other ways, for example, in choosing the place they worked part time. For more detail on character of Harris and Klebold see Briggs and Blevins (1999) and Simpson et al. (1999).

2. White House Conference . . . (1999). Chapter 2 discusses the conference in greater detail.

3. According to the U.S. Census Bureau, on August 1, 1998, there were 70,000,000 Americans (26 percent of the population) under eighteen.

4. Later in this chapter literature on the effects of trauma will be cited.

5. See Chapter 7 for more details about Eric Harris and Luvox, and for the effects of antidepressants and stimulants on children.

6. Lacayo (1999), p. 872.

7. Farhi (1999) compares the extensive media coverage of the Columbine High School shootings to the relatively limited coverage of the Atlanta office building shootings on July 29, 1999, when Mark O. Barton killed nine adults after already killing his wife and two children. Some of the most painful feelings captured by the media were evoked by Barton's murder of his own two children.

8. Verhovek (1999).

9. There are variations in the time line from different sources. *Newsweek's* (1999), p. 28, unsigned report starts the alarm at 11:15 A.M. and the first entry of the SWAT teams at 12:30 P.M., and completes the rescue at 4:30 P.M. The *Washington Post* (Kenworthy, 1999, p. A10) times the initial alarm at 11:30 A.M. and, like most reports, sets the arrival at the library at 4:00 P.M. A postmortem on the role of the SWAT teams by the *Washington Post* (Vobejda et al., 1999) times the alarm at 11:25 A.M., the initial shootout in the parking lot at 11:28 A.M., the first "makeshift six-member SWAT team" entrance into the school at 11:46 A.M., and the arrival at the library at 3:30 P.M. This is one of the shorter time lines, indicating an interval of four hours and five minutes from the alarm to the arrival at the library.

10. Vobejda et al. (1999).

11. Scanlon (1999).

12. Von Drehle and LeDuc (1999).

13. The police say they stayed with Mr. Sanders and called for help, and that the paramedic who arrived told them he was dead (Massaro, 1999).

14. Shore (1999).

15. Rimer (1999).

16. Simpson (1999).

17. Rotbart (1999), p. 24.

18. Kenworthy and Suro (1999).

19. Cloud (1999).

20. ABCNEWS.com (1998).

21. Sack (1999). The word "glitzy" is his.

22. ABC *Nightline* and several cable news stations provided continuous coverage.

23. Mays (1999). For example, she describes the police telling people to take cover for fear of a sniper picking them off.

24. Steinberg (1999).

25. Jones (1999).

26. Ingold (1999).

27. Robinson and Chronis (1999).

28. Robinson and Chronis (1999).

29. Cloud (1999).

30. Meredith (1999).

31. Cohen, A. (1999).

32. Dedman (1999).

33. Cooper and Russakoff (1999). Michael had been taking Dexedrine for attention deficit / hyperactivity disorder.

Chapter 2

1. Office of Mrs. Gore (1999).

2. Office of the Press Secretary (1999).

3. *New York Times* (1999, May 8), p. A10; also, Connolly (1999).

4. Kaufman (1999).

5. No definitive evidence has surfaced concerning the timing of Kip Kinkel's use of psychiatric drugs. Sometimes the media have reported he was taking Prozac and Ritalin, or Prozac alone, at the time of the shootings. However, a source close to the surviving family communicated with me via an intermediary, and reported that a family member said Kip was taking Ritalin at the time of the shooting and Prozac sometime earlier. It is unfortunate that more exact information has been kept from the public.

6. O'Meara (1999). Kelly Patricia O'Meara is one of the few reporters to cover the story relating psychiatric drugs to some of the school shootings.

7. O'Meara (1999).

8. Myths and facts . . . (1999).

9. This truth was confirmed in the final report of the National Institutes of Health (1998) Consensus Development Conference on attention deficit hyperactivity disorder (ADHD) and its treatment. After hearing all the scientific evidence, the panel concluded that there is no "data to indicate that ADHD is due to a brain malfunction. Further research to establish the validity of the disorder continues to be a problem." But then, to diminish the impact, the panel added in the next sentence: "This is not unique to ADHD, but applies as well to most psychiatric disorders, including diseases such as schizophrenia." The panel's statement was such an embarrassment to establishment psychiatry that, after the panel was disbanded, the National Institute of Mental Health edited the remarks about brain malfunction out of the statement.

10. Brain scans cannot distinguish a depressed person from a nondepressed person and they have not located a cause for any psychiatric disorder. Instead, they are mainly used in biopsychiatry to promote the profession to lay audiences by giving the false impression that radiological technology can distinguish between normal people and those with psychiatric diagnoses. The usual sleight of hand involves comparing photographs of a brain scan of a depressed patient and a nondepressed patient where there happen to be *other* differences between the two brains. Sometimes the differences simply reflect normal variation and sometimes they reflect drug damage. Brain scans cannot show differences between the brains of depressed and normal patients because no such differences have been demonstrated. See Breggin (1991, 1997a) and Breggin and Breggin (1994) for more detailed analyses.

11. The scientific literature confirms that there is no known genetic or biological cause for any psychiatric disorder and that brain scans have contributed nothing to our understanding of what causes them. For critiques of biological psychiatry, see Breggin (1991, 1997a, 1998a), Breggin and Breggin (1994, 1998), Caplan (1995), Fisher and Greenberg (1989, 1997), Joseph (1999), Mender (1994), Mosher and Burti (1994), and Ross and Pam (1995).

12. White House Announces . . . (1999) describes planned clinical trials involving children at NIMH.

13. In Breggin (1998a) I further document the government's push to open the pediatric market to psychiatric drugs.

14. I read Dr. Koplewicz's remarks with special interest because I'd been deprived of the opportunity to discuss them more directly with him. In the previous two weeks, both CNN and Fox Cable News had invited him to debate me on the subject of what our children need—drugs or human services—but he pulled out each time. He is director of the Division of Child and Adolescent Psychiatry at the New York University Medical Center and Bellevue Hospital Center.

15. See Chapter 7 for detailed discussion of antidepressant efficacy and adverse effects.

16. Koplewicz (1996), pp. 180–181.

17. Ibid., p. 234. The bad seed theory will be discussed at greater length in Chapter 6.

18. Ibid., p. vi.

19. Koplewicz (1996). Dr. Koplewicz's lengthy chart fails to inform parents of many of the most common serious dangers of the drugs that he recommends. For example, his chart fails to note that the tranquilizer Xanax is addictive; he leaves blank the box for "serious" effects for this dangerous drug. His chart does not mention that any of the stimulants, such as Ritalin and amphetamine (Dexedrine, Adderall), are highly addictive. It omits that neuroleptic drugs such as Prolixin, Haldol, and Orap cause *permanent* severe neurological disorders (tardive dyskinesia) in a high percentage of children and that they can also cause neuroleptic malignant syndrome, a potentially lethal disorder that mimics a viral inflammation of the brain. By contrast, the labels approved by the FDA for these same drugs contain prominent "Warning" sections for these adverse effects. Any parent reading Dr. Koplewicz's seemingly comprehensive chart would be extremely misled and misinformed about the supposed safety of these and other highly dangerous psychiatric drugs.

20. According to the cover of the paperback edition of Koplewicz's book, he received the 1997 Exemplary Psychiatrist Award from the National Alliance for the Mentally Ill. For discussions of NAMI's politics, see Breggin (1991, 1998a), Breggin and Breggin (1998), and Mosher and Burti (1994).

21. Though Koplewicz did not specifically mention sexual abuse when he stated at the White House Conference that "serious childhood trauma" could not cause mental disorders, his meaning was clear in this regard. In his 1996 book *It's Nobody's Fault* (pp. 6–8) he said that "sexual abuse" and "abuse," as well as "divorce" or "death of a loved one," cannot by themselves cause a "psychiatric disorder" in children. He stated, "But unless he has the brain chemistry that makes him vulnerable to a psychiatric disorder, the child will not end up with a disorder." That is, children with normal brains don't get seriously depressed or anxious over *any abuse or trauma*, including sex abuse or the death of a parent. Koplewicz does not even include posttraumatic stress disorder in his list of thirteen major mental disorders in children, yet it is probably the most common of all. He is literally claiming that our children's anger, frustration, anxiety, sadness, and rebellious or disordered conduct are always caused by brain diseases comparable to a tumor or encephalitis.

22. There is voluminous research on the role of stress and trauma in the development of "mental illness," including recent reviews and analyses by Bloom (1995), Bloom and Reichert (1998), and Herman (1997). Alice Miller (1983) vividly describes the aftermath of childhood abuse and trauma. John Bowlby (1973) studied and reviewed the effects of deprivation and abandonment in infancy and early childhood. Many studies are presented in comprehensive volumes such as Eth and Pynoos (1985); Herman (1997); Miller (1989); Marsella et al. (1996); Ochberg (1988); and van der Kolk et al. (1996). For studies of the specific effects of sexual trauma see Wyatt and Powell (1988) and for the effects of overall child abuse see Wolfe (1987). Green (1989) reviewed the literature on the relationship between trauma and most psychiatric disorders. A compendium edited by Miller (1989) presents research on the role of trauma in the development of the most severe disorders, including "schizophrenia." The literature is vast and constantly evolving, and can be reviewed through any medical library or index. There are a number professional journals devoted to the subject. Also see Breggin (1992) for a discussion of the impact on adult life of trauma and stress endured in childhood. Disturbances in relationships have also been demonstrated to impact negatively on the psychosocial development of chimpanzees (Goodall, 1983) and gorillas (Fossey, 1983), producing syndromes indistinguishable from so-called major depressive disorder in humans (discussed in Chapter 6 of Breggin, 1991). The animal studies also document the emotional healing of primates through relationships with other primates, including humans (also see Mowat, 1987). Ironically, animal research, such as Jane Goodall's, has taken a more "human" perspective on the importance of love and relationship in creating and maintaining healthy lives among the creatures, while biological psychiatry has become less human, denying the importance of these same factors in human life.

23. Stein et al. (1988). This is a relatively low overall rate for reported sexual abuse. In more in-depth surveys, most women report childhood sexual abuse. Peters (1988) found that 60 percent of women endured at least one episode of sexual abuse before age eighteen and that 51 percent had experienced abuse from two or more separate perpetrators.

24. Bloom and Reichert (1998), p. 109.

25. Italics added.

26. Jennings (1999).

27. Chapter 7 of this book summarizes some of the many adverse effects of neuroleptic (antipsychotic) medication. Much more detailed information about adverse drug effects can be found in Breggin and Cohen (1999) and especially Breggin (1997a).

28. For a description and scientific critique of ACT, see Gomory (1997). Also see Breggin (1999e). For a coalition of patient rights groups opposed to ACT and to involuntary treatment, see Oaks (1999). ACT is strongly advocated by the National Alliance for the Mentally Ill (NAMI), a parents group that supports coercive measures toward its own children and has considerable influence through Mrs. Clinton and Mrs. Gore.

29. Discussed further in Chapter 7.

30. Obmascik et al. (1999).

31. Belluck and Wilgoren (1999).

32. Kane (1996).

33. Baldwin (1997). Baldwin also notes that the Department of Defense recognizes the dangers of soldiers taking addictive substances, such as Ritalin and the amphetamines: "Because Ritalin is a controlled drug with considerable abuse potential, we cannot allow it to be possessed by our recruits while in basic or advanced training."

34. Counseling is sometimes defined as focusing more on the positive aspects of human potential while therapy is defined as being concerned with "pathology," problems, or difficulties. Most therapists actually focus on both. I don't find the distinctions between therapy and counseling particularly useful and will use the terms interchangeably.

35. More details of the program can be found on the Internet at "President Clinton announces . . . "(1999).

36. Tedford (1999) describes the program in Houston, Texas, run by the Harris County Psychiatric Center. It claims to be the first of its kind. Under Clinton's plan, a central program from Washington, D.C., would be piped into all the schools of the nation.

37. The Bush administration's Violence Initiative, and all of the surrounding implications, were thoroughly described and documented in our book *The War Against Children* (1994); this material was updated in the second edition, retitled *The War Against Children of Color* (1998).

38. Breggin and Breggin (1998).

39. Goodwin (1992). Made available on demand to Congressman John Conyers and the Black Caucus of the U.S. Congress, and then passed on to the Breggins.

40. Department of Health and Human Services Press Office (1999, June 7).

41. Olinger et al. (1999).

42. Achenbach and Russakoff (1999).

43. Callahan (1999); Belluck and Milgoren (1999).

44. Ibid.

45. Barron (1999); Brooke (1999a, 1999b).

46. Imse and Kass (1999).

47. For more details on Eric Harris and Luvox, see Chapter 7.

48. Boyle (1999).

49. On the other hand, the boys were good at putting up a facade. Classmates who knew them well and talked with them shortly before the assault said that the two boys were behaving normally, even planning future events (Kiely and Fields, 1999).

50. See Firestone (1999) and Cloud (1991) for early profiles.

51. I wish to thank Drs. James P. McGee and Caren R. DeBernardo (1999a, 1999b) for making their informative unpublished paper available to me. It describes an additional four school shootings in 1993 and 1995 involving one to two deaths each. Both doctors are psychologists at Sheppard Pratt Hospital in Baltimore, Maryland. Dr. McGee is the chief psychologist of the Baltimore County Police Department and director of the Critical Incident Program for the Maryland State Police. Dr. DeBernardo is a member of the Maryland State Police Critical Incident Stress Debriefing Team and the Baltimore County Police Department's Hostage Negotiation Team.

52. DeBernardo and McGee (1999).

53. Ibid. DeBernardo and McGee concluded that "referral for psychiatric treatment may initially be appealing although it may not be the most effective course of action. These individuals are difficult clients, hold a poor prognosis and are unlikely to participate in therapy." Instead, they recommend tightening police measures in the schools to prevent wholesale violence much as antihighjacking measures have succeeded for airplanes originating out of the United States. They do not suggest that these measures would improve the well-being of most students.

54. See for example, Breggin and Breggin (1994), the first edition of what became the *War Against Children of Color* (1998).

55. Schulte (1999).

Chapter 3

1. Stolberg (1999).

2. Dylan Klebold's maternal grandfather was Jewish (Belluck and Wilgoren, 1999).

3. McGee and DeBernardo (1999b).

4. The summary data is taken from Cloud (1999) with two additional shooting incidents added from McGee and DeBernardo (1999b). In some cases, we obtained the school population by contacting the school.

5. Adapted from Breggin (1998a).

6. Smart (1999).

7. U.S. Census Bureau data.

8. Armour (1999).

9. Data on domestic abuse compiled by Bloom and Reichert (1998), who provide the original sources.

10. The phrase was originated by Straus and Steinmetz (1973).

11. Data on child abuse and neglect compiled by Bloom and Reichert (1998), who provide the original sources.

12. Paula Caplan (1995) originated the relevant concept of "delusional dominating personality disorder." See page 178 of this book.

13. For readable, readily available discussions of sexism and male domination in relation to psychological development and psychiatric diagnosis and treatment, see Caplan (1995), Chesler (1997), Gilligan (1982), and Herman (1989). I have also discussed these issues in a chapter entitled "Suppressing the Passion of Women" in *Toxic Psychiatry* (1991).

14. Keirsey (1998).

15. For a discussion of parentification, see Helms (1999).

16. Caldwell (1999).

17. A commentary by Rob Long (1999) focused my attention on this detail.

18. Mifflin (1999).

19. See Chapter 12 for a discussion of treatment centers that do provide genuine help through the kinds of relationships that children need.

20. This is also confirmed by Herman (1997) and almost any textbook on child abuse.

21. Oldenburg (1999).

22. Mifflin (1999).

23. The U.S. government (and the Bureau of the Census) define poverty for a family of four as an annual income of $16,400 or less. For a good, short summary and analysis, see Rook (1999). For more data, see *Young Children in Poverty: A Statistical Update*, available from the National Center for Children in Poverty at (212) 304–7100 or visit www.cpmcnet. columbia.edu/dept/nccp/.

24. See Chapter 7 for research on psychoses induced by psychiatric drugs.

25. Of course, the figures would be much higher if the survey had included children who were using prescribed stimulants that are also "used, kept and sold" in middle schools around the country.

26. McGee and DeBernardo (1999b).

27. Walsh (1999).

28. Stolberg (1999).

29. Cooper (1999).

30. Brooke (1999).

31. Sam Yette (1971) first warned that the United States would either fully integrate its black population or feel compelled to exterminate it. Bertram Karon (1975) wrote the first scientific study of the effects of racism, and Grier and Cobbs (1980) wrote the well-known psychological analysis of the problem. Kotlowitz (1991) and Bell (1992) have portrayed the personal traumatization of black youth. Andrew Hacker (1991) has reminded us that apartheid is getting worse in America. Amos N. Wilson (1991) delved deeply into white culture to demonstrate its destructive impact in humiliating the black male. Jonathan Kozol (1991) has described racism's degrading effects on schoolchildren. With my wife, Ginger, I have written about the subject in *The War Against Children of Color* (Breggin and Breggin, 1998).

Chapter 4

1. Often children are already taking psychiatric drugs when I begin to treat them, and I may have to prescribe drugs in the process of withdrawing them. However, I do not believe that psychoactive substances are ever a proper response to a child's emotional suffering or conflicts with adults, and I do not start children on them.

2. The genetic and biological basis of childhood emotional and behavioral problems is a matter of political policy rather than scientific inquiry at NIMH. To suppress contrary information, NIMH has fired scientists with contrary beliefs. NIMH even suppressed the conclusion drawn by one of its own conferences (see endnote 9, chapter 2).

3. In *Talking Back to Ritalin* (1988), I devote an entire chapter to the possible medical causes for behavior problems in children. I also document that "authorities" on behavioral problems in children often completely overlook the many real biological causes in favor of the mythological "biochemical imbalance." Often they promote fad biological causes, such as allergies, sugar, or food additives, that have little scientific basis. In a routine practice in a middle-class or affluent community where children receive adequate health care, very few behavior problems have any physical basis. In communities where head injuries, malnutrition, and untreated medical illnesses abound, the behavior of many children may be commonly adversely affected by physical disorders.

Chapter 5

1. Quoted from Ansbacher and Ansbacher (1956), p. 397. The bracketed explanation is in the original. Like Carl Jung, Alfred Adler became one of Freud's students and then broke with him. Consistent with my focus in this book on meaningful relationships, Adler emphasized the social interest of children and adults as the most important motivating factor in humans.

2. Modern researchers concerned with intelligence have almost universally failed to realize that critical intelligence requires virtues such as courage and determination. Even when discussing creativity, wisdom, insight, or critical thinking, these researchers do not recognize that the expression of these faculties entails grave risks. This failure to understand the connection between intelligence and courage is typified by commonly cited works in the field such as Gardner (1983, 1993), Levy (1997), Sternberg (1988, 1990), and Sternberg and Davidson (1996).

3. Abigail Adams's letter to her husband John Adams, dated June 17, 1782, quoted in Bennett (1997), pp. 40–41.

4. Clemmont Vontress, professor emeritus of counseling at George Washington University, pioneered the field of cross-cultural counseling and courageously broke down barriers against blacks taking leadership positions in the academic community. He continues to give seminars on the necessity of black children and youths grasping the oppression they inevitably encounter, often on a daily basis, in America.

5. In *Cross-Cultural Counseling*, Dr. Vontress and the coauthors, Dr. Jake Johnson and Dr. Lawrence Epp (1999), focus on the importance of examining the effects of racism in the counseling process.

6. Masson (1996).

7. Jeffrey Moussaieff Masson's books about animals include *When Elephants Weep* and *Dogs Don't Lie About Love*.

8. Samuels (1999).

9. Cooper and Russakoff (1999).

Chapter 6

1. Wender (1973), p. 9.

2. Wender (1973), p. 42: "It is the child's behavior that is likely to make his parents behave inconsistently."

3. Wender (1973), p. 114.

4. Wender (1995), p. 10.

5. Barkley (1981), p. 4.

6. Barkley (1995), p. 76.

7. See Chapter 2.

8. For the effects of child abuse, see Wolfe (1987) and Wyatt and Powell (1988). For a more lengthy list of sources, see endnote 21, chapter 2.

9. Isaacson (1999).

10. Chua-Eoan (1999).

11. Drug company funding of the APA is described in Breggin (1991).

12. If the behaviors last for six months or more, then the child qualifies for the official diagnosis. In actual clinical practice, however, the diagnosis is usually made without regard to the duration of the problem or, for that matter, the actual number of criteria that are met. Usually, the doctor makes a diagnosis on the basis of an impression that only somewhat reflects any particular official description of the diagnosis.

Chapter 7

1. For example, Robert L. Findling, director of child and adolescent psychiatry at Case Western Reserve University in Cleveland, said: "Do these medicines cause violence? The answer absolutely is no" (Price, 1999).

2. The July 30, 1999, MSNBC show was "Now and Again." It gave details about the life of Eric Harris without making any mention of his psychiatric treatment. The occasion of the television report was Mark O. Barton's July 29 murderous rampage at two stock day trading firms in Atlanta, Georgia.

3. The Jefferson County coroner announced that toxicology tests of Eric Harris's body showed a "middle therapeutic range" of Luvox in his system (Kenworthy and Thompson, 1999). I have confirmed this by means of documents obtained from the FDA through the Freedom of Information Act. I received a copy of an Adverse Event Report (labeled "intentional injury, suicide attempt") that Solvay Pharmaceuticals (1999), the manufacturer of Luvox, sent to the FDA. It refers unmistakably to one of the boys (unnamed) involved in the April 20 school shooting in Littleton (it cites the date, the number killed, and other relevant facts). The drug company report said that Solvay had contacted the chief deputy officer of the (name deleted) County Coroner's Office who "confirmed the presence of a Luvox blood level at autopsy—therapeutic." In other words, the blood level was in the expected range for someone receiving a clinically effective dose. The blood level of Luvox drops by one half in approximately fifteen hours, so Harris probably took the Luvox shortly before the autopsy, within a day or less of the assault, and was under its influence at the time he died.

4. Belluck and Wilgoren (1999). The reporters do not make the connection between the start of drug treatment and the start of the journal. Of course, depending on the timing, it is possible that the same distress that led to the journal writing also led to the prescription of Luvox.

5. O'Meara (1999).

6. As mentioned earlier in the book, a friend of the family sent information to me, through a third party, indicating that Kip Kinkel was taking Ritalin at the time of the shooting, and that he had stopped taking Prozac several months earlier.

7. O'Meara (1999).

8. The current review may be extensive enough to convince most readers; if not, much more extensive scientific information about violence produced by stimulant and antidepressant drugs is presented in Breggin and Breggin (1994) and Breggin (1997a, 1998a). Those sources also document a much broader range of adverse reactions to these drugs than the ones enumerated here.

9. The Prozac-like antidepressants are called selective serotonin reuptake inhibitors (SSRIs) because they inhibit the removal of the neurotransmitter serotonin from the synaptic cleft (the space between nerve cells).

10. Emslie et al. (1997), p. 1033. The data are hidden in the section on why patients were discontinued from the study. It mentions that 3 out of 44 children taking Prozac dropped out of the clinical trials because they developed what were termed "manic symptoms." None of the controls developed mania. The report paid no attention to this serious finding. When Emslie gave a pre-publication paper on his study, I responded with a published letter in a psychiatric newspaper (Breggin, 1995) and raised issues about the high rate of mania, and about increased aggression on Prozac, which was also reported by Emslie prior to official publication. At the bottom of my published letter, the newspaper noted that Dr. Emslie "declined to respond." Furthermore, Emslie left out of the official publication his earlier acknowledgment of Prozac-induced aggression in children taking part in the study. Drug advocates like Emslie persistently cover up the devastating effects of drugs on children.

11. Moore (1998) calculated that, at the admitted rate of 1 percent for causing mania in adults treated for depression, Prozac was producing 7,500 cases of mania per month in March 1996. Moore's estimate is drawn from the Prozac manufacturer Eli Lilly's data that 754,000 new prescriptions were written for the drug in March 1996. Moore adds, "However, there is simply no way of knowing how many cases of mania—moderate or severe—are being triggered by antidepressant drugs."

12. *Physicians' Desk Reference* (1999), p. 3122, under the heading of "Precautions" for Luvox. This is the FDA-approved label for the drug. The "precautions" section of any drug label, according to the FDA, "shall contain information regarding any special care to be exercised by the practitioner for the safe and effective use of the drug . . . " (*Code of Federal Regulations, 21,* CFR 201.57).

13. It is well known that rates for adverse effects will be higher in routine practice than in clinical trials (discussed at length in Breggin, 1997a, 1998b).

Not only are the trials very short and closely monitored, they usually exclude children who have any history of mania or violence, as well as anyone who is acutely suicidal. In clinical trials the doctors are more sophisticated about adverse effects, rules governing experiments require the parents to be informed about adverse effects, doses are given in more moderate dose ranges, and drug combinations are generally discouraged.

14. Schrader (1999). The expert was Robert Davies from the University of Colorado.

15. The research is reviewed in Breggin (1991).

16. Solvay Pharmaceuticals, Inc., and Upjohn Company (1994).

17. It was actually reported in the press that the autopsies showed no drugs, legal or illegal, in either of the boys' bodies (O'Driscoll and Fields, 1999; Brooke, 1999). For some reason, they had not initially been tested for Prozac-like drugs.

18. The article promoted the speculative, simple-minded idea that violence is related to a gene that controls neurotransmission in the serotonergic system (Manning, 1999). The brain-scan photographs are on the front page; the article, on the second page. These claims have not been remotely proved. There's no evidence that individual differences in violence level are genetic (reviewed in Breggin and Breggin, 1998).

19. Begley (1999).

20. Many illustrations of Prozac-induced violence are reviewed in Breggin and Breggin (1994). Also see Breggin (1997a).

21. Confirmation that antidepressants cause mania, as well as the nature of mania, will be described further in the chapter.

22. The well-known biological psychiatrist Ronald Fieve (1973), for example, makes these claims for mania and creativity.

23. Achenbach and Russakoff (1999).

24. American Psychiatric Association (1994), p. 329. Also see p. 331, which states, similarly, "Symptoms like those seen in a Manic Episode may also be precipitated by antidepressant treatment such as medication. ..." Drug-induced mania falls into the official diagnostic category of substance-induced mood disorders.

25. Ibid., p. 329; see also p. 330. The *DSM-IV* makes clear that mania can be associated with violence or "assaultive behavior" that can get a person into trouble with the law.

26. Ibid., pp. 328 and 332.

27. One post-Littleton newspaper report (Luke, 1999) described how a sixth-grader was being treated for depression when it was discovered that he "really" had bipolar disorder. Very possibly, this "manic" part of the supposed bipolar disorder was a product of taking antidepressants.

28. Food and Drug Administration (1999).

29. Breggin (1997a and 1998b) discuss the FDA position on the use of the spontaneous reporting system with citations from FDA publications.

30. A health professional sent in a very similar report, probably about the same person but without mentioning aggression.

31. The patient was also taking perphenazine, a neuroleptic, and the brief description looks more like a neuroleptic malignant syndrome. The reference in the literature is not cited in the summary.

32. See discussion in Breggin and Cohen (1999).

33. I was a medical expert on behalf of the plaintiffs against the drug company, and did the original research for the many unified cases against the drug company, nearly all of which have been settled out of court. Sometime toward the end of the Wesbecker trial, Eli Lilly & Co. probably concluded that they might lose, because the drug company fixed the trial while it was still going on. Eli Lilly & Co. paid the plaintiffs a huge but undisclosed amount of money in return for which the plaintiffs watered down the remainder of their case and their closing remarks in the trial. The plaintiffs got the money and Eli Lilly & Co. manipulated a close verdict in its favor, protecting itself from adverse publicity that would have injured the sales of Prozac and the company's reputation and profits. When the trial was over, the presiding judge, J. W. Potter, realized he had been misled. In an extremely unusual turn of events, the Kentucky Supreme Court handed down a unanimous opinion about Eli Lilly & Co., stating, "In this case, there was a serious lack of candor with the trial court and there may have been deception, bad faith conduct, abuse of judicial process or perhaps even fraud" (Trial court's authority . . . , 1996; also see Gibeaut, 1996, p. 18). Judge Potter changed the outcome of the trial from a jury verdict in favor of Eli Lilly & Co. to "settled with prejudice" by the drug company (Breggin, 1997a, gives more details. See also Castellano, 1995; Gibeaut, 1996; Potter, 1995; Scanlon, 1995; Varchaver, 1995; and my Website, www.Breggin.com, for further information.)The major media reported the victory of the drug company before it was known that the trial had been faked, but did not report the later disclosures of the manipulation and possible fraud, as well as the nullification of the jury verdict. The drug company got away with a public relations triumph. Once again the public remained in the dark about the dangers of Prozac and related antidepressants.

34. King et al. (1991). Frank was designated "F." in the report.

35. Ibid. Susie was designated "S." in the report.

36. It is not uncommon for people to continue to get worse for a while after discontinuing the offending drug. In fact, withdrawal itself can cause serious problems (Breggin and Cohen, 1999).

37. Riddle et al. (1990–91). At the time, Riddle was at Yale. He is now at Johns Hopkins.

38. Jain et al. (1992). The terms "hypomania" (a lesser version of mania) and "manic-like" are use by Jain and his colleagues to describe the collection of symptoms caused by Prozac. However, the syndrome described in the report much more resembles a full-blown manic reaction or mania.

39. Temple (1991). Through the Freedom of Information Act (FOIA), I obtained a copy of the actual memorandum in which the FDA decided to delete from the label that "depression" was a commonly or frequently reported adverse effect of Prozac during the company-sponsored clinical trials. Thus, depression as an adverse effect went from common to nonexistent on the official label, and physicians and patients then had no warning about this extremely important adverse effect. When patients become more depressed on Prozac, the drug dosage is often increased instead of stopped. This episode is further discussed in Breggin (1997a).

40. See Sommers-Flanagan and Sommers-Flanagan (1996) and Fisher and Fisher (1996). Also see Baker (1995).

41. Gugliotta (1999). Of course, the drug companies could be sued if they made false claims that caused damage to consumers, but this is a very poor protection for the consumer. As an expert in product liability cases against drug companies, I can say that my experience demonstrates that even now it is difficult to hold them legally responsible for giving out misleading information. The new ruling will make it much harder.

42. P. 373.

43. A total of 2,821 reports were submitted to the FDA, mostly by physicians and pharmacists who believed they had identified an unusual or serious adverse reaction to Ritalin. I published the data in Breggin (1998a&d and 1999a&c).

44. Breggin (1998a, 1998d, 1999a, 1999b, 1999c).

45. More information is available in my books *Talking Back to Ritalin* (1998) and *Your Drug May Be Your Problem* (1991) (coauthored with David Cohen), and my recent articles published in scientific journals (Breggin 1999a, 1999b, 1999c).

46. See Breggin and Breggin (1994) for a discussion of depression and serotonin. For critiques of other biochemical speculations see Breggin (1991, 1997a, 1998a).

47. Gerhardt (1999).

48. The brain-disabling principle of drug treatment is discussed in detail in my medical textbook, *Brain-Disabling Treatments in Psychiatry* (1997a).

49. See Melega et al. (1997a, 1997b). I have reviewed the scientific studies in peer-reviewed journals (Breggin, 1999b, 1999c).

50. Ellinwood and Lee (1996), p. 14.

51. Nasrallah et al. (1986).

52. Lambert (1998).

53. Fuller (1994). At my suggestion, lawyers questioned under oath Fuller and other top researchers at Eli Lilly & Co. as to whether they conducted any animal studies to test for recovery from well-documented Prozac-induced brain dysfunctions. They said they had not. If any such studies have been done anywhere, no one is acknowledging their existence or releasing the data.

54. Clozaril is an old drug newly marketed in the United States.

55. For withdrawal procedures, see Breggin and Cohen (1999).

56. Neuroleptics cause tardive dyskinesia in a high percentage of children (probably at least 5 to 7 percent a year, the rate in adults) and often with severe symptoms that impair posture and gait (literature reviewed in Breggin, 1997a). They also cause neuroleptic malignant syndrome, a severe and potentially lethal condition similar to a viral encephalitis in its effects.

57. For tardive dyskinesia in children see Gualtieri and Barnhill (1988) and Gualtieri et al. (1984). The subject is reviewed and updated in Breggin (1997a). Also see page 310 n14.

58. My 1998 book, *Talking Back to Ritalin*, is the most accessible source of data on adverse effects of Ritalin. Also see Breggin (1998d, 1999a, 1999b, 1999c).

59. International Narcotics Control Board (1995). Reported by Crossette (1995) in the *New York Times*.

60. International Narcotics Control Board (1999).

61. Drug Enforcement Administration (1995).

62. O'Meara (1999).

63. Goldsmith (1997a, 1997b, 1997c, 1997d); Weber (1998).

Chapter 8

1. There have been several cycles of escalating Ritalin prescription. In the early 1970s and then again in the late 1980s it peaked, met considerable public criticism, and reach plateaus for a while.

2. For critiques of the concept of learning disabilities, see Armstrong (1995), Breggin (1998a), and Coles (1987, 1998).

3. Gardner (1993), p. 7. That the concept of IQ has been highly criticized for decades is demonstrated in the essays in Block and Dworkin (1976). Biological psychiatry is anything but scientific. It tends, instead, to use very outmoded concepts in the furtherance of justifying drugs and electroshock for the control of behavior.

4. For confirming data and opinions, see Coles (1987, 1998) and Dumont (1999).

5. The data in this section are from Vobejda (1998).

Chapter 9

1. Harmon (1999).
2. *New York Times* (1999).
3. Brener et al. (1999). Newspaper coverage in Cooper (1999).
4. Shear and Salmon (1999).
5. Schulte (1999).
6. See interviews of Columbine High School students (*New York Times*, 1999, April 3).
7. Foster (1999).
8. Cloud (1999).
9. Cloud (1999), chart on pp. 36–37.
10. McGee and DeBernardo (1999a, 1999b).
11. For a more extensive examination of shame, see Breggin (1992).
12. See Chapter 2 for quotes from Eric Harris's Website.
13. Mauro (1999).
14. Quotes from Gorney (1999).
15. Many useful details are taken from Mauro (1999).
16. Biskupic (1999). The quote is from Biskupic.
17. Bronner (1999).
18. Gorney (1999) discusses programs for discouraging peer harassment in the schools.
19. Adams and Russakoff (1999).
20. For an examination of the negative effects of competition, see Kohn (1986).
21. Miedzian (1991), p. 199.
22. Gilligan et al. (1990), p. 298.
23. Azar (1999).
24. Caplan (1995).
25. Gilligan (1982), p. 25.
26. White (1999).
27. Quoted in Bronner (1999).
28. In *Beyond Conflict* (1992) I review some of the earlier feminist literature by women and men who, from a variety of perspectives, were calling for an amelioration of male competitiveness and aggression, and for increased male cooperativeness and sensitivity. Recent books include Garbarino (1999), Gurian (1999), Kindlon and Thompson (1999), and Pollack (1998).

Chapter 10

1. I know several students who have attended the schools described in this chapter. In order to protect their privacy, I have combined their stories in

ways that do not specifically pertain to one or another individual person. But the stories are based on common occurrences in my practice and in the community.

2. Smith (1998), p. 77.

3. U.S. Department of Education (1998).

4. Maslow (1970), p. 52.

5. For example, see Lewin (1999).

6. Mosteller (1999).

7. Seymour (1999).

8. Data in this paragraph from Applebome (1999).

9. Ibid.

10. Nodding (1992), p. xiv. Nodding lists principles for running a good school that parallel many in this chapter. Also see Bloom (1995).

11. U.S. Department of Education (1998).

12. Alcoholics Anonymous (1976); see p. 59 for the Twelve Steps and p. 564 for the Twelve Traditions.

13. Ibid. *Alcoholics Anonymous* speaks of a "loving God" in stating the Second Tradition.

14. Associated Press (1999).

15. David (1992).

16. Hacker (1992), p. 74.

17. National Center on Institutions and Alternatives (NCIAA, 1992). Under the direction of Jerome Miller, the NCIAA conducted studies in Baltimore and Washington, D.C.

18. See Kozol (1991) for vivid descriptions of these schools, which are mostly in districts with ethnic or racial minorities.

19. In consultations with Lieutenant Colonel Collier and Dr. Ronald David, I had urged that they bring volunteers into the schools.

20. Kozol (1981). Also see bell hooks (1994) and Paulo Freire (1998) for a discussion of education in service of conformity and of resistance to oppressive authority.

21. Granat (1995).

22. Ibid. One such conference, held January 24–25, 1995, was sponsored by the National Institute of Mental Health and the Food and Drug Administration with active drug company participation. Conference sponsors sought to promote the increased psychiatric drugging of children under the guise of "more research."

23. Chrisjohn and Young (1997), p. 4.

24. The White House program is described in Chapter 2.

25. Christian (1999).

26. Ibid.

27. Gatto (1992).

Chapter 11

1. Reported by Connie Erikson (1999), school program director, Suicide Prevention, Yolo County, Davis, California.

2. McGee and DeBernardo (1999b).

3. U.S. Department of Education (1998). The organizations included the American Counseling Association, the American Association of School Administrators, the National Education Association, and the American Federation of Teachers.

4. Sharon Collins, M.D., is a pediatrician who is associated with the International Center for the Study of Psychiatry and Psychology. In her practice, she does not start children on stimulant drugs for ADHD.

5. Murray (1996). Also see Breggin (1998a), Chapter 20, which has a section on home schooling.

6. Many books provide extensive guidance about how to resolve conflicts between adults and children. In addition to my own books *Talking Back to Ritalin* and *Beyond Conflict*, I would recommend starting with two excellent older works, Ginott's (1969) *Between Parent and Child* and Gordon's (1970) *P.E.T.: Parent Effectiveness Training*. Books that focus on conflict resolution can also be very useful, such as *Difficult Conversations: How to Discuss What Matters Most* (Stone et al., 1999), an outgrowth of the Harvard Negotiation Project.

Chapter 12

1. All the interviews in this chapter were conducted specifically for this book in June and July 1999.

2. See Bowlby (1973) for a review.

3. For chimpanzees, see Goodall (1993). For apes, see Fossey (1983) and Mowat (1987). Animal researchers describe how infant and young animals are dependent on the affection and devotion of adult animals for their survival and will become depressed, withdrawn, and stop eating when that companionship is lost. Mowat describes how Fossey nursed an infant ape back to health after its parent had been lost. See endnote 22, Chapter 2.

4. Stanton (1999). Some of the quotes are from his report and others from my interview with him.

5. Stanton (1999).

6. See Ansbacher and Ansbacher (1970), pp. 380ff., and Ansbacher and Ansbacher (1956), pp. 392ff., for discussions of Alfred Adler's child clinics.

7. I want to thank Jackie Cook of Beaver, West Virginia, for directing me to the existence of contemporary Adlerian clinics. The North American Society of Adlerian Psychology is located at 65 East Wacker Place, Suite 400,

Chicago, IL 60601; (312) 629-8801. There are several functioning programs around the country.

8. To get more information about Adlerian Open Forum Counseling contact Parent Encouragement Program, 10100 Connecticut Avenue, Kensington, MD 20895. Website: www.ipo.net/parenting.

9. See, for example, Ansbacher and Ansbacher (1956), p. 394, for the emphasis on therapists admitting to families and children that they too have faults and make mistakes.

10. See Breggin and Stern (1996) for essays by various therapists and researchers, and Karon and Vandenbos (1981).

11. It is a myth that the use of antipsychotic drugs emptied the mental hospitals. The drugs begin working in minutes; the abrupt decline in the hospital census in North America didn't begin until ten or more years later. At that time, the hospitals were compelled, owing to overcrowding and declining funds, to discharge patients without regard for what happened to them. Many went to even worse nursing and board and care homes, and many went onto the street. Many now flood the jails. Very few ended up with better living conditions or lives. I have reviewed this subject and cited background sources in *Toxic Psychiatry* (Breggin, 1991).

12. For the commission report see Joint Commission (1961). Our book about the program is Umbarger et al. (1962). I've written about the volunteer program in Chapter 1 of *Toxic Psychiatry* (Breggin, 1991).

13. Mosher (1996) and Mosher and Burti (1994). I also describe his work in Breggin (1991).

14. The most common neurological disorder caused by the neuroleptic or antipsychotic drugs is tardive dyskinesia. It occurs at rates of 5 to 7 percent per year, cumulative. Thus, a patient who takes these drugs for five years has approximately a 25 to 35 percent chance (5 to 7 percent times five years) of developing an untreatable, irreversible disease that involves twitches and other involuntary muscle movements that can cause pain, disfigurement, and sometimes severe disability (see Breggin, 1997a, for a thorough review of relevant literature). These drugs can also cause many other very dangerous and even potentially fatal disorders.

15. I discuss therapy, including the grateful therapist, in *The Heart of Being Helpful: Empathy and the Creation of a Healing Presence* (Breggin, 1997b).

16. For more about healing presence, see ibid.

17. *Your Drug May Be Your Problem: How and Why to Stop Taking Psychiatric Medications,* by Breggin and Cohen (1999), describes how to withdraw from psychiatric drugs.

18. Psychiatric survivor alternatives are described in Breggin (1991). Also see Chamberlin (1978). David Oaks (1999) publishes a newspaper, *Dendron,* as part of a support network for psychiatric survivors.

19. For a history of moral psychiatry, see Bockoven (1963). I evaluate the moral era in *Toxic Psychiatry* (1991), pp. 381–84.

20. The International Center for the Study of Psychiatry and Psychology holds conferences of this kind on a regular basis. It can also provide the names of professionals who can join or even lead such a conference. For information on contacting ICSPP, see Appendix B.

21. The Ritalin controversy in the early 1970s is described by Schrag and Divoky (1975) in *The Myth of the Hyperactive Child*.

22. For a history of the controversy surrounding stimulant drugs for the control of behavior see Breggin (1998a).

23. The International Center for the Study of Psychiatry has been monitoring and opposing the practice of inflicting electroshock and psychosurgery on children. In recent years, organized psychiatry, including the American Psychiatric Association and the National Alliance for the Mentally Ill (NAMI), has lobbied to increase the numbers of children given shock treatment. Only a few states ban the practice on children (Breggin, 1997a). My reform work began in the 1970s in large part in reaction to psychosurgical projects that inflicted multiple electrical mutilations in the brains of children, most of them African American, by means of implanted electrodes (Breggin and Breggin, 1998, *The War Against Children of Color*).

24. However, the concerted effort being made by government agencies to get more psychiatric drugs approved for children will almost surely lead to the development of "positive" studies and eventual FDA approval.

25. For an elaboration on this viewpoint that schools and mental health facilities should provide the same quality of sanctuary, see the work of the psychiatrist Sandra Bloom (1995, 1997).

Chapter 13

1. For a detailed discussion of conflicts between liberty and love, and their potential resolution, see Breggin (1992).

2. Gilbert (1999).

3. Glasser (1998).

4. Glaberson (1999b).

Bibliography

ABC News. 1999. *Nightline*, May 10: Why kids turn violent—a search for answers. Official transcript #4683, available from ABC News, 47 West 66th Street, New York, New York 10023.

ABCNEWS.com. 1998. School shooting in Oregon. From Website (May 21): http://abcnews.go.com/sections/us/DailyNews/school980521.html.

Achenbach, J., and D. Russakoff. 1999. Portrait of a teen at war. *Washington Post*, April 29, p. A1.

Adams, L., and D. Russakoff. 1999. Dissecting Columbine's cult of the athlete. *Washington Post*, June 12, p. A1.

Alcoholics Anonymous. 1976. *Alcoholics Anonymous*, 3rd ed. New York: Alcoholics Anonymous World Services.

American Psychiatric Association. 1976. Amicus curiae brief, *Tarasoff vs. Regents of the University of California* 551 P.2d 334.

American Psychiatric Association. 1994. *Diagnostic and statistical manual of mental disorders, 4th edition*. Washington, D.C.: American Psychiatric Association.

Ansbacher, H. L., and R. R. Ansbacher, eds. 1956. *The individual psychology of Alfred Adler: A systematic presentation in selections from his writings*. New York: Basic Books.

———. *Alfred Adler: Superiority and social interest*. Evanston, Ill.: Northwestern University.

Applebome, P. 1999. Two words behind the massacre in Colorado. *New York Times*, May 2, section 4, p. 1.

Armour, S. 1999. Family-friendly work policies get cold shoulder. *USA Today*, April 30, p. 1B.

Armstrong, L. 1993. *And they call it help: The psychiatric policing of America's Children*. New York: Addison-Wesley.

Armstrong, T. 1995. *The myth of the A.D.D. child*. New York: E. P. Dutton.

Associated Press. 1999. Children's Rights Council calls Maine best place to raise kids. *USA Today*, July 28, p. 3A.

Athens, L. 1989. *The creation of dangerous violent criminals*. New York: Routledge.

At-Home Dad. A quarterly newsletter, c/o Peter Baylies, 61 Brightwood Avenue, North Andover, Massachusetts 01845.

Azar, B. 1999. Boys to men: Emotional miseducation. *APA Monitor*, July–August, p. 1.

Baker, B. 1995. Though data lacking, antidepressants used widely in children. *Clinical Psychiatry News*, March, p. 16

Baldwin, J. 1997. Military policy on Ritalin use under examination. *Psychiatric Times*, April, p. 30.

Barkley, R. A. 1981. *Hyperactive children: A handbook for diagnosis and treatment*. New York: Guilford Press.

———. 1995. *Taking charge of ADHD: The complete authoritative guide for parents*. New York: Guilford Press.

Barron, J. 1999. Warnings from a student turned killer. *New York Times*, May 1, p. A10.

Barshinger, C. E., L. E. LaRowe, and A. Tapia. 1995. *Christianity Today*, August 14, pp. 35–37.

Begley, S. 1999. Why the young kill. *Newsweek*, May 3, p. 32.

Bell, D. 1992. *Faces at the bottom of the well*. New York: Basic Books.

Belluck, P., and J. Wilgoren. 1999. Caring parents, no answers, in the Columbine killers' pasts. *New York Times*, June 29, p. A1.

Bennett, W. J. 1997. *The spirit of America: Words of advice from the Founders in stories, letters, poems, and speeches*. New York: Simon & Schuster.

Biskupic, J. 1999. Schools liable for harassment: High court limits ruling to student misconduct that harms an education. *New York Times*, May 25, p. A1.

Block, N. J., and G. Dworkin, eds. 1976. *The IQ Controversy*. New York: Pantheon.

Bloom, S. L. 1995. Creating sanctuary in the school. *Journal for a Just and Caring Education* 1:403–433.

———. 1997. *Creating sanctuary: Toward the evolution of sane societies*. New York: Routledge.

Bloom, S. L., and M. Reichert. 1998. *Bearing witness: Violence and collective responsibility*. New York: Haworth Press.

Bockoven, S. 1963. *Moral treatment in psychiatry*. New York: Springer.

Bowlby, J. 1973. *Attachment and loss*. Volume 2: *Separation, anxiety and anger*. New York: Basic Books.

Boyle, P. 1999. Killers bluffed through diversion program. *Youth Today*, June, p. 16.

Bradley, C. 1937. The behavior of children receiving benzedrine. *American Journal of Psychiatry* 94:577–585.

Breggin, P. R. 1991. *Toxic psychiatry: Why therapy, empathy and love must replace the drugs, electroshock and biochemical theories of the "new psychiatry."* New York: St. Martin's Press.

———. 1992a. A Case of fluoxetine-induced stimulant side effects with suicidal ideation associated with a possible withdrawal syndrome ("crashing"). *International Journal of Risk and Safety in Medicine* 3:325–328.

———. 1992b. *Beyond conflict: From self-help and psychotherapy to peacemaking.* New York: St. Martin's Press.

———. 1994. Testimony, October 17–19, in *Fentress et al. vs. Shea Communications et al.* ("the Wesbecker case"), volume 16. Jefferson Circuit Court, Division one, Louisville, Kentucky, case no. 90-CI–06033.

———. 1995. Prozac "hazardous" to children. *Clinical Psychiatry News*, September, p. 11.

———. 1997a. *Brain-disabling treatments in psychiatry: Drugs, electroshock, and the role of the FDA.* New York: Springer.

———. 1997b. *The heart of being helpful: Empathy and the creation of a healing presence.* New York: Springer.

———. 1998a. *Talking back to Ritalin: What doctors aren't telling you about stimulants for children.* Monroe, Me: Common Courage Press.

———. 1998b. Analysis of adverse behavioral effects of benzodiazepines with a discussion of drawing scientific conclusions from the FDA's Spontaneous Reporting System. *Journal of Mind and Behavior* 19:21–50.

———. 1998c. Psychotherapy in emotional crises without resort to psychiatric medication. *The Humanistic Psychologist* 25:2–14, 1998.

———. 1998d. Risks and mechanism of action of stimulants. *NIH consensus development conference program and abstracts: Diagnosis and treatment of attention deficit hyperactivity disorder,* pp. 105–120. Rockville, Md.: National Institutes of Health.

———. 1999a. Psychostimulants in the treatment of children diagnosed with ADHD. Part 1: Acute risks and psychological effects. *Ethical Human Sciences and Services* 1(1):13–33.

———. 1999b (in press). Psychostimulants in the treatment of children diagnosed with ADHD. Part 2: Adverse effects on brain and behavior. *Ethical Human Sciences and Services* 1(3).

———. 1999c. Psychostimulants in the treatment of children diagnosed with ADHD: Risks and mechanism of action. *International Journal of Risk and Safety in Medicine* 12(1):3–35.

———. 1999d. To love them is to drug them? We must stop using psychiatric drugs to control our children—and take back the responsibility of raising them. *Dr. Laura Perspective*, pp. 8–9ff.

————. 1999e. Psychiatry's reliance on coercion. *Ethical Human Sciences and Services* 1(2):115–118.

Breggin, P. R., and G. Breggin. 1994. *Talking back to Prozac: What doctors aren't telling you about today's most controversial drug*. New York: St. Martin's Press.

————. 1994. *The war against children*. New York: St. Martin's Press.

————. 1998. *The war against children of color*. Rev. ed. Monroe, Me.: Common Courage Press.

Breggin, P. R., and D. Cohen. 1999. *Your drug may be your problem: How and why to stop taking psychiatric medications*. Reading, Mass.: Perseus Books.

Breggin, P., and E. M. Stern, eds. 1996. *Psychosocial approaches to deeply disturbed persons*. New York: Haworth Press.

Brener, N. D., T. R. Simon, E. G. Krug, and R. Lowry. 1999. Recent trends in violence-related behaviors among high school students in the United States. *Journal of the American Medical Association* 282 (August 4):440–446.

Breton, D., and C. Largent. 1996. *The paradigm conspiracy*. Center City, Minn.: Hazeldon.

Briggs, B., and J. Blevins. 1999. Harris, a consummate actor, his secret yen for revenge. *Denver Post*, May 2, p. 18A.

Bronner, E. 1999. Assurance and anxiety after ruling. *New York Times*, May 25, 1999, p. A24. This ruling was the U.S. Supreme Court ruling on school harassment.

————. 1999. Rethinking America's schools of hard knocks: Ugly rites of passage. *New York Times*, May 30, section 4, p. 1.

Brooke, J. 1999a. Diary of a high school gunman reveals a plan to kill hundreds. *New York Times*, April 27, p. A1.

————. 1999b. Little was done on complaints in Littleton file. *New York Times*, May 1, p. A1.

————. 1999c. A new hint of missed signals in Littleton. *New York Times*, May 5, p. A14.

————. 1999d. Congressman from Littleton explains vote for gun control. *New York Times*, June 21, p. A10.

Bruni, F. 1999. Senate votes gun curbs, hours after school shooting. *New York Times*, May 21, p. A1.

————. 1999a. The new politics of gun control. *New York Times*, May 30, section 4, p. 3.

————. 1999b. Tipper Gore keeps cautious watch at door she opened. *New York Times*, June 7, p. A16.

Byers, J. A. 1999. Play's *the* thing. *Natural History*, July–August, pp. 40ff.

Caldwell, C. 1999. Levittown to Littleton. *National Review*, May 31, pp. 30–32.

Califano, J. A. 1998. A weapon in the war on drugs: Dining in. *Washington Post*, October 19, p. A21.

Callahan, P. 1999. Killers' parents were warned. *Denver Post*, May 7, p. 1B.

Caplan, P. 1995. *They say you're crazy: How the world's most powerful psychiatrists decide who's normal*. New York: Addison-Wesley.

Carnegie Council on Adolescent Development. 1989. *Turning Points: Preparing American youth for the 21st century*. New York: Carnegie Corporation.

Carney, J., and J. F. Dickerson. 1999. Political gunplay. *Time*, May 31, p. 53.

Castellano, M. 1995. Kentucky fried verdict up for grabs. *New Jersey Law Journal*, May 15, p. 39.

Chamberlin, J. 1978. *On our own: Patient-controlled alternatives to the mental health system*. New York: Hawthorn.

Chesler, P. 1987. *Women and madness*. New York: Harcourt Brace.

Chrisjohn, R., and S. Young. 1997. *The circle game: Shadows and substance in the Indian residential school experience in Canada*. Penticton, British Columbia: Theytus Books.

Christian, N. 1999. Is smaller perhaps better? *Time*, May 31, p. 43.

Chua-Eoan, H. 1999. Escaping from the darkness. *Time*, May 31, p. 44.

Clinical Psychiatry News. 1995. Prozac for kids: "Landmark" study affirms drug's use. July, p. 1.

Cloud, J. 1999. Just a routine school shooting. *Time*, May 31, p. 34.

Code of Federal Regulations (CFR), Food and Drugs. 1990. Washington, D.C.: Office of the Federal Register, National Archives and Records Administration.

Cohen. A. (1999). Criminals as copycats. *Time*, May 3, p. 38.

Colbert, T. C. 1996. *Broken brains or wounded hearts: What causes mental illness*. Santa Ana, CA: Kevco Publishers

Coles, G. 1987. *The learning mystique: A critical look at "learning disabilities."* New York: Pantheon.

———. 1998. *Reading lessons: The debate over literacy*. New York: Hill & Wang.

Connolly, C. 1999. Tipper Gore details depression treatment. *Washington Post*, May 8, p. A2.

Cooper, K. J. 1999. Youth violence declines: CDC's national studies defy public perceptions. *Washington Post*, August 4, p. A1.

Cooper, K. J., and S. A. Pressley. 1999. Florida House approves school vouchers; Senate votes today. *Washington Post*, April 29, p. A2.

Cooper, K. J., and D. Russakoff. 1999. "Columbine Hysteria," or smart policy? *Washington Post*, May 25, p. A1.

"Court TV." 1999. Psychologist: Georgia school shooter said he only wanted to cause panic. From Website (August 11): www.courttv.com/trials/solomon/081099 ctv.html.

Covey, S. R. 1997. *The 7 habits of highly effective families*. New York: Golden Books.

Crossette, B. 1995. Agency sees risk in drug to temper child behavior. *New York Times*, February 29, p. A14.

David, R. 1992. The health crisis in African American communities: Rethinking the diagnosis and the prescription. *Harvard Journal of African American Public Policy* 1:1–9.

DeBernardo, C. R., and J. P. McGee. 1999. Preventing the classroom avenger's next attack: Safeguarding against school shootings. Unpublished manuscript.

Dedman, B. 1999. Secret Service is seeking pattern for school killers. *New York Times*, June 21, p. A10.

Department of Health and Human Services Press Office. 1999. The Department of Health and Human Services on mental health issues. HHS fact sheet. From Website (July 7): www.hhs.gov/news/press/1999press/990607.html.

Dinkmeyer, Sr., D., G. D. McKay, and D. Dinkmeyer, Jr. 1997. *The parent's handbook*. Circle Pines, Minn.: AGS.

Drug Enforcement Administration (DEA). 1995. *Methylphenidate (A background paper)*. Washington, D.C.: Drug and Chemical Evaluation Section, Office of Diversion Control, DEA, U.S. Department of Justice.

Dumont, M. 1999. Book review of *Reading Lessons*, by G. Coles. *Ethical Human Sciences and Services* 1:107–108.

Eisler, R. 1987. *The chalice and the blade*. New York: Harper & Row.

Ellinwood, E. H., and T. H. Lee. 1996. Central nervous system stimulants and anorectic agents. In M. N. G. Dukes, ed., *Meyler's side effects of drugs: An encyclopedia of adverse reactions and interactions*, 13th ed. New York: Elsevier, pp. 1–30.

Emslie, G. J., A. J. Rush, W. A. Weinberg, R. A. Kowatch, C. W. Hughes, T. Carmody, and J. Rintelmann. 1997. A double-blind, randomized, placebo-controlled trial of fluoxetine in children and adolescents with depression. *Archives of General Psychiatry* 54:1031–1037.

Erikson, C. 1999. Littleton lessons. Letter to the editor. *Youth Today*, July–August, pp. 5–6.

Eth, S., and R. S. Pynoos, eds. 1985. *Post-traumatic stress disorder in children*. Washington, D.C.: American Psychiatric Association Press.

Fahri, P. 1999. The tragedy that didn't seize TV: Why was Columbine a bigger story than the massacre in Atlanta? *Washington Post*, July 31, p. C1.

Farber, S. 1999. *Unholy madness: The church's surrender to psychiatry*. Downers Grove, Ill.: InterVarsity Press.

Faber, A., and E. Mazlish. 1980. *How to talk so kids will listen and listen so kids will talk*. New York: Avon.

Fernando, S. 1993. Psychiatry and racism. *Changes: An International Journal of Psychology and Psychotherapy* 11 (March):46–48.

Fieve, R. R. 1973. *Moodswing: The third revolution in psychiatry.* New York: Bantom.

Firestone, D. 1999. An affinity for weapons, but no signs of anger. *New York Times*, May 21, p. A18.

Firestone, P., L. M. Musten, S. Pisterman, J. Mercer, and S. Bennett. 1998. Short-term side effects of stimulant medications in preschool children with attention-deficit / hyperactivity disorder: A double-blind placebo-controlled study. *Journal of Child and Adolescent Psychopharmacology* 8:13–25.

Fisher, S., and R. Greenberg. 1989. *The limits of biological treatments for psychological distress: Comparisons with psychotherapy and placebo.* Hillsdale, N.J.: Lawrence Erlbaum.

———. 1997. *From placebo to panacea: Putting psychiatric drugs to the test.* New York: John Wiley.

Fisher, R., and S. Fisher. 1996. Antidepressants for children: Is scientific support necessary? *Journal of Nervous and Mental Disease* 184:99–102.

Food and Drug Administration. 1999. Adverse Event Reporting System for Luvox (Fluvoxamine) for November 1, 1997 - July 2, 1999. Rockville, Md.: Center for Drug Evaluation and Research, Office of Training and Communication, Freedom of Information Staff.

Fossey, D. 1983. *Gorillas in the mist.* Boston: Houghton Mifflin.

Foster, D. 1999. Harassment common at Columbine. *Denver Rocky Mountain News*, May 7, p. 49A.

Fowler, M. 1992. *Educators' manual.* A project of the CH.A.D.D. National Education Committee. Plantation, Fla.: CH.A.D.D.

Fried, J. P., and B. Harden. 1999. Officer guilty of helping torture immigrant. *Time*, June 9, p. A1.

Freire, P. 1998. *Pedagogy of the oppressed.* New York: Continuum. Originally published in 1970.

Fromm, E. 1950. *Psychoanalysis and religion.* New Haven: Yale University Press.

———. 1956. *The art of loving: An inquiry into the nature of love.* New York: Harper Colophon.

Fuller, R. 1994. Deposition, April 14, in *Fentress et al. vs. Shea Communications et al.* ("the Wesbecker case"), volume 1. Jefferson Circuit Court, Division One, Louisville, Kentucky, case no. 90-Cl–6033.

Garbarino, J. 1999. *Lost boys: Why our sons turn violent and how we can save them.* New York: Free Press.

Gardner, H. 1983. *Frames of mind: The theory of multiple intelligences.* New York: Basic Books.

———. 1993. *Creating minds*. New York: Basic Books.

Gatto, J. T. 1992. *Dumbing us down: The hidden curriculum of compulsory schooling*. Gabriola Island, British Columbia: New Society Publishers.

Gerhardt, P. 1999. Running at Ritalin: Studies say alternative drug may be
more convenient. *The Washington Post Health*, May 25, p. 9.

———. 1999. New drugs show promise in relieving depression, *The Washington Post Health*, July 13, p. 5.

Gibeaut, J. 1996. Mood-altering verdict. *American Bar Association Journal*,
August, p. 18.

Gilbert, S. 1999. Bully or victim? Studies show they're much alike. *New York
Times*, August 10, p. D7.

Gilligan, C. 1982. *In a different voice: Psychological theory and women's development*. Cambridge, Mass.: Harvard University Press.

Gilligan, C., N. P. Lyons, and T. J. Hanmer, eds. 1990. *Making connections:
The relational worlds of adolescent girls at Emma Willard School*. Cambridge,
Mass.: Harvard University Press.

Ginott, H. 1969. *Between parent and child*. New York: Avon.

Glaberson, W. 1999. Right to bear arms: A second look. *New York Times*,
May 30, section 4, p. 3.

———. 1999b. Town rides to the rescue of its young inmates. *New York
Times*, August 7, p. A6.

Glasser, William. 1998. *Choice theory: A new psychology of personal freedom*.
New York: HarperCollins.

Golding, W. 1954. *Lord of the flies*. New York: Berkley.

Goldsmith, S. 1997a. Medicating foster care: Unmonitored stream of mood
drugs imperils children entrusted to state. *Seattle Post-Intelligencer*, March
31, p. 1.

———. 1997b. A drug poisoning: 6-year-old died while in state's hands.
Seattle Post-Intelligencer, April 1, p. 1.

———. 1997c. Drugs and doubt in Wenatchee: Medications cloud investigation of sex cases. *Seattle Post-Intelligencer*, April 2, p. 1.

———. 1997d. Boy's death spurs Oregon act. *Seattle Post-Intelligencer*, April
3, p. 1.

Goldstein, A. 1999. Shooter used often-prescribed drug. *Washington Post*,
April 30, p. A5.

Gomory, T. 1999. Programs of assertive community treatment (PACT): A
critical review. *Ethical Human Sciences and Services* 1, 147–63.

Goodall, J. 1983. *The chimpanzees of Gombe*. Cambridge, Mass.: Harvard University Press.

Goodwin, F. K. 1992. Partial transcript of address, February 11, to the National Mental Health Advisory Council, pp. 115–120. Unpublished.

Gordon, T. 1970. *P.E.T.: Parent Effectiveness Training*. New York: Peter H. Wyden.

Gorney, C. 1999. Teaching Johnny the appropriate way to flirt. *New York Times Magazine*, June 13, pp. 43ff.

Grace, J. 1997. When the silence fell. *Time*, December 15.

Granat, D. 1995. The young and the restless. *Washingtonian*, April, p. 60.

Green, A. 1989. Physical and sexual abuse of children. In H. Kaplan and B. Sadock, eds., *Comprehensive textbook of psychiatry*. Baltimore: Williams & Wilkins, pp. 1962–1970.

Greenhouse, L. 1999. Sex harassment in class is ruled schools' liability. *New York Times*, May 25, p. A1.

Grier, W. H., and M. Cobbs. 1980. New York: Basic Books.

Gualtieri, C. T., and L. J. Barnhill. 1988. Tardive dyskinesia in special populations. In M. E. Wolf and A. D. Mosnaim, eds., *Tardive dyskinesia: Biological mechanisms and clinical aspects*. Washington, D.C.: American Psychiatric Press, pp. 135–154.

Gualtieri, C. T., D. Quade, R. E. Hicks, J. P. Mayo, and S. R. Schroeder. 1984. Tardive dyskinesia and other clinical consequences of neuroleptic treatment in children and adolescents. *American Journal of Psychiatry* 141:20–23.

Gugliotta, G. 1999. Judge curbs FDA role on "off-label" therapy: Drug firms more free to push new uses. *Washington Post*, July 29, p. A1.

Gurian, M. 1999. *A fine young man: What parents, mentors, and educators can do to shape adolescent boys into exceptional men*. San Francisco: T. J. Tarcher.

Hacker, A. 1992. *Two nations: Black and white, separate, hostile, and unequal*. New York: Charles Scribner's Sons.

Harmon, A. 1999. Theme song on the Internet: The pain of social ostracism. *New York Times*, April 24, p. A12.

Hartocollis, A. 1999. Private school choice plan draws a million aid-seekers. *New York Times*, April 21, p. A1.

Hauser, K. 1999. Letters to the editor. *Youth Today*, July–August, p. 4.

Herman, J. 1997. *Trauma and recovery*. New York: Basic Books.

Helms, A. D. 1999. When Mom and Dad trade places with kids. *Washington Post*, April 20, p. C4.

Hernandez, R. 1999. Legislators near accord on special education overall. *New York Times*, June 12, p. A14.

Hiatt, F. 1999. A Littleton massacre every day. *Washington Post*, April 25, p. B7.

Hooks, Bell. 1994. *Teaching to transgress: Education as the practice of freedom*. New York: Routledge.

Huffington, A. 1997. Exit Joe Camel, enter Joe Prozac. From Website (July 17): http://ariannaonlinecom/columns/files/071797/html.

———. 1999. Are we fueling the demons in kids? *Los Angeles Times*, May 10.

Hunter, M. 1999. Work work work work! It's taking over our lives—invading our homes, haunting our holidays, showing up for dinner. Should we care? *Modern Maturity*, May–June, pp. 37ff.

Imse, A., and J. Kass. 1999. Columbine killers robbed van. *Denver Rocky Mountain News*, May 4, p. 7a.

Ingold, J. 1999. 4 Adams teens to be tried as adults. *Denver Rocky Mountain News*, May 15, Mile High Suburbs section, p. 1.

International Center for the Study of Psychiatry and Psychology (ICSPP), 4628 Chestnut Street, Bethesda, MD 20814. Website: www.Breggin.com.

International Narcotics Control Board (INCB). 1995. Dramatic increase in methylphenidate consumption in US: Marketing methods questioned. *INCB Annual Report 1995: Background Note No. 2.* February 28. Vienna, Austria: United Nations Information Service.

———. 1999. Europeans taking "downers"; Americans taking "uppers." *INCB Annual Report 1998: Release No. 4.* February 23. Vienna, Austria: United Nations Information Service.

Isaacson, W. 1999. Covering the violence. *Time*, May 31, p. 6.

Jain, U., B. Birmaher, M. Garcia, M. Al-Shabbout, and N. Ryan. 1992. Fluoxetine in children and adolescents with mood disorders: A chart review of efficacy and adverse reactions. *Journal of Child and Adolescent Psychopharmacology* 2:259–265.

Jennings, C. 1999. Press briefing, June 7, on White House Conference on Mental Health. Jennings is deputy assistant to the President for health policy. From Website (June 7): www.mentalhealth.gov/jennings.asp.

Joint Commission on Mental Illness and Health. 1961. *Action for Mental Health: Final report.* New York: Basic Books.

Jones, J. (Reuters). 1999. School shooting hits Canada. From Website (April 28): http://abcnews.go.com/sections/world/DailyNews/canadashooting 990429.html.

Kane, G. (Cox News Service). 1996. Ritalin puts military careers out of bounds: Rejection of would-be enlistees a problem for recruiters. *Roanoke Times*, November 30, p. A1.

Karon, B. 1975. *Black scars: A rigorous investigation of the effects of discrimination.* New York: Springer.

Karon, B., and G. Vandenbos. 1981. *The psychotherapy of schizophrenia: The treatment of choice.* New York: Jason Aronson.

Katz, J. 1999. Report from Hell High. *Brill's Content*, July–August, pp. 71–72.

Kaufman, M. 1999. Are psychiatric drugs safe for children? *Washington Post Health*, May 4, p. 7.

————. 1999. White House decries stigma. *Washington Post Health*, June 8, p. 7.

Keirsey, D. 1998. *Please understand me, II*. Amherst, New York: Prometheus.

Kenworthy, T. 1999. Up to 25 die in Colorado school shooting. *Washington Post*, April 21, p. A1.

Kenworthy, T., and R. Suro. 1999. 9 days after rampage, police still under fire. *Washington Post*, April 30, p. A1.

Kenworthy, T., and C. W. Thompson. 1999. Colorado man linked to killers' handgun. *Washington Post*, May 4, p. A6.

Kiely, K., and G. Fields. 1999. Colo. killers' last days gave no hint of plans. *USA Today*, May 3, p. 7A.

Kindlon, D., and M. Thompson. 1999. *Raising Cain: Protecting the emotional life of boys*. New York: Ballantine.

King, R. A., M. A. Riddle, P. B. Chappell, M. T. Hardin, G. M. Anderson, P. Lombroso, and L. Scahill. 1991. Emergence of self-destructive phenomena in children and adolescents during fluoxetine treatment. *Journal of the American Academy of Child and Adolescent Psychiatry* 30 (March):179–186.

Kocrner, B. J. 1999. From way cool to out of control. *U.S. News & World Report*, May 3, p. 20.

Kohn, A. 1986. *No contest: The case against competition*. Boston, Mass.: Houghton Mifflin.

Koop, C. E. 1992. Violence in America: A public health emergency. *Journal of the American Medical Association* 275:3075–3076.

Koplewicz, H. 1996. *It's nobody's fault: New hope and help for difficult children*. New York: Random House.

Kotlowitz, A. 1991. *There are no children here*. New York: Anchor Books.

Kozol, J. 1981. *On being a teacher*. Oxford, U.K.: Oneworld.

————. 1991. *Savage inequalities: Children in America's schools*. New York: Crown.

Kramer, P. 1993. *Listening to Prozac*. New York: Viking.

Kuhn, T. S. 1976. *The structure of scientific revolutions*. 3rd ed. Chicago: University of Chicago Press. First published in 1962.

Lacayo, R. 1999. Why do schoolkids kill? In *Time Almanac*. Boston: Time Inc., p. 872.

Lambert, N. 1998. Stimulant treatment as a risk factor for nicotine use and substance abuse. In *NIH consensus development conference program and abstracts: Diagnosis and treatment of attention deficit hyperactivity disorder*. Rockville, Md.: National Institutes of Health, pp. 191–200.

Lamont, C. 1977. *The philosophy of humanism*. New York: Frederick Ungar.

Lang, L. H. 1999. Newest depression medications widely prescribed for children. Press release, April 22, School of Medicine, University of North Carolina at Chapel Hill. Press release embargoed until May 1.

Levy, D. A. 1997. *Tools of critical thinking: Metathoughts for psychology*. Boston: Allyn & Bacon.

Lewin, T. 1999. Arizona high school provides glimpse inside cliques' divisive webs. *New York Times*, May 2, p. 26.

Long, R. 1999. Hollywood, Littleton, and us: How to think about the violence debate. *National Review*, July 26, pp. 44–46.

Los Angeles Times. 1999. Prozac surge among kids. Editorial, May 1.

Luke, S. K. (Associated Press). 1999. Kids' mental health getting more notice. *USA Today*, June 14, p. 11A.

Manning, A. 1999. Chemistry of a killer: Is it in the brain? *USA Today*, April 29, p. 2A.

Marsella, A. J., M. J. Friedman, E. T. Gerrity, and R. M. Scurfield, eds. 1996. *Ethnocultural aspects of posttraumatic stress disorder: Issues, research, and clinical applications*. Washington, D.C.: American Psychological Association.

Maslow, A. 1970. *Religions, values, and peak-experiences*. New York: Penguin Books.

Mason, W. 1994a. Drugs for kids sparks parental concern. *Philadelphia Tribune*, March 29.

———. 1994b. Ritalin furor rages. *Philadelphia Tribune*, May 27.

Massaro, G. 1999. Police say teacher was not abandoned. *Denver Rocky Mountain News*, April 30, p. 71A.

Masson, J. M. 1996. *The wild child: The unsolved mystery of Kaspar Hauser*. New York: Free Press.

Mauro, T. 1999. Will every childish taunt turn into a federal case? *USA Today*, May 25, p. 1A.

Mayes, S. D., D. L. Crites, E. O. Bixler, F. J. Humphrey, and R. E. Mattison. 1994. Methylphenidate and ADHD: Influence of age, IQ and neurodevelopmental status. *Developmental Medicine and Child Neurology* 36: 1099–1107.

Mays, P. J. 1999. (Associated Press). Terror intrudes on day at the office: Shock more than panic marks workers' escapes. *USA Today*, July 30, p. 2A.

McGee, J. P., and C. DeBernardo. 1999a. The classroom avenger. *Forensic Examiner*, May–June, pp. 16–18.

———. 1999b. The classroom avenger. Unpublished. (An expanded version of their 1999a paper.)

Melega, W. P., M. J. Raleigh, D. B. Stout, S. C. Huang, and M. E. Phelps. 1997a. Ethological and 6-[18F]fluoro-L-DOPA-PET profiles of long-term vulnerability to chronic amphetamine. *Behavioural Brain Research* 84:258–268.

Melega, W. P., M. J. Raleigh, D. B. Stout, G. Lacan, S. C. Huang, and M. E. Phelps. 1997b. Recovery of striatal dopamine function after acute amphetamine- and methamphetamine-induced neurotoxicity in the vervet monkey. *Brain Research* 766:113–20.

Mender, D. 1994. *The myth of neuropsychiatry*. New York: Plenum Press.

Mercer, P. 1999. Failures hold new fear for Florida schools. *New York Times*, May 2, p. 27.

Meredith, R. 1999. Bomb, arrests and school plot unnerve small Michigan city. *New York Times*, May 18, p. A12.

Miedzian, M. 1991. *Boys will be boys: Breaking the link between masculinity and violence*. New York: Doubleday.

Mifflin, L. 1999. Many researchers say link is already clear on media and youth violence. *New York Times*, May 9, p. 23.

———. 1999. Pediatricians urge limiting TV watching. *New York Times*, August 4, p. A1.

Miller, A. 1983. *For your own good: Hidden cruelty in child rearing and the roots of violence*. New York: Farrar Straus Giroux.

Miller, T. W., ed. 1989. *Stressful life events*. Madison, Conn.: International Universities Press.

Moore, T. J. 1998. *Prescription for disaster: The hidden dangers in your medicine cabinet*. New York: Simon & Schuster.

Mosher, L. R. 1996. Soteria: A therapeutic community for psychotic persons. In P. R. Breggin and E. M. Stern, eds. *Psychosocial approaches to deeply disturbed persons*. New York: Haworth Press, pp. 43–58.

Mosher, L. R., and L. Burti. 1994. *Community mental health: Principles and practice*. New York: Norton.

Mosteller, F. 1999. The case for smaller classes *Harvard Magazine*, May–June, pp. 34–35.

Mowat, F. 1987. *Woman in the mists*. New York: Warner Books.

Murray, B. 1996. Home schools: How do they affect children. *Monitor*, December, p. 24.

Myths and facts about mental illness. 1999. Press release, June 7, from the White House Conference on Mental Health. From Website: www.mentalhealth.gov.myths.asp.

Nasrallah, H., J. Loney, S. Olson., M. McCalley-Whitters, J. Kramer, and C. Jacoby. 1986. Cortical atrophy in young adults with a history of hyperactivity in childhood. *Psychiatry Research* 17:241–246.

National Center for Children in Poverty. 1990. *Five million children: A statistical profile of our poorest young citizens*. New York: Columbia University Press.

National Center on Institutions and Alternatives (NCIAA). 1992. *Hobbling a generation: Young African American males in the criminal justice system of*

America's cities. Baltimore, Md.: NCIAA. Publication available from NCIAA, 635 Slaters Lane, Suite G–100, Alexandria, Virginia 22314.

National Commission on Children. 1991a. *Beyond rhetoric: A new American agenda for children and families.* Washington, D.C.: National Commission on Children.

————. 1991b. *Speaking of kids: A National survey of children and parents.* Washington, D.C.: National Commission on Children.

National Institutes of Health. 1998. Diagnosis and treatment of attention deficit hyperactivity disorder. National Institutes of Health Consensus Development Conference Statement (draft), issued following the conference that took place on November 16–18, 1998.

Newsweek. 1999. Anatomy of a massacre. May 3, pp. 25ff.

New York Times. 1999. Town in Texas discusses own school crisis, April 27, p. A21; Columbine students talk of the disaster and life, April 30, p. A25; Tipper Gore says she took treatment for depression, May 8, p. A10; Word for word/Columbine High School: How carnage in our hallways scarred us, and made us better people, May 23, p. 7.

Nodding, N. 1992. *The challenge to care in our schools: An alternative approach to education.* New York: Teachers College Press.

Novak, V. 1999. Picking a fight with the N.R.A. *Time*, May 31, p. 54.

Oaks, D., ed. 1999. *Dendron.* Newspaper available from P.O. Box 11284, Eugene, OR 97440. Website: dendron@ efn.org.

Obmascik, M., P. G. Chronis, and M. Robinson. 1999. Marines reject Harris: Killer on psychiatric medication. *Denver Post*, April 28, p. 1.

Ochberg, F. M. 1988. *Post-traumatic therapy and victims of violence.* New York: Brunner/Mazel.

O'Driscoll, P., and G. Fields. 1999. 3 teens detained during massacre cleared. *USA Today*, April 29, p. 1A.

Office of Mrs. Gore. 1999. Press Release, May 19: Tipper Gore to chair White House Conference on Mental Health, to take place on June 7, 1999. The White House. From Website: www.mentalhealth.gov/media4.asp.

Office of the Press Secretary. 1999. Radio address, June 5, by the President and Mrs. Gore to the nation. The Oval Office, the White House. From Website: www.pub.white.gov/uri-res/12 . . . :pdi://oma.eop.gov.us/1999/6/7/14.text.1

Office of the *Federal Register.* 1990. *Code of Federal Regulations (CFR), Food and Drugs* 21, parts 200–299. Rev. ed. Washington, D.C.: National Archives and Records Administration.

Oldenburg, A. 1999. Parents see violence, not sex, as biggest concern with media. *USA Today*, May 6, p. 1D.

Olinger, D., M. Robinson, and M. Eddy. 1999. Harrises demand immunity. *Denver Post*, May 1, p. 1A.

O'Meara, K. P. 1999. Doping kids: Though shocked by bizarre shootings in schools, few Americans have noticed how many school shooters were among the 6 million kids now on psychotropic drugs. *Insight*, June 28, pp. 10–13.

Physicians' Desk Reference. 1999. Montvale, N.J.: Medical Economics.

Pollack, W. 1998. *Real boys: Rescuing our sons from the myths of boyhood*. New York: Henry Holt.

Potter, J. W. 1995. Corrected Judgment and Court's Motion Pursuant to Civil Rule 60.01 and Notice, April 19, in *Fentress et al. vs. Shea Communications et al.* ("the Wesbecker case"), volume 1. Jefferson Circuit Court, Division One, Louisville, Kentucky, case no. 90-CI–06033.

President announces national school safety training program for teachers and educational personnel. 1999. White House Conference on Mental Health, June 7. From Website: www.mentalhealth.gov/school.asp.

Psychiatric News. 1999. White House announces bold plans to help mentally ill, eradicate stigma. July 2, p. 1.

Quinn, P. O., and J. M. Stern. 1991. *Putting on the brakes: Young people's guide to understanding attention deficit hyperactivity disorder (ADHD)*. New York: Magination Press.

Rapoport, J. L. 1989. *The boy who couldn't stop washing*. New York: E. P. Dutton.

Reuters News Report. September 1, 1999. Police find Prozac in Atlanta shooter's car.

Riddle, M. A., R. A. King, M. T. Hardin, L. Scahill, S. I. Ort, P. Chappell, A. Rasmusson, and J. F. Leckman. 1990–91. Behavioral side effects of fluoxetine in children and adolescents *Journal of Child and Adolescent Psychopharmacology* 1:193–198.

Rimer, S. 1999. Another great escape for massacre's "boy in window." *New York Times*, May 8, p. A10.

Robinson, M., and P. Chronis. 1999. High school freshman held in Columbine copycat plot. *Denver Post*, May 15, p. 3B.

Rook, A. 1999. Economy's rising tide lets kids sink. *Youth Today*, July–August, p. 9.

Rogers, C. 1961. *On becoming a person*. New York: Houghton Mifflin.

Ross, C. A., and A. Pam. 1995. *Pseudoscience in biological psychiatry: Blaming the body*. New York: John Wiley.

Rotbart, D. 1999. An intimate look at covering Littleton. *Columbia Journalism Review*, May–June, pp. 24–25.

Sack, K. 1999. Youth with 2 guns shoots 6 at Georgia school. *New York Times*, May 21, p. A1.

Sack, K. 1999. Gunman in Atlanta slays 9, then himself: His wife and 2 children also killed. *New York Times*, July 30, p. A1.

Samuels, C. A. 1999. Pr. William schools ban bulky coats in buildings. *Washington Post*, May 27, p. A24.

Scanlon, B. 1999. In memory of Dave Sanders. *Denver Rocky Mountain News*, May 2, p. 43A.

Scanlon, L. 1995. Secret deal struck at trial not to appeal Prozac verdict. Move halted evidence on 2nd drug, judge thinks. *Courier-Journal* (Louisville, Kentucky), April 20, p. B1.

Schachar, R. J., R. Tannock, C. Cunningham, and P. V. Corkum. 1997. Behavioral, situational, and temporal effects of treatment of ADHD with methylphenidate. *Journal of the American Academy of Child and Adolescent Psychiatry* 36:754–763.

Schmued, L. C., and J. F. Bowyer. 1997. Methamphetamine exposure can produce neuronal degeneration in mouse hippocampal remnants. *Brain Research* 759:135–140.

Schrag, P., and D. Divoky. 1975. *The myth of the hyperactive child*. New York: Pantheon.

Schrader, A. 1999. Drug found in Harris body. *Denver Post*, May 4.

Schulte, B. 1999. After Littleton, Montgomery schools rethink safety. *Washington Post*, July 12, p. A1.

Segal, D. 1999. Drugmaker readies fen-phen settlement. *New York Times*, September 18, p. A1.

Seymour, L. 1999. Cherishing their schoolhouses: In western Loudoun, older buildings mean smaller, more intimate classes. *Washington Post*, June 6, p. C1.

Shear, M. D., and J. L. Salmon. 1999. An education in taunting: Schools learning dangers of letting bullies go unchecked. *Washington Post*, May 2, p. C1.

Sheng, P., B. Ladenheim, T. H. Moran, X.-B. Wang, and J. L. Cadet. 1996. Methamphetamine-induced neurotoxicity is associated with increased striatal AP–1 DNA-binding activity in mice. *Molecular Brain Research* 42:171–174.

Shore, S. 1999. Columbine victim's faith eulogized nationwide. *Denver Post*, May 15, p. 3B.

Siebert, A. 1999. Brain disease hypothesis for schizophrenia disconfirmed by all evidence. *Ethical Human Sciences and Services* 1:179–189.

Simpson, K. 1999. Victim recounts his leap. *Denver Post*, May 8, p. 1A.

Simpson, K., P. Callahan, and P. Lowe. 1999. Dylan Klebold's dark side a shock to friends, classmates. *Denver Post*, May 2, p. 19A.

Smart, T. 1999. Six survival tips. *Modern Maturity*, May–June, p. 41.

Smith, S. D. 1999. Mr. Dad: Stay-at-home fathers find fulfillment. *Gazette* (Cedar Rapids, Iowa), June 20, p. 1D.

Solvay Pharmaceuticals, Inc. 1999. Adverse Event Report FLUV-00299000121, May 14, to the FDA concerning Luvox blood levels from an autopsy of one of the April 20, 1999, school shooters. Rockville, Md.: FDA Medical Products Reporting Program. Obtained through Freedom of Information Act.

Solvay Pharmaceuticals, Inc., and Upjohn Company. 1994. Press release (December 6): New hope for the estimated five million people suffering from obsessive compulsive disorder. Marietta, Ga.: Solvay Pharmaceuticals, Inc.

Sommers-Flanagan, J., and R. Sommers-Flanagan. 1996. Efficacy of antidepressant medication with depressed youth: What psychologists should know. *Professional Psychology: Research and Practice* 27:145–153.

Sonsalla, P. K., N. D. Jochnowitz, G. D. Zeevalk, J. A. Oostveen, and E. D. Hall. 1996. Treatment of mice with methamphetamine produces cell loss in the substantia nigra. *Brain Research* 738:172–5.

Stanton, T. 1999. Seneca Center: A resident treatment program without psychiatric drugs. *Ethical Human Sciences and Services* 1:103–106.

Stein, J. A., J. M. Golding, J. M. Siegel, M. A. Burnam, and S. B. Sorenson. 1985. Long-term psychological sequelae of child sexual abuse: The Los Angeles epidemiological catchment area study. In G. E. Wyatt and G. J. Powell, eds. *Lasting effects of child sexual abuse*. Newbury Park, Calif.: Sage Publications, pp. 135–154.

Steinberg, J. 1999. 13-year-olds charged in bomb threat were elite. *New York Times*, April 30, p. A27.

Steinmetz, S. K., and M. A. Straus. 1973. The family as the cradle of violence. *Society* 10(6):50–56.

Sternberg, R. S., ed. 1988. *The nature of creativity*. Cambridge, U.K.: Cambridge University Press.

———. 1990. *Wisdom: Its nature, origins, and development*. Cambridge, U.K.: Cambridge University Press.

Sternberg, R. S., and J. E. Davidson, eds. 1996. *The nature of insight*. Cambridge, Mass.: MIT Press.

Stolberg, S. G. 1999. Columbine shootings unpredictable, unpreventable, scientists say. *Denver Rocky Mountain News*, May 9, p. 45A.

Stone, D., B. Patton, and S. Heen. 1999. *Difficult conversations: How to discuss what matters most*. New York: Viking.

Tagliabue, J. 1999. Shoring up satan, closing limbo. *New York Times*, January 31, p. A4.

Tedford, D. 1999. New program seeks to identify the truly troubled students. *Houston Chronicle*, July 12, p. 13A.

Temple, R. 1987. Memorandum: Fluoxetine label. Memorandum dated December 28 from the director, Office of Drug Research and Review, to the director, Division of Neuropharmacology Drug Products. Internal Document of the Department of Health and Human Services, Public Health Service, Food and Drug Administration, Center for Drug Evaluation and Research.

Trafford, A. 1999. Confronting mental illness. *Washington Post Health*, June 8, p. 6.

Trial court's authority to investigate and determine the correctness and veracity of judgments. 1996. Hon. John W. Potter, Judge vs. Eli Lilly and Company (95-SC–580-MR). Appeal from Court of Appeals; opinion, May 30, by Justice Wintersheimer, reversing, rendered May 23, 1996. 43 K.L.S.5, pp. 33–35.

Twomey, S. 1999. Civil offense: Cursing on the river goes to trial. *Washington Post*, June 6, p. A1.

Umbarger C. C., A. P. Morrison, J. S. Dalsimer, and P. R. Breggin. 1962. *College students in a mental hospital: Contribution to the social rehabilitation of the mentally ill.* New York: Grune & Stratton.

U.S. Department of Education. 1998. *A guide to safe schools*. Washington, D.C.: U.S. Department of Education, Special Education and Rehabilitative Services. Obtainable From Website: www.ed.gov/offices/OSERS/ OSEP/earlywrn.html.

Valenstein, E. S. 1998. *Blaming the brain: The truth about drugs and mental health*. New York: Free Press.

van der Kolk, B. A., A. C. McFarlane, and L. Weisaeth, eds. 1996. *Traumatic stress: The effects of overwhelming experience on mind, body and society*. New York: Guilford.

Varchaver, M. (American Lawyer News Service). 1995. Prozac verdict was a sure thing. *Fulton County Daily Report* (Atlanta), September 25.

Verhovek, S. M. 1999. Sounds from a massacre: "Oh God, kids, stay down." *New York Times*, April 24, p. A1.

Vobejda, B. 1998. Too much time on the job perils teens' future, panel says. *Washington Post*, November 6, p. A3.

Von Drehle, D., and D. LeDuc. 1999. Heroism amid the terror. *Washington Post*, April 22, p. A1.

Vontress, C. E., J. A. Johnson, and L. R. Epp. 1999. *Cross-cultural counseling*. Alexandria, Va.: American Counseling Association.

Wagner, G. C., G. A. Ricaurte, C. E. Johanson, C. R. Schuster, and L. S. Seiden. 1980. Amphetamine induces depletion of dopamine and loss of dopamine uptake sites in caudate nucleus. *Neurology* 30:547–550.

Washington Post. 1999. Gun fever in the House. Editorial, June 17, p. A34.

Waters, R. 1999, June 17. Johnny get your pills: Are we overmedicating our kids? From Website (June 17): www.salon.com/health/feature/1999/06/17/antidepressants.

Weber, T. 1998. Widespread drugging found among Calif. foster children. *Arizona Republic*, May 23, p. A20.

Weis, R. 1999. N.Y. research centers faulted in child study: Patient protection is found lacking. *Washington Post*, June 12, p. A2.

Welch, E. 1999. Gun victims' medical care costs billions. *Washington Post*, August 4, p. A11.

Wender, P. 1973. *The hyperactive child: A handbook for parents*. New York: Crown.

Wender, P. 1995. *Attention deficit hyperactivity disorder in adults*. New York: Oxford University Press.

White House, Oval Office, Office of the Press Secretary. 1999b. Press release on White House Conference on Mental Health, June 7: Myths and facts about mental illness. From Website: www.mentalhealth.gov. myths.asp.

White House announces bold plans to help mentally ill, eradicate stigma. 1999. *Psychiatric News*, July 2, p. 1.

White House Conference on Mental Health. 1999. Remarks by the President, the first lady, the Vice President, Mrs. Gore, and others. Howard University, Washington, D.C., June 7. Distributed to the press by the Office of the Press Secretary.

White, J. 1999. Women dies of injuries from beating. *Washington Post*, July 2, p. B1.

Wilson, A. N. 1991. *Understanding black adolescent male violence: It's remediation and prevention*. New York: African World Infosystems.

Wolfe, D. A. 1987. *Child abuse: Implications for developmental psychopathology*. Newbury Park, Calif.: Sage Publications.

Wood, G. H. 1993. *Schools that work: America's most innovative public education programs*. New York: Penguin.

World Almanac and Books of Facts 1999. Mahway, N.J.: Primedia References.

Wyatt, G. E., and G. J. Powell G. J., eds. 1988. *Lasting effects of child sexual abuse*. Newbury Park, Calif.: Sage Publications.

Yette, S. F. 1971. *The Choice: The issue of black survival in America*. Silver Spring, Md.: Cottage Books.

Zaczek, R., G. Battaglia, J. F. Contrera, S. Culp, and E. G. De Souza. 1989. Methylphenidate and pemoline do not cause depletion of rat brain monoamine markers similar to that observed with methamphetamine. *Toxicology and Applied Pharmacology* 100:227–233.

Index

Abuse
  emotional, 23–24, 51, 52, 56
  medical, 279
  physical, 51–52, 56
  sexual, 24, 51–52, 56, 295n21,
    296n23
  See also Peers
Accidents, 58
ACT (Assertive Community
  Treatment), 26
Adams, John, 88
Adderall, 139. *See also* Stimulants
ADHD (Attention Deficit
  Hyperactivity Disorder), 22,
  116, 293n9, 299n2
Adler, Alfred, 86, 264–65
Adoption, 78
Adults
  meaningful relationships with,
    83
  stressors and, 48, 56
  See also Parents
African Americans, 38–39, 60,
  66–67, 212–217
  humiliation and, 184
  "pathologizing" and, 218
Alcoholics Anonymous (AA), 207,
  272
Alienation, 65, 67, 205

American Psychiatric Association,
  121, 132
Amphetamines. *See* Stimulant
  drugs
Antidepressant drugs, 18, 137, 140,
  143, 274
  Koplewicz and, 22
  Luvox, 19, 127, 129, 130, 133,
    138, 301n3
  mania and, 303n11
  Prozac, 19, 128, 134–38, 302n10,
    303n11, 305n39
  Remeron, 140
  Zoloft, 134
Antipsychotic drugs, 26, 311n13
Anxiety, 171
Assertive Community Treatment
  (ACT), 26
Athens, Lonnie, 172
Athletes, 175–76
Atlanta, Georgia, 11
"At-risk" children (violence prone)
  identifying, 33–34, 36–38, 43–44
  profiling, 45–46
Attention Deficit Hyperactivity
  Disorder (ADHD), 22, 116,
  293n9
  National Institute of Mental
    Health and, 299n2